FOLLOWING CHRIST AND CONFUCIUS

LIU INSTITUTE SERIES IN CHINESE CHRISTIANITIES

Series Editor: Alexander Chow, University of Edinburgh

LIU INSTITUTE
FOR ASIA AND ASIAN STUDIES

Christianity is the fastest growing religion in both mainland China and a large, linguistically and culturally diverse Chinese diaspora, which encompasses more than a fifth of the world's population. Any consideration of the future of world Christianity must now take into account the role of Chinese Christians and their distinctly Chinese interpretation of the Christian faith. Despite the development and influence of this tradition, the academic world has been slow to invest in this timely subject. This series features titles that offer new perspectives on the vast and expanding field of Chinese Christianities in all its diverse forms, providing a forum for cross-disciplinary conversation. Books are welcome from a variety of disciplinary approaches, including but not limited to historical, theological, social scientific, and sinological perspectives. The University of Notre Dame's Liu Institute for Asia and Asian Studies is pleased to support sustained quality research on this rich and varied religious tradition that merits greater understanding.

UNIVERSITY OF NOTRE DAME | KEOUGH SCHOOL OF GLOBAL AFFAIRS

FOLLOWING CHRIST AND CONFUCIUS

Wang Mingdao and Chinese Christianity

CHRISTOPHER PAYK

University of Notre Dame Press

Notre Dame, Indiana

University of Notre Dame Press
Notre Dame, Indiana 46556
undpress.nd.edu

Published in the United States of America

Library of Congress Control Number: 2023946556

ISBN: 978-0-268-20824-0 (Hardback)
ISBN: 978-0-268-20826-4 (WebPDF)
ISBN: 978-0-268-20827-1 (Epub3)

For her countless contributions to see this book come to print, the detailed list of which would nearly double the page count, this work is lovingly dedicated to Terri.

CONTENTS

ACKNOWLEDGMENTS

I would like to recognize and thank the following people for their contributions to this book:

Dr. Alexander Chow, thank you for spending so much time reading the original manuscript, providing many helpful suggestions, and recommending this book to the University of Notre Dame Press.

Dr. Emily King, for her many efforts to see this book come to print and her high level of professionalism.

Dr. Joyce H. S. Li, for her outstanding editing of this book.

For sharing many resources, connections, and their expertise with me, I want to thank Miss Yang Tingting, Dr. Clement Yung Wen, Dr. Kao Chenyang, Dr. Gene Ng, Dr. Iap Sian-Chin, Dr. Matsutani Yosuke, Dr. Wang Peter Chen-Main, Dr. Chin Ken-Pa, Dr. Wang Cheng-Wen, and Dr. Tsai Yuan-Lin.

Dr. Tsai Yen Zen for his constant encouragement and kindness. You are missed.

Dr. Ying Fuk Tsang for sharing a digital copy of *Wang Mingdao's Last Confession*, Wang's Shanghai sermons, and many articles with me. You are a model scholar.

To Kenny and Anna, for always asking about how Dad's book is going.

My heartfelt thanks to you all.

A NOTE ON CHINESE NAMES

Currently, the standard way to transliterate a Chinese name from Chinese characters into English is to use the Hanyu Pinyin system of transliteration. However, there is a growing sentiment among nonmainland Chinese scholars that the "Mandarinization" of their names is a type of cultural pressure to suppress their cultural identity. In light of this, I have tried, where I am aware of the preferred transliteration, to use the spelling of an author's name in English that they themselves have used in their written works. In order to be consistent, I have also done this with authors from the past. Therefore, for example, the name 趙紫宸 has been translated as T. C. Chao, as he preferred to write his name in his English writings, instead of the Hanyu Pinyin transliteration Zhao Zichen. This creates some difficulty from a standardization perspective, but it makes things easier from a recognition perspective, especially for non-Chinese readers, since the standardized names are not used in any works that have been published.

CHAPTER ONE

Wang Mingdao's Story Told Thus Far

After his release in 1980, Wang Mingdao's 王明道 (1900–91) life story had become so well known that he was visited in his small Shanghai home by a steady stream of Chinese and foreign visitors, including Billy Graham, who wanted to see the man who had taken on legendary status as a spiritual father in the unregistered Chinese Protestant Church. His name was familiar enough in the city at the time that it has been said that when taxi drivers at the Shanghai train station heard that their customer wanted something related to "Christianity" or "church," they would drive the person to Wang Mingdao's residence.[1] His home became known as a mecca for both Chinese and Western Christians.[2]

In later chapters, the major events of Wang's life will be described in detail. However, for introductory purposes, a brief biography will establish the topic of this study. In this outline of his story, I indicate the five major periods of Wang's life, changing at the natural turning points in his story, which will form the historical backbone of this study: the "dependent years: 1900–21," the "independent years: 1921–37," the "conflict years: 1937–55," the "prison years: 1955–80," and the "spiritual father years: 1980–91." The ideal way to study Wang's thought is to take account of his theology within the historical context in which it was formed in order to understand him as a Chinese theologian.

Shortly before Wang Mingdao was born on July 25, 1900, Wang's father, a Chinese doctor's assistant at the Peking Methodist Hospital, committed suicide out of fear of imminent torture and death at the hands of the Boxers. Subsequently, Wang Mingdao grew up with his widowed mother and older sister in the lower economic stratum of Beijing. He was dependent on the Christian missionary community for his education during these "dependent years" as he was able to attend London Missionary Society (LMS) and Methodist schools. At the LMS's Tsui Wen Academy, he received instruction in both the Christian and Chinese classics. He attended missionary schools until he completed his first year of postsecondary studies but was forced to drop out due to family circumstances.

In 1914, a significant change took place in his life when he converted to Christianity. After the collapse of the Qing dynasty (1911) and the subsequent search among the Chinese for the national way forward and despite the pressure exerted on religious Chinese in the wake of May Fourth Movement's exaltation of science (1919), Wang Mingdao persisted in his Christian faith: after delaying his original intention of a university education, he taught at a Presbyterian school in Baoding until he was fired in 1921 due to his insistence on being rebaptized; at this, he finally abandoned his dream of a university education. Thus began his "independent years," independent of missionary Christianity, which started with a difficult phase of soul searching and individual Bible study until February 1925, when an elderly woman who was well connected in the Beijing Christian community advised him and connected him to that network. He followed her advice, and his ability as a public speaker sparked a preaching ministry that later allowed him to travel to twenty-four of China's provinces, speaking in hundreds of locations.

After the May Thirtieth Movement in 1925, a tense situation arose for Chinese Christians due to the connection Chinese made between the Christian missionary movement and cultural imperialism. However, it was subsequent to this period that Wang carved out a reputation as an outstanding independent Chinese preacher. In 1927, Wang, drawing on the connections he made through his itinerant preaching ministry, began his quarterly journal, *The Spiritual Food Quarterly*, which he published continuously from 1927 to 1955. This further extended his influence among Protestant Christians throughout China. In 1950, he published his autobiography, *The Last Fifty Years*, which covered the initial fifty years of his life.

Wang had begun to conduct worship services in his home in 1925. In 1933, he began to have regular church meetings in Beijing. By August 1, 1937, just weeks after the Marco Polo Bridge incident on July 7, which set off the Second Sino-Japanese War, at the beginning of his "conflict years," Wang began services at the newly constructed Christian Tabernacle, a church he led and that grew to become one of the largest churches in Beijing at the time of his first imprisonment in 1955. The Sino-Japanese War period was an extremely challenging time for Wang due to the intense pressure he was under by the Japanese to head the North China Christian Union Group, a group designed by the Japanese to separate Chinese Christians from the Western church and political connections and to exercise control over the Chinese church. Through an amazing series of events and inspired by both biblical and Chinese heroes, Wang was the only Christian leader able to resist the demand to participate in the group. After the departure of Japan from occupied territory in China, due to his resolve, he became one of the most famous Protestant Christians in China.

During the Chinese civil war, Wang maintained his usual political distance by neither endorsing the Nationalists nor the Communists. In 1949, after the Chinese Communist Party's (CCP's) victory, due to what he saw as the restraint and discipline exhibited by the CCP army, Wang was initially optimistic about the new government and believed that the CCP would continue to grant religious freedom in China. He was asked to join the newly formed Three Self Reform Movement (TSRM), which eventually became the Three Self Patriotic Movement (TSPM). The group was formed through the efforts of leaders in both the Chinese church and in the CCP. Wang refused to join mainly because he did not think it was right for Christians to join any organization in which "unbelievers" were members. This eventually set off a war of words chronicled in Wang's *Spiritual Food Quarterly* and the TSPM's journal *Tianfeng*. After initially trying to woo Wang into participating in the organization, by 1954, the leaders of the TSPM changed tactics and verbally attacked him. The conflict eventually became so heated that after the publication of Wang's most influential article, "We Are for the Faith!" he was arrested, which brought his independent phase to an end.

Wang Mingdao was imprisoned from August 8, 1955, thus beginning his "prison years." On September 29, 1956, he was released after he promised to attend the TSPM meeting in Beijing and signed what he later described as a false confession. He read the "confession" at a TSPM meeting at the Beijing YMCA on September 30. During his release period, he experienced intense anguish over what he considered was his moral failure of lying and making the false confession; because of this, he regularly thought of committing suicide. After passively refusing to attend the TSPM meetings, which was an understood condition of his release, he was rearrested on April 29, 1957. In prison, he faced his greatest challenge due to being physically and psychologically tortured by fellow inmates under the direction of prison officials.

In July 1963, he was sentenced to life imprisonment. The news first devastated him, but after January 1965, he "stood back up" and recovered his life through inspiration from Micah 7:7–9. At this point, he no longer desired to leave prison. This was a major turning point in his life because he felt he no longer lived in fear and sensed that his relationship with God was restored.

In 1966, at the beginning of the Cultural Revolution, he was transferred to the Datong Labor Reform Camp. In 1968, he was again transferred, this time to Yingying Labor Camp, both of which were in Shanxi Province. It was here in Yingying, where his conditions were more relaxed, that he was able to engage in significant personal study through newspapers and the over five hundred books and articles his son had sent or brought him. During his elementary education, Wang had memorized significant portions of the Bible and the *Four Books* of Confucianism (*Analects*, *Mencius*, *The Great Learning*, and *The Doctrine of the Mean*). In Shanxi, he added to that foundational study *Xunzi*, *The Records of the Grand Historian*, and the historiographic poetry of Wen Tianxiang, among other works. As will be discussed in subsequent chapters, he interpreted the events of his day in continuity with the Chinese "spirit of righteousness" that has guided many Chinese for millennia. This period of study in Shanxi was crucial to that development.

After Mao Zedong died and Deng Xiaoping became paramount leader, there was a subsequent opening up of Chinese society. In 1980, after being tricked into leaving prison without his case being rectified to his satisfaction, Wang reunited with his wife, Liu Jingwen, and his son, Wang Tianduo, in Shanghai, which began his "spiritual father" years.

To his surprise, not only had he not been forgotten while in prison, but he was revered by the unregistered Chinese and global Christian community as a father figure to the Chinese house church movement due to his years of suffering. He consistently maintained that he had been imprisoned for over two decades for no criminal activity but simply for opposing the TSPM. From 1982 to 1983, he wrote his final major work, a request for his case to be reviewed by the president of the Supreme People's Court of China in order to seek "rehabilitation," which would officially restore his reputation and that of those who had been implicated with him. This "Rehabilitation Request Manuscript"[3] is, in fact, fifteen separate documents and twenty loose pages preserved by his son, Wang Tianduo, which were entrusted to and edited by Ying Fuk Tsang, professor of Chinese Christianity at Chung Chi College, Chinese University of Hong Kong. In these documents, the full development of Wang's thought is displayed: nearly every page of this manuscript refers to an ancient Chinese story that relates to a modern Chinese context. Every page includes idioms or fixed expressions that reveal Wang's intellectual formation as a largely self-taught Chinese intellectual. In the "Rehabilitation Request Manuscript," we see Wang interpreting twentieth-century Chinese history from a Confucian Christian perspective and commenting on what he saw was the way forward for Chinese society.

In addition to his writing, Wang also reengaged in house church ministry in July 1984 until the end of his life. He and his wife held weekly house church meetings on Sundays in his Shanghai apartment and received throngs of visitors throughout the week. On July 2, 1991, Wang became ill and a few weeks later, on July 28, 1991, died due to blood clots that had damaged his brain. His ashes were buried along with those of his wife in Dongshan Cemetery on a hill near Tahu Lake, forty-five kilometers southwest of Suzhou, Jiangsu Province.

WANG'S STORY TOLD THUS FAR

Wang Mingdao's life story has already been documented in various ways. A significant aspect of his story was told through his own writings. Beginning in 1926 with *The Bride of Christ*, he published various books and pamphlets until he was imprisoned for the first time in 1955 with his last publication being the 1955 essay "We Are for the Faith!"[4] Many of these books, along with several of his sermons,[5] were published in sections of his quarterly journal, *The Spiritual Food Quarterly*, which Wang almost exclusively wrote[6] and published from 1927 to 1955 in 114 quarterly volumes.[7] He also kept a diary from 1915 to 1955 totaling forty-one volumes, which were confiscated in 1955 but later returned with the exception of the 1954 volume. His diary was written in "easy classical" Chinese as opposed to the rest of his writings, which were written in the vernacular. Xerox copies of these diaries were entrusted by Wang's son to the Hong Kong Jiandao (Alliance Bible) Theological Seminary's Christianity and Chinese Culture Research Center in order to copy and eventually publish them.[8] Currently, the only diary by Wang Mingdao in publication is the Hong Kong Lingshi Publishing House's *Selections from Wang Mingdao's Diaries*, which was published in 1997. However, as noted by Ying Fuk Tsang, the published material accounts for only a very small percentage of the forty-one diaries.[9] As previously mentioned, while in prison, Wang wrote what he described as a "false confession" in 1956.[10] Later while in prison in 1963, after receiving a life sentence, he wrote hundreds of pages refuting his previous confession.[11] These docu-ments, if they still exist, have not been released to the public. The "Rehabilitation Request Manuscript," which makes up part of *Wang Mingdao's Last Confession* that he wrote from 1982 to 1983,[12] was published in 2013 by Logos Publishers after painstaking effort by Ying Fuk Tsang to collect, edit, and footnote it.[13] There is also a collection of audio CDs that contain several of the sermons that Wang preached when he began house church meetings in his home in Shanghai from July 1984 until his death.[14] Some of these have been transcribed into Microsoft Word documents and were generously shared with me by Ying Fuk Tsang for the purpose of completing this research. Also, some of the sermons from this period are available for viewing on YouTube.[15]

In terms of significant biographical studies, in 1950, Wang himself published an autobiography titled *The Last Fifty Years*. In 1981, it was translated into English by Arthur T. F. Reynolds, an English Christian missionary to China from 1933 to 1955 who knew Wang personally.[16] Reynolds's translation has provided the non-Chinese-reading public with a significant contribution since so few English translations of Wang's works have been made.[17] However, Reynolds's translation of *The Last Fifty Years* is haphazard in that much of Wang's original story, including some significant Chinese elements, have been edited out.[18]

Throughout the 1960s and 1970s when little was published on Christianity in China due to the aggressive stance taken by the CCP against Christianity, a number of former missionaries to China, including Reynolds, Francis P. Jones, and Leslie Lyall, continued to provide English readers with information on the Chinese church and Wang Mingdao. In 1962, Francis P. Jones wrote *The Church in Communist China*, which discussed Wang Mingdao's imprisonment.[19] In 1963, Jones translated a significant number of articles related to the Three Self movement including Wang Mingdao's 1955 article, "We Are for the Faith!" and his 1956 "Self Examination," which Wang had described as a false confession.[20] In 1968, Reynolds published *Pathway to Glory: The Voice of China's Christians* in which he recounted Wang's story.[21] In 1973, Leslie Lyall wrote *Three of China's Mighty Men*, which focused on Wang Mingdao, Watchman Nee, and David Yang. In 1951, Lyall, an Englishman with a long missionary career with the China Inland Mission, was forced to leave China after the CCP victory. He went to work for the home office of his mission and produced several important works on the unregistered churches in China. Lyall, who was a well-respected "China watcher," with his firsthand experience in China and personal acquaintance with several of the people he wrote about including Wang Mingdao, interpreted for English readers around the world some of what happened to Chinese Christians. His inclusion of Wang as one of the "mighty men" or "giants" of Chinese Christianity bolstered Wang's recognition around the world.

After Wang was released from prison in 1980, an old friend, Stephen Wang, conducted a series of interviews of Wang Mingdao and his wife, Liu Jingwen, from 1989 to 1990 in order to write a biography that continued the story from 1950 to 1991. These interviews were smuggled out of China[22] and published in 1997 as *Another Forty Years*.[23] Stephen oversaw the translation of this work into English, which was published in 2002 as *The Long Road to Freedom: The Story of Wang Mingdao*.[24]

In 2001, an important perspective on Wang Mingdao was provided through Liu Jingwen in the book *Sixty-Three Years: Walking the*

Narrow Road with Mr. Wang Mingdao. This book is a series of recollections by Liu Jingwen on her life with Wang Mingdao as collected and edited by Shi Meiling.[25] In 2006, an informative biography was written by Lin Chiu-Hsiang and Chang Kuan-Ing titled *An Injured Brave*.[26] This biography is significant because Chang lived with Wang Mingdao and Liu Jingwen in Shanghai after Wang's unsuccessful eye surgery in September 1982, so it provides a helpful firsthand account of Wang's later years in Shanghai.

However, it was in 2013, when *Wang Mingdao's Last Confession* was published, that the study of Wang Mingdao's thought advanced by a great leap forward. This book is the culmination of Ying Fuk Tsang's efforts to collect and edit fifteen documents and twenty loose papers that Wang Mingdao wrote as his appeal to have his sentence reversed and clear his name from the conviction of "counterrevolutionary crimes." Also, Wang wrote this "Rehabilitation Request Manuscript" in an attempt to clear those who were implicated with him in the Wang Mingdao counterrevolutionary clique.[27] This clique was a group of people who had been punished in varying degrees of severity by the CCP after 1955 for their connection and loyalty to Wang Mingdao and resistance to joining the TSPM. In the *Last Confession*, which is, in fact, a collection of smaller booklets and loose pages, we can see Wang Mingdao's mature thought as a Confucian Christian who was deeply influenced by Chinese history and sage stories, which informed his vision for Chinese social life.

THE FORMATION OF A CONFUCIAN CHRISTIAN

Since there are already such extensive writings on Wang Mingdao's life and theology, what more is there to say?[28] More importantly, what further *original* contributions on the life and work of Wang Mingdao can be added to the field? Chloë Starr, professor of Chinese theology at Yale Divinity School, notes that the theology of Watchman Nee and John Sung, two men who are often mentioned along with Wang Mingdao as being among the most influential of Fundamentalist Protestant Christians in twentieth-century China, could be read without knowing anything of the situation in China.[29] However, when reading

Wang's autobiography, *The Last Fifty Years*, the biography *Another Forty Years*, and *Wang Mingdao's Last Confession*, knowledge of the twentieth-century Chinese historical context and ancient stories of the Chinese past are crucial for understanding. An in-depth analysis of the influence of these "Chinese elements," as Starr describes them, on Wang and the impact he believed Confucian Christians could have on society, within the social network of his time as his thought developed over the five stages of his life, is the contribution of this book. In this study, "Chinese elements" refers to the Confucian stories of the past understood within the Chinese social context of twentieth-century China. Thus far, no scholar has analyzed in detail how the ancient stories from the Chinese classics, sages, and histories informed Wang Mingdao's writing and sermons throughout his entire life including his later prison and Shanghai years. In the examples of men such as Confucius, Qu Yuan, Xunzi, Wei Zheng, Zhang Xun, Wen Tianxiang, and others, Wang saw a spirit of righteousness that he believed pervaded Chinese history and provided the Chinese people with knowledge of how to live upright moral lives both individually and socially. Stemming from this, the focus of this book is on how the Chinese classics, sages, and histories shaped Wang Mingdao's Christian theology within his twentieth-century social context and thus qualified him to be considered a significant Chinese theologian.

WANG MINGDAO AS CHINESE THEOLOGIAN

In 2012, based on his field research from 2004 to 2005 in China,[30] Kao Chen-yang wrote an article titled "The House Church Identity and Preservation of Pentecostal-Style Protestantism in China"[31] in which he describes Wang Mingdao as being recognized by many in China as the "spiritual leader" of the unregistered house church movement.[32] Kao argues that Wang's anti-TSPM ideology legitimizes the ministry of house church leaders outside of the TSPM. As a result, many modern unregistered house church leaders believe, in part due to Wang's writings and example, that the unregistered church is not an alternative to the official one but is the *only* divinely sanctioned church in China.[33] Wang Mingdao, known as a "giant" of Chinese Christianity,[34] a "pioneer in indigenous

Chinese church planting,"[35] the "Dean of the House Churches,"[36] a "hero and martyr of the faith,"[37] and the "symbol,"[38] and "spiritual leader"[39] of the house church movement, has firmly established his position as a significant Chinese Christian leader.

However, his credentials as a significant Chinese *theologian* are not as well established. In 2003, Richard Cook wrote his PhD dissertation on Wang Mingdao titled "Fundamentalism and Modern Culture in Republican China: The Popular Language of Wang Mingdao, 1900–1991" in which he described Wang as neither a theologian nor a profound thinker but rather an effective speaker and writer who used the popular ideas and language of his era in China.[40] Cook says that Wang is best remembered as "a stalwart emblem of conservative Christian orthodoxy and as a Christian martyr"[41] but notes that Wang did not create a comprehensive or systematic theology.[42]

In 2007, Cook also wrote "Wang Mingdao and the Evolution of Contextualized Chinese Churches."[43] Following the model of missiologist Andrew Walls, Cook describes three stages of the contextualization of Christianity: missions, indigenization, and contextualization. Cook believes that Wang did not reach the third stage of comprehensively contextualized theology but remained at the second transitional stage of indigenization. He notes that Wang's significant contributions were his establishment of an indigenous preaching ministry, a Chinese-led Christian quarterly journal, and an independent church but that he did not significantly contribute to the development of a Chinese theology; rather, Wang Mingdao "remained, for the most part, an American-style fundamentalist."[44] Cook's conclusion is particularly important for this study: "Wang is probably best remembered by conservative Protestants . . . as a hero and a martyr for the faith. Yet his most important contribution may have been his role in serving in the transition from the missionary Church to the indigenous Church in China. It will be from a later generation of Church leaders that will emerge an 'Origen' or an Augustine in China who is able to produce a contextualized theology that is equally conversant in Chinese culture and thinking as well as Christian biblical studies and systematic theology."[45]

As will be argued in the following chapters, I disagree with Cook's conclusions that Wang was not a fully contextualized theologian because he was not conversant with academic Christian theology. Cook's comments were written before *Wang Mingdao's Last Confession* was published in 2013, and so he was unable to read Wang's more mature theological thought at the time of publication of his article. Perhaps if he could have read *Wang Mingdao's Last Confession*, Cook would have rethought his position.

Scholars have argued that Wang Mingdao's theology provides no help to those who are seeking to change the world[46] and shows a lack of social consciousness.[47] Also, some see Wang as "neither a theologian, nor a profound thinker"[48] as well as basically being an "American-style fundamentalist,"[49] or even worse, "a pawn of foreign reactionary forces,"[50] which reveals that not everyone agrees that Wang was an outstanding Chinese theologian.

Although it is true that Wang was not an academic or systematic theologian, he should still be considered a significant theologian. Comparatively, in 1964, Albert Outler made the case that John Wesley, the influential English founder of the Methodist Church, was not appreciated as a theologian on the same level as academic or systematic theologians but nevertheless deserved recognition as a major theologian. Outler argued that Wesley's theology was that of a "folk theologian."[51] Wesley's theological genius was not in academic speculative theology but in clearly communicating the essentials of Christian theology to laypeople.[52] Wang's theological genius is similar to that of Wesley. One need not be an academic or systematic theologian like Thomas Aquinas, John Calvin, or Karl Barth to be a significant theologian. Martin Luther and John Wesley were both nonsystematics who are now universally recognized as being significant theologians. Wang's theological genius was in his clear explanation of Christian theology from a perspective that took the Bible, as well as Chinese Confucian history and morality, seriously. His intellectual formation in the Confucian classics, sages, and histories shaped his Christian theology. What Archie C. C. Lee has pointed out about other Asian Christians attempting to do biblical hermeneutics and fashion Christian theology can also be applied to Wang's connection to Confucianism: "The whole problematic of Asian hermeneutics is largely that while the newly-acquired Christian Bible began to provide them with a new meaning of life, Asian Christians could not completely sever their connection with their community and its cultural-religious texts, which had nurtured and shaped their lives and continued to sustain and nourish their well-being."[53] What Lee sees as crucial in Asian hermeneutics—the lack of detachment from the theologian's historical and social context—is also true of Wang Mingdao. He never severed his connection to the Confucian tradition when he became a Christian. Wang believed that the Confucian revelation was for Chinese fulfilled by the Christian revelation.[54] He recognized that he did not have a long or thorough education, so treasured among Chinese, but that his talent was rather in his ability to write and speak in ways that communicated the Way, or *Dao*, of God, attested to throughout Chinese history in the teachings of Confucius and his subsequent followers in China, in ways that were simple to understand.[55] Wang's well-attested life of high moral integrity provided the important connection in Christianity between theology and praxis. The shift away from the extreme valuation of academic or systematic theology toward the valuation of a theology like Wang's that was deeply connected to the life of Chinese Christian believers is an ongoing process.[56] I hope this work will contribute to a reevaluation of Wang Mingdao, particularly of him in his later Shanghai years, as a significant Chinese Christian *theologian*.

This discussion of Wang as a significant Chinese theologian brings up an important point: How should "theology" be defined? In 1948, a Christian journal reported that a student once asked Wang Mingdao, "What theology did you study?" to which Wang responded, "Bitter toil theology" 苦力神學.[57] Wang did not like the idea of studying theology due to his perception, common among Chinese Fundamentalists at the time, that the major theological seminaries and departments of religion in China were dominated by theological Modernists, or as he called them, "unbelievers" 不信派, since they did not believe as he did in the same fundamental Christian doctrines.[58] However, he certainly engaged in theological reflection and wrote theological works as even a cursory reading of *The Spiritual Food Quarterly* reveals. To define theology with regard to Wang Mingdao, the term means Wang's reflection on God and God's interaction with the creation, as recorded in his writings and audiovisual recordings. As will be revealed in the subsequent chapters of this book, Wang's theology was largely based on Christian scripture but was also shaped by reason, Confucian tradition, and experience. A sort of "Wangian Quadrilateral" emerges when Wang's theology is analyzed.

To rigorously engage with how Wang Mingdao was simultaneously a thoroughly Chinese and a thoroughly Christian theologian necessitates a comprehensive and in-depth analysis of each of the five major stages of his life, within his social context, in order to trace at what points he was introduced to the Chinese classics, sages, and histories and to analyze how these influenced him as a Christian theologian. To do this, the following chapters contain a reevaluated biography of Wang Mingdao, relying mainly on the autobiographical and biographical sources and supplemented by secondary sources, referenced as abundantly as possible with the Chinese classics, sages, and histories to show that Wang Mingdao was a significant Chinese Christian "folk theologian." Wang Mingdao's story begins at the very beginning of the twentieth century with an event that was both catastrophic for China and for Wang personally: the Boxer Uprising.

CHAPTER TWO

The Dependent Years

1900–1921

Autobiographies are calculated expressions of self-revelation for a reading audience in which the author has intended goals. Religious experience contained within an autobiography is already interpreted in the retelling of the account. Autobiographical narratives are thus attempts to make sense of these experiences and convey meaning.[1] Wang Mingdao's *The Last Fifty Years* is no exception. He began his writing of *Fifty Years* in 1948 and published it for the first time in 1950 with the inclusion of his 1947 memorial essay for his mother. In 1951, he added details about his father in a republishing of *Fifty Years*. Wang stated that the goal of his autobiography was to help other people by candidly sharing his experience of achievements, endurance, and temptation in order to encourage and comfort them.[2] Another goal of Wang's autobiographical writings and interviews was to show that he was a thoroughly *Chinese* Christian. Time and again, he references Chinese stories and events that show that his early formative years were thoroughly Chinese in cultural context. He begins *Fifty Years* in 1900, the beginning of the twentieth century that was unimaginably painful for millions of Chinese, by recounting how he was born in the fire of what he described as an extremely painful and shameful event, the Boxer Uprising.[3] Due to this event, he never knew what his ancestral village was or much information about his paternal family line.[4] What was the cause of such a pitiful lack of knowledge among a people so proud of history and lineage?

THE BOXER UPRISING

The Boxer Uprising was the result of many factors.[5] In previous decades, the Qing government had suffered several humiliating defeats at the hands of foreign armies. The Chinese people's resentment toward foreign Christian missionaries and local Chinese Christians further increased when Christians took advantage of favorable tax agreements and extraterritorial rights. At the same time, groups of men known as Boxers, or *Yihequan* 義和拳, translated as "Boxers united [in] righteousness," had grown desperate on the North China Plain due to drought and economic disruption. These Boxers, who practiced martial arts and spiritual possession practices, believed the problems China faced were due to deviation to Christianity from proper religious patterns laid out in Chinese traditions. Consequently, the Boxers decided the solution was to expunge foreign and local Christians and thus restore the heavenly balance on earth. On June 21, 1900, Empress Dowager Cixi 慈禧太后 (r. 1861–1908) declared war on the foreign powers and gave imperial backing to the Boxers. Soon, assaults on Chinese Christians began to include attacks on missionaries and other foreigners. As a result, foreign residents and many thousands of Chinese Christians sought shelter from the Boxers in the fortified Legation Quarter of Beijing.[6]

To seek protection, Wang Mingdao's father, Wang Zihou 王子厚, mother, Li Wenyi 李文義, and older sister, Wang Enrong 王恩榮, entered the Dongjiao Minxiang 東交民巷,[7] a street to the south of the Forbidden City that led to the Legation Quarter during the Boxer Uprising. Both Wang Zihou and Li Wenyi were members of the London Missionary Society (LMS), which would have enabled them access to the Legation Quarter since the LMS had been issuing cards to Chinese members reading, "L.M.S. Christian Please Admit."[8] At this time, Wang Mingdao was still in his mother's womb. In *Fifty Years*, Wang reports that his father went up on a ladder to look over the Legation wall and saw countless Boxers and Qing soldiers surrounding the Legation Quarter. As Paul Cohen has observed, among Christians, the anxiety of death at the hands of the Boxers was powerful at the time.[9] Many reports circulating at the time spoke of the Boxers mutilating Chinese Christians.[10] Figuring that an excruciating death was inevitable, Wang Zihou told his wife that it would be better to avoid suffering by committing suicide. On June 22, 1900, a person informed Li Wenyi that her husband had hung himself in the garden of the Su Prince's Mansion 肅王府花園;[11] her husband's death left Li Wenyi with a young daughter and yet-unborn son.[12]

Then and for many years to come, Wang Zihou's suicide had profound effects on his family and Wang Mingdao in particular. Social scientific studies show that the children of people who commit suicide are much more likely to commit suicide themselves.[13] Over five decades after the Boxer Uprising, Wang Mingdao's wife, Liu Jingwen, demonstrated intuitive knowledge of this fact when she expressed her fear that like his father, Wang Mingdao would try to commit suicide when faced with the humiliation he had endured in writing a false confession and lying in order to be released after being first arrested on August 8, 1955. During his release from September 29, 1956 to April 29, 1957, Wang fixated on a plan to bring Liu Jingwen back to her home in Hangzhou 杭州, Zhejiang Province and for him to commit suicide by drowning himself in the West Lake 西湖, a beautiful body of water rich in historical meaning for Chinese poets,[14] the beauty of which Wang Mingdao had heard about since childhood.[15] However, his plan was foiled when he was not permitted to leave Beijing. Liu Jingwen believed that Wang Mingdao's intention to commit suicide was related to his father's suicide more than half a century earlier.[16]

PEKING METHODIST HOSPITAL

Years before his death, at some unknown date, Wang's father, Wang Zihou, had migrated to Beijing and had been working as a Chinese assistant to Western doctors at what was then known as Peking Methodist Hospital 同仁醫院, or simply, Peking Hospital. The hospital was destroyed during the Boxer Uprising[17] and was rebuilt from funds provided by a donation from the Hopkins family in the United States around 1900, when it became known as Hopkins Memorial Hospital. The Peking Methodist Hospital had been established in 1886 by the Methodist Episcopal Church (MEC)[18] and was located originally in the MEC's mission compound in the Legation Quarter, but after it was rebuilt, it was moved just southeast of the Forbidden City.[19] Wang Mingdao reports that at that time in China, no programs for teaching Western medicine or Western-style medical schools existed except for Christian hospitals like the Peking Methodist Hospital. Wang Zihou was one of three Chinese men who worked closely with foreign doctors to study Western medicine, and he gradually became a Chinese doctor's apprentice.[20] Since there were only two to three foreign doctors at the Peking Methodist Hospital who were training Chinese assistants like Wang Zihou,[21] by researching the history of the hospital, it is possible to reasonably ascertain the identity of the doctors who were involved in training the Chinese assistants.

Two doctors in particular are likely candidates to have been involved in Wang Zihou's training. One doctor is Dr. Nehemiah Somes Hopkins,[22] an MEC missionary eye doctor who arrived in China in 1886.[23] Another is Dr. George Davis Lowry,[24] an MEC medical missionary who arrived in China on November 8, 1894.[25] Both Dr. Hopkins and Dr. Lowry spent many years of service at Peking Methodist and were active during the time Wang Zihou was being trained there. Dr. Lowry was among those listed during the Boxer Uprising who sought shelter in the Legation Quarter along with Wang's family.[26] The interest and experience of these two doctors in training Chinese assistants is revealed in their 1906 report on medical work in Peking where they write, "There can be no more important work coming to the foreign physician than that of giving a knowledge of medicine to the Christian men of this nation and no one should be as competent to do this work as the medical missionary."[27] The significance of this connection of Wang Zihou's job at Peking Methodist to the foreign Christian community and foreign missionaries is that it put Wang and his family in great danger during the Boxer Uprising. Although it cannot be proven, his membership in the LMS and the opportunity to train to become a doctor's assistant make it likely that Wang Zihou was a Chinese convert to Christianity[28] since foreign missionary doctors in China at the time said, "We are to give our instruction to those who are likely to use their abilities for the extension of Christ's kingdom."[29] Possibly, Wang Zihou's religion but certainly his foreign Christian connections would make him a target during the Boxer Uprising. The anxiety of this threat convinced him that suicide was preferable to torture and death at the hands of the Boxers.

A MOTHER'S STRENGTH

After her husband's suicide, Li Wenyi did not abandon her family. On July 25, 1900, after being widowed for just over a month, Li Wenyi delivered Wang Mingdao.[30] His maternal grandmother delivered the newborn and was overjoyed to see that he was a stout baby boy; she gave him the nickname Iron. He did not like this name as a boy but gradually came to appreciate its connection to the iron will that Old Testament prophets such as Jeremiah were given by God.[31] When her husband was alive, Li Wenyi had lived with him in the dormitories of the Peking Methodist Hospital. However, once the Boxer Rebellion had subsided, the fatherless family had to leave the Beijing legation and seek housing elsewhere. The now matriarchal family found a small house to rent on East Beijing's Dry Fish Lane, which would later become known as Sweet Rain Lane, a short distance away from the Forbidden City.[32]

Wang Zihou's connection to Peking Methodist Hospital and his suicide sparked by the Boxers qualified the family to receive compensation from the Qing government. After the uprising, as punishment for supporting the Boxers and the resultant killing of foreign and Chinese Christians, the Eight-Nation Alliance that provided military forces created the Boxer Protocol, which stipulated that the Qing government pay an enormous 450 million taels of silver as indemnity payments.[33] There were also untold losses in looting by foreigners, missionaries included, with Beijing being described by some observers as "a carnival of loot" after the uprising. Some of this indemnity money was given to churches by the foreign governments; the churches, in turn, gave "a few hundred taels of silver" to Chinese Christians such as Wang Mingdao's mother. Li Wenyi saved some of that money and later purchased the housing unit she was renting on Sweet Rain Lane.[34] To make adequate money for the family to live on, she began renting out rooms.

Li Wenyi had studied for a few years at an LMS girls elementary school.[35] Wang Mingdao, in his memorial essay for his mother, recalled that she was not highly intelligent but had a very strong memory, even in her senior years.[36] During her elementary school education in the LMS school, she had memorized sections of the *Four Books* 四書; *Poems of One Thousand Writers*千家詩, an anthology of poems from the Tang to the Song dynasties; and other quotations from ancient Chinese books that she could recite even into her eighties.[37] That Wang Mingdao knew this indicates that she would quote these passages to Wang when he was a child. She had a violent temper and was stubborn in her opinions, which caused many difficulties for her in her role as a landlady. Even in this entrepreneurial position, however, the rent Li Wenyi collected was not enough to support herself and her two children. This was partly due to the fact that her renters took advantage of her widowed situation: they often would not pay her the rent that was due since they thought that there was nothing she could do about it. To reduce one expense for his family, Wang Mingdao began to collect unused charcoal from other homes' garbage piles, a task that he continued until he was twelve years old, when he began boarding at school.[38]

BICULTURAL EDUCATION

From an early age, Wang Mingdao showed an academic inclination in that he enjoyed reading, and the selection of books he read from as a child reveals his immersion in a bicultural Chinese Christian heritage that began even before he went to school. He recalls that in his early years, he read the *Three Character Classic* 三字經, the *Hundred Family Names* 百家姓, the *Thousand Characters Text* 千字文, and the *Collection of Writings of Famous Worthies* 名賢集, the first three of which have been central to Chinese elementary education since the Song dynasty.[39] He also notes that he read another set of texts: John Bunyan's *Pilgrim's Progress* 天路歷程 and *Pilgrim's Progress Part II* 續天路歷程, the Christian classic which had been fully translated into Mandarin in 1866;[40] Favell Lee Mortimer's *The Peep of Day* 正道啟蒙, a collection of Christian religious instruction for children written in 1833 and translated into Chinese in 1864;[41] and the Old and New Testaments of the Bible. Wang's maternal grandmother was a Christian and taught her grandson Christian songs when he was a child.[42] Through reading both Chinese and Christian texts as a child, the intellectual foundation was laid early on for Wang's later self-identification as a Confucian Christian.[43]

Coupled with his academic propensity, Wang was a curious, thoughtful child who, somewhere from 1906 to 1909 between the ages of six and nine, became very concerned about the question of what happens to a person after they die. He had a maternal uncle 舅父[44] who knew many stories and would often share these tales with Wang Mingdao and his older sister. Wang asked him, "Uncle, is there a way not to die?" His uncle responded, "There is a way." His uncle told him that the way to immortality was to retreat into the mountains and seek the Way, forsake the world of mortals, abandon fame and profit, put an end to the pursuit of pleasure, meditate in mountain caves, drink the dew from grass and leaves, unearth mushrooms for food, practice austerities, and eventually become an immortal, thus avoiding death. This possibility filled Wang Mingdao with great joy and comfort.[45] His uncle's advice has some interesting parallels with the adventures recorded in the Chinese classic *The Journey to the West* 西遊記. For example, the Chinese phrase his uncle uses, "to practice austerities and become an immortal 修煉成仙," is used in *The Journey to the West* in reference to the Monkey King who "became an immortal" and that "within the three regions, all creatures endowed with the nine apertures can, through exercise, become immortals."[46] A man with such extensive knowledge of Chinese novels and stories such as Wang Mingdao's uncle was surely familiar with *The Journey to the West*, one of the most famous books in Chinese literature, and used his knowledge of such stories to reply to his young nephew's question about immortality. Wang Mingdao wanted to leave immediately for the mountains to pursue what would likely have been the path of a Daoist hermit or priest, although his uncle evaded his request. Still, the hope of this path to escape death provided Wang with comfort for several years until his second year of school.

TSUI WEN PRIMARY ELEMENTARY SCHOOL

Wang's thoroughly bicultural Chinese and Christian education continued in 1909 when, at nine years of age, he began his studies at Tsui Wen Primary Elementary School (Tsui Wen Academy) 萃文初等小學,[47] which had been established by the LMS. Tsui Wen appears to have been reestablished after the Boxer Uprising led to the destruction of a previous LMS boys boarding school in West City of Beijing.[48] The school was located in the LMS compound on Lilu Hutong in West Beijing and contained the primary school, separate boarding schools for boys and girls, a clinic, and three mission houses.[49] According to Wang Mingdao, the school was halfway between an older-style private school 私塾 and a modern Christian school. Despite the fact that in 1905, the Qing government abolished the imperial examination system, Confucian-style education still persisted in China for at least another decade. Although there was great eagerness in China to learn from the foreign powers and adopt elements from foreign education systems, a strong desire also remained to preserve the best aspects of Chinese history and literature in education, and there were very few teachers in China who had the skills and experience to provide alternative education options other than a Confucian-style education.[50] Wang notes that Tsui Wen Elementary School's curriculum included arithmetic, history, geography, moral cultivation, and Chinese literature, yet the main emphasis was on memorizing the *Four Books and Five Classics* 四書五經, the authoritative books of the Confucian tradition in China.[51] The study of the Confucian classics had been the path to upward social mobility for even commoners like Wang since the Han dynasty.[52] Despite the changes in the education system in 1905 and the inclusion of other elements in the curriculum at Christian schools, Wang was given a Confucian-style elementary education at Tsui Wen.

He began by memorizing *The Analects* 論語, then worked through *Mencius* 孟子, *The Great Learning* 大學, and *The Doctrine of the Mean* 中庸, completing the *Four Books* as well as *Mr. Zuo's Commentary on Chun Qiu* 左傳. He memorized significant sections of these books as evidenced by the fact that when he was writing his "Rehabilitation Request Manuscript" in 1982, he used many quotations from the *Four Books*.[53] Tsui Wen Elementary School had only one teacher, but this man had a significant impact on Wang Mingdao. His name was Xu Zhichen 徐質臣,[54] and Wang notes that his teacher was well versed in literature. Since Xu was in his fifties when he taught Wang at the LMS-sponsored school, it is almost certain that Xu had received a traditional Chinese education since he taught a Classical Chinese literature curriculum focused on the *Four Books and Five Classics*. Curriculum in all elementary mission schools at the time, despite being established by Christian missionaries, still had a significant Classical Chinese orientation, with the curriculum largely dependent on the instructor's background[55] with even the poorest of families whose children were enrolled in mission schools desiring adherence to the traditional Confucian curriculum.[56] Xu was encouraging of Wang Mingdao's strong academic ability but also strict when he noticed Wang was negligent in his studies. The great care his teacher showed Wang Mingdao prompted him to describe Xu Zhichen as his "strict teacher 嚴師,"[57] a term of endearment and reference to the *Book of Rites*' 禮記 record on the subject of education in which the author advises that proper reverence for a worthy teacher or master is crucial to education.[58]

Around 1911, the year the Qing dynasty began to crumble, the comfort Wang derived from his uncle's idea of retreating to the mountains to become an immortal also disintegrated due to what he was learning at school. In the course of his studies, he learned about how the emperors Qin Shihuang 秦始皇 and Han Wudi 漢武帝 had both pursued the elixir of immortality without success. Although Wang does not reveal the source of the information about the emperors, the search by Qin Shihuang, the first emperor of a unified China, for the elixir of immortality is recorded in *The Grand Scribe's Records* 史記.[59] That these two emperors, with the unlimited resources of the entire Chinese Empire available to them, could not find the path to immortality made Wang Mingdao despair that a poor boy like him could never find it. He asked his uncle about this, and his uncle admitted that he had deceived him. The realization that his path to immortality had collapsed combined with his fear of death filled Wang with a terrible sense of dread. He recalled that his feeling at the time was described perfectly in the poem titled "On a Gate Tower at Yuzhou" by Tang dynasty poet Chen Ziang 陳子昂 (661–702 CE),

> Where before me are the ages that have gone?
> And where behind me are the coming generations?
> I think of heaven and earth, without limit, without end,
> And I am all alone and my tears fall down.[60]

Wang Mingdao, as will be shown in the following chapters, was deeply touched by Chinese poetry that could express his feelings as captured in the writing of past poets. Although it is not clear where Wang picked up his love of poetry, it is likely that his education at Tsui Wen Academy included poetry in his literature classes, and poetry became a lifelong delight. In 1980, upon being released from prison and awaiting travel arrangements to his new home in Shanghai, an old friend Zeng Pingdao 甄品道 had come with Wang's son Wang Tianduo 王天鐸 to celebrate his release. As they waited for the paperwork for Wang's release to be processed, the two old friends talked about the past, prayed, read the Bible, and discussed poetry with the two taking turns reciting verses of their favorite poems.[61]

TSUI WEN SENIOR ELEMENTARY SCHOOL

In the course of his diligent study and memorization of the *Four Books*, Wang encountered Mencius's statements that human nature is good.[62] However, his home life provided an alternative perspective on human nature. His mother's renting out her housing complex units to Beijing's lower socioeconomic class brought Wang Mingdao into contact with tenants who abused one another and engaged in prostitution and gambling. Wang lamented that if his mother followed Mencius's mother's example to move until she could find a suitable environment for her son's proper moral development,[63] his family would starve to death because no such upstanding renters could be found among Beijing's lower socioeconomic class.[64] He originally thought the problem of human nature was due to a lack of a proper education. However, in 1912, the same year that the Qing dynasty finally ended, he concluded that the problem with humankind's degenerate moral state was a problem of human nature. Now twelve years of age and entering adolescence, Wang moved up to Tsui Wen Senior Elementary School 萃文高等小學 and began to board at the school. He was surprised to discover that some of his older classmates, those who had received a higher level of education than he had, were just as morally degenerate as the poor Beijing residents he had grown up with in his mother's housing complex: vicious bullying, lewd sexual storytelling, and coarse language were common at the school of around thirty-five students. Wang himself felt that his morality had degenerated from living at the school.[65] Beginning in the senior elementary level, since he now had higher fees due to living at the school and his mother did not earn enough money through her rental income to pay his fees, Wang relied on merit scholarships from the LMS.[66] Thus began Wang's dependence on missionary Christianity that lasted until his break with missionary churches in 1921.

He was allowed to go home only on Saturday afternoons, and he spent the rest of his time living on the school campus. Being a physically weak and sickly child, certain aspects of Wang's personality were revealed at this time that would come out more clearly later in his life, including an "iron" strong will. When he was bullied by older and stronger classmates, he would not yield, even when beaten. Also, he would not follow other people blindly if he was not clear on the issue. However, if his conviction was set on an issue, no matter who opposed him, he would persist in his conviction. Looking back three decades later, Wang Mingdao described himself as having both radical and conservative aspects to his personality.[67] In this duality, Wang reveals himself to be a young man well suited to the early twentieth-century Chinese context as many Chinese at the time wanted to see radical change, while others hoped to conserve the best of Chinese culture. Some, like Wang Mingdao, wanted both. On February 12, 1912, with the forced abdication of the child emperor Puyi 溥儀, who reigned as the Xuantong emperor 宣統帝, a new postimperial age had dawned in China. Many Chinese hoped to see the benefits of radical change with the formation of the Republic of China under Sun Yat-sen's 孫中山 Guomindang Party (KMT) 國民黨, but they were also hopeful that they could conserve the best aspects of Chinese civilization.[68] There was a greater consciousness of the need for fundamental change among Chinese who were hopeful to see a "new China" emerge.[69] Wang was one among many "radical conservatives" of the time.[70]

CHANGE IS IN THE AIR

At the beginning of his autobiography *Fifty Years*, Wang reveals himself to be a young man of his time: hoping to preserve the best of Chinese culture, while at the same time eager for the hope that change can bring. His early formation in the Chinese and Christian classics provided the intellectual formation for him to develop into the Chinese Christian theologian he would later become. However, he was not yet a Christian: by 1914, with his fear of death still not waylaid and now combined with rapid social changes on the outside and his guilt over his moral degeneration inside, the conditions were right for a significant change in Wang Mingdao's life. In 1913, Yuan Shikai 袁世凱, the commander of the Beiyang Army, was elected president of the Republic of China. Shortly thereafter, he dissolved the KMT and did not abide by the provisional constitution that the young republic had proposed, instead declaring himself the emperor of China in 1915. He also attempted to dissolve the provincial system of China to create a strong central government to control the country. However, this created an enormous backlash, which resulted in several provinces degenerating into warlord states. Yuan abdicated in 1916 and died shortly thereafter of natural causes.[71] This volatile national situation corresponded with Wang Mingdao's volatile personal situation.

Wang recalled that at this time, both his home environment and his school environment were morally poor. The fine instruction of his beloved "strict teacher" Xu Zichen at the primary level of Tsui Wen Elementary School had been replaced by inferior instructors at the senior level of the elementary school. Wang states that although he still had a class on cultivating moral character 修身, the emphasis of the class was on the literature aspect of the lessons and not actually on the cultivation of a superior moral life. The teachers at Tsui Wen Senior Elmentary School emphasized good hygiene and etiquette, but it was not until he was fourteen years of age that he paid careful attention to moral improvement.[72]

His mother and father were both members of the LMS, and he could recall attending Christian worship services with his mother since he had been a young child. After he entered school at nine years of age, he attended daily Christian meetings. Once he began boarding at the school at twelve years of age, he attended upward of ten Christian meetings a week. The students from both his boys' school and the affiliated girls' school[73] met together in corporate worship in the early morning for half an hour every day from Monday to Saturday. On Wednesday afternoons, he attended a prayer meeting. On Sunday mornings, he attended Sunday school and a large-scale worship service, in the afternoon an "encouragement group," and in the evening a meeting for young people. In addition to all this, he also attended three or four Bible classes a week.[74] Wang Mingdao received both a thorough Chinese education and a thorough Christian education. Therefore, it is curious as to why some scholars do not see Wang as having grown up in the Christian faith since he was immersed in Christian teaching and activities from his earliest years.[75]

Later, Wang recalled that attendance at these meetings had been mandatory and that the Bible classes' content was tested for grades, which therefore resulted in mechanical memorization that led to the content soon being forgotten after the test. Wang lamented that no one was interested in the "truths of the Bible" and that the preachers lacked both ability and interest, which resulted in students detesting going to the meetings. When attendance became voluntary during holidays, the students were "rare as morning stars."[76] Correspondingly, in the spring of his fourteenth year, Wang described himself as having no religious beliefs. However, this was soon to change.

During the spring of 1914, a student who was three years older initiated a conversation with Wang.[77] This student's moral conduct and care for others had earlier impressed Wang and had given him a good impression of his older schoolmate. Wang describes the student as first leading him "to know God"[78] and then taking up the role of mentor by guiding Wang on how to revere God through the practice of Christian religious disciplines such as prayer, Bible reading, daily self-examination, and diary keeping. Although Wang would later experience other significant moments in his religious life, including his rebaptism,[79] his acceptance of the doctrine of salvation by faith,[80] and his "standing up again" through repentance after an eight-year-long period of lying in prison,[81] Wang consistently looked back at this moment when he was fourteen years old as his conversion to Christianity. When Wang was eighty-two years old, in his "Rehabilitation Request Manuscript," he wrote that "at 14 years of age, due to the leading of an older schoolmate, I became a Christian."[82] This reveals something significant about Wang's theology: he consistently believed that it is the point where a person expresses faith in Jesus Christ that he or she becomes a Christian, not a further act of cognitive recognition of correct doctrine or further obedience to the will of God that marks the change.

Wang's conversion to Christianity was a significant turning point for him as it opened a path that would eventually resolve his concern about life after death, and it also provided him with a way to achieve the moral cultivation that the Confucian tradition called for.[83] His mature thought on the subject as an octogenarian describes what was beginning to transpire in the thoughts of the young teenager:

> I gradually felt that the lessons in the *Four Books* were consistent with the truth in the Bible, and I began to understand the statement in the *Great Learning*: "Their thoughts being sincere, their hearts were then rectified. Their hearts being rectified, their persons were cultivated. Their persons being cultivated, their families were regulated. Their families being regulated, their states were rightly governed. Their states being rightly governed, the whole kingdom was made tranquil and happy."[84] I was a primary school student at the time, and of course I could not say anything about "Their families being regulated, their states were rightly governed. Their states being rightly governed, the whole kingdom was made tranquil and happy." But I was able to learn the lesson of "Their thoughts being sincere, their hearts were then rectified. Their hearts being rectified, their persons were cultivated." Therefore, I started to pay attention to "thoughts being sincere, hearts being rectified, and persons being cultivated" from that day, and I made progress in the future. The Bible and the *Four Books* laid the foundation for my life. No matter what I read, I paid careful attention to ethics.[85]

Clearly, Wang Mingdao saw no inconsistency between the ethical demands of the Bible and the *Four Books* but rather saw the two as representing largely harmonious views on the moral requirements for human beings. This is another important facet of Wang Mingdao's theology. It is well known that Modernist theologians such as T. C. Chao (Zhao Zichen) 趙紫宸 thought that the Confucian and Christian traditions were largely consistent,[86] but it is less well known that some self-described Fundamentalists such as Wang Mingdao also saw Confucian thought as being compatible with Christian religious beliefs. This harmonization between the two traditions, Confucianism and Christianity, began in Wang's thought when he converted in 1914 and continued throughout his life.

H. L. ZIA AND THE YMCA

This harmonization of traditions was not the product of Wang's thoughts alone, though. The older schoolmate who was such an influential mentor gave Wang a copy of H. L. Zia's (Xie Honglai) 謝洪賚 book, *Friendly*

Talks to Students 修學一助, which had a profound effect on Wang. In fact, Wang was so impressed by this work that he proceeded to buy every book he could find written by the author.[87] H. L. Zia (1873–1916) was born into a Christian family in Shaoxing, Zhejiang Province, and at seven years old, he began a traditional education at a private school, where he learned the Confucian classics. At eleven years old, he left home to attend the Buffington Institute and was baptized into the MEC at the age of thirteen. In 1895, Zia graduated from the institute as top student, went on to work at the Anglo-Chinese College in Shanghai, and eventually moved into publishing with the YMCA.[88] He became fluent in English and Japanese and was particularly interested in training young people, which led him to become the head of the YMCA's publishing department and its secretary of the national board in China in 1904, a position he held until his death from tuberculosis in 1916.[89] In his dozen years with the YMCA, Zia published or translated over 106 titles, becoming possibly "the greatest pioneer Chinese Christian writer in early twentieth century China."[90] By the time Wang read *Friendly Talks to Students* in 1914, the book had already gone through four editions with Zia being a recognized author in China.[91]

Friendly Talks with Students, first published in 1912, is actually a compilation by several authors. H. L. Zia wrote five and translated twelve of the twenty-nine sections.[92] The book covers several practical topics such as "How to Use a Dictionary" and "How I Learned to Read English." There are also more philosophical topics such as the section on "The Aim of Education" in which the author states that the goal of education is moral cultivation, to rectify or correct thinking, and for the student to become a mature person.[93] The author in the section on "The Object of Study" states that the purpose of study is to pursue self-perfection to the greatest degree. Consequently, one should obtain the highest useful position one can reach to be the person God wants one to become through seeking wisdom, self-control, excellence, and application through what one has learned.[94] The section on "Books and How to Read Them" contains an interesting idea about moral integrity. Zia advises readers to only recommend a book to others after reading it fully as only then can a reader truly understand the argument of the book instead of simply trying to appear learned.[95] Wang would remember this lesson and described himself in the 1980s as a person who does not speak about a book unless he has read it.[96] In the section "How to Spend a Vacation Properly," Zia states that when a student returns home from summer vacation and there is no set schedule, it is easy to lose self-discipline. He encourages students to pray and read the Bible every day, with the first week after returning home being especially crucial for this, before one becomes undisciplined. If there is no place to worship, Christian students should gather and conduct worship or meet in groups together and that the summer break is a good opportunity to train one's faith.[97] The "Student's Decalogue" at the book's conclusion is comprised of ten commandments for students to frame their thinking about life and education. The final three commandments are instructive on how Zia approved of a disciplined Christianity:

8. Love your friends more than yourself. Love your school more than your friends. Love your homeland more than your school. Love God more than anything.
9. In self-cultivation use the finest as your expectation. When you find a person of virtue, you should follow that example.
10. Be rigorous in self-discipline with every day's self-governance becoming stricter.[98]

Chinese Christians like Wang received Zia's works well because Zia emphasized practical methods that students could use to improve themselves. Zia did this in a way that combined a Confucian sense of morality and self-discipline with his own deep commitment to the Christian scriptures, along with a desire to learn from the best of what the West could provide Chinese students, thus creating his own modern Confucian Christian thought that Wang Mingdao deeply admired.[99]

TSUI WEN MIDDLE SCHOOL

Wang indicates that after his conversion, with the instruction from his older schoolmate and that from the works of H. L. Zia, over the next few months, his mental state and life began to change significantly.[100] He started to become clear on the meaning and responsibility of life.

He became very interested in reading the Bible, praying, and attending Christian worship meetings. At the same time, he developed a revulsion for what he considered immoral behavior and vile language, both of which he had engaged in previously. On April 12, 1914, Easter Sunday, Wang was baptized at an LMS worship service. He graduated from Tsui Wen Senior Elementary School in the summer of 1914 and entered Tsui Wen Middle School 萃文中學 that fall, which at that time offered a four-year academic program. His older schoolmate, who was in his fourth and final year of middle school, continued to mentor Wang through his first year of middle school until the older student graduated in 1915.[101] One evening in the fall of 1914 before his mentor left the school, Wang and this student went for a walk on the school campus. His older schoolmate asked him what career he aspired to. Wang responded that he had no particular ambitions and was rebuked by his mentor that a young person must have ambition. His older mentor quoted Zhu Xi's 朱熹 (1130–1200 CE) comment on *Analects* 7.6 that "in order to learn, one must first be determined"[102] and from the *Book of the Later Han* 後漢書that "a truly determined person will find a solution"[103] to Wang.[104] This conversation prompted Wang to begin to think about his career. In spite of his negative assessment of the quality of religious life at Tsui Wen Elementary School, Wang Mingdao was deeply influenced by his first teacher, Xu Zhichen, who was most likely a Confucian Christian. Also, H. L. Zia's Confucian Christian instruction, which, according to Wang, paired commitment to all essential points of Christian scripture with emphasis on Christian behavior, and was written in an accessible way for young people, had a deep impact on his life.[105] The influence of these two important teachers, combined with his older schoolmate's mentorship, conveyed Christianity to Wang in a way that he could embrace with his bicultural Confucian Christian background. His years at Tsui Wen Elementary School and his first year at Tsui Wen Middle School with his older schoolmate provided some foundational concepts and examples that Wang would later build on to become a Christian leader in the future. This was, in fact, one of the goals of Christian education at the time in China with teachers attempting to influence Chinese students by example to provide the lessons and morals to become the future leaders of the Chinese church.[106]

In his second year of middle school, at the age of fifteen, Wang was now without a personal mentor to help him navigate his new religious life. Research on religious life at Christian middle schools in China during this time reveals that most students went unconverted, to the disappointment and concern of missionaries. The majority of families desired their children to go to Christian middle schools such as Tsui Wen Middle School not for Christian religious instruction but simply for their children to learn English,[107] which would increase academic and employment opportunities in the postimperial examination period of China.[108] YMCA statistics reveal that in 1915, there was a significant drop in the number of Christian students at Tsui Wen. Out of eighty-eight students, only three were Christians.[109] However, Wang looked back from his later perspective and saw the low quality of moral and religious life at Tsui Wen Middle School as being providential. In 1915, during his second year of studies at the middle school, there were several new students who came from government official and successful business families. Several of these students not only had poor behavior, but some of them had contracted venereal diseases, indicating fornication, which was in violation of behavior policies of Christian schools. Wang was concerned that these students were leading others who had formerly exhibited good behavior to regress. He spoke with the school's directing teacher[110] to rein in these students and was shocked by the teacher's response that if he were to expel them, the school's finances would suffer, leading to the school's closure, and so he would not do it. Infuriated by this statement, Wang responded that it would be better to close the school than to have a school run by morally incompetent teachers who lead young people astray and that to have Christians running a school that allows students to be immoral loses the propriety of Christ.[111]

In Wang's statement to his teacher, we encounter for the first time in Wang Mingdao's postconversion life an internal principle that he consistently maintains until 1955: it would be better to lose everything than to compromise righteousness. His exposure to both the Christian and Confucian traditions nourished this principle, as will be displayed in the research on the years to follow. One of the offending students overheard Wang's outburst to the supervising teacher and shared the information with other students, which caused them to detest Wang. For the next few years of middle school, these classmates, hoping to catch him in misbehavior, carefully examined everything Wang did. He believed this was providential and thought that God used these students to improve his moral behavior; by the time he was to graduate from middle school, Wang was a model student.[112]

Looking back on his life, Wang recalled that at fifteen, he was thankful to his mentor for guiding him to revere God and to have faith in Christ. Nevertheless, in Wang's opinion, his older schoolmate had not helped him to understand Christian salvation or the promises of the afterlife. This lack of certainty resulted in Wang continuing to fear death despite his conversion.[113] To resolve this tension and prompted by the earlier conversation with his mentor about a career, Wang began to think about becoming a politician. Looking back, the desire to live on through reputation and become a politician made sense to him at fifteen years of age because, at that time, he followed the logic of the Chinese proverb that "after death, a tiger leaves to later generations it's fur, but a man, his reputation."[114] In the same way, Wang hoped to develop a name for himself as other great men such as Abraham Lincoln had done to live on in the memories of other people. Wang had read a biography of Lincoln and was impressed that like him, Lincoln had grown up in poverty, and yet he had risen to great fame throughout the world. Wang longed to become the "Lincoln of China."[115] Upon reflection, he later realized that his motivation to become a politician was not due to political aspirations, even though news of Beijing's political situation surely reached him living in the capital, but rather because he saw politics as a pathway to escape death through his name living on in fame.[116]

In spite of his career plans, during the first half of 1915, Wang began to sense "God's call" on his life to enter Christian ministry. He immediately resisted this call as he saw political life as being glorious and the life of a preacher being petty and low. To communicate how he felt about going from pursuing a political career to an ecclesial career, he referred to Mencius's statement that a bird does not descend from a lofty tree to enter a dark valley.[117] The reason for this revulsion toward Christian ministry was the fact that he saw Chinese preachers as not being useful people. In his young opinion, they were the lowly assistants of Western missionaries or second-class students who were not intelligent enough to go into medicine or teaching, and so without other options, they entered theological training and church work. Since during his education thus far he had always scored among the top students, which provided him with scholarships, he did not think a lowly career as a preacher was appropriate for such a talented person like himself. Therefore, he rejected God's initial overtures for him to become a preacher.[118] He recalled that he resisted God's call on his life for more than three years from the ages of fifteen to eighteen, which made up the majority of his time at Tsui Wen Middle School. The middle school program at Tsui Wen still operated on the old four-year middle school system, and he was scheduled to graduate from the school in the summer of 1918.[119]

However, in the spring before graduation, he had to determine what to study in university. He resolved that he was going to major in political studies feeling that "man can conquer heaven."[120] He later concluded that to resist God's call on his life was like "striking a stone with an egg"[121] and was a useless battle that he could not win. During the middle of March 1918, he became extremely ill with symptoms of fatigue, dizziness, and high fever and spent over a month sick in bed at home and could only return to school on May 7 but remained ill. He had a relapse and returned home on May 23, getting worse by the day. Still, he went to take the Christian universities' entrance examination for middle school students, which was scheduled for June 3–7. However, he was only able to test for the first two days, so severe was his illness, and on the third day, he could not get out of bed. Fearing his death was imminent since an LMS hospital doctor told his sister that his condition was beyond hope, and still having a terrible fear of death, he finally gave up his aspiration of becoming a famous politician and promised to no longer resist God's call on his life, realizing that the idiom "man can resist heaven" was nonsense. By the end of June, his health returned. On June 27, 1918, since his academic performance had been excellent up until he became ill, Wang was allowed to graduate from Tsui Wen Middle School with the rest of his class.[122]

UNIVERSITY DREAMS AND THE MAY FOURTH MOVEMENT

Since Wang was still quite weak after his illness, many people encouraged him to take a year off to recuperate. However, to continue his formal education without delay, he resumed his study schedule and began his studies in the middle of July 1918 at what became known as Chong Wen

Middle University Preparatory School 崇文中學預科班.[123] The story of his post–middle school education is quite complicated as is the whole story of education in China during the May Fourth Movement. According to Wang, when he was in middle school, the Beijing region had two Christian universities. Xiehe University 協和大學, also known as North China College (founded 1867), was located in Tong County 通縣 of Beijing and was operated as a cooperative effort by the Presbyterians, Congregationalists, and LMS. The other was Hweiwen (Huiwen) University 匯文大學, also known as Methodist Peking University (founded 1870), which was located in Beijing and was operated by the MEC. Since Wang had graduated from an LMS middle school, he would have gone to Xiehe University to begin his university career. However, in the fall of 1918, the church missionary societies decided to amalgamate the two schools into what would eventually become Yenching University 燕京大學 in Beijing.[124] The university was to have a six-year program with two years for a university preparatory course (預科) and four years for the undergraduate degree course (本科). Since Wang had just graduated from middle school, he had to first take the preparatory course before he could begin his undergraduate degree.[125] The undergraduate course was to be conducted in the east part of Beijing while the preparatory course was to be conducted on the old campus of Huiwen University in Beijing, which continued to be known in English as (Methodist) Peking University.[126]

In July 1918, Wang entered his first year of studies in the two-year university preparatory course.[127] He never reveals what program he decided to study, but one can assume, due to his resignation to God's call on his life to prepare for Christian ministry, that he enrolled in a liberal arts program geared toward eventual acceptance into Yenching University's prestigious religion program.[128] However, after the initial three thousand students from Beijing institutions gathered at Tiananmen on May 4,[129] Wang reports near the end of the academic year on May 19, 1919, that all university students in Beijing began to skip classes due to the influence of the May Fourth Movement. From that point on, students did not attend classes, and so an early summer vacation began on June 3 and Wang returned home. On June 5, he received news that the university preparatory school he attended would no longer be offering courses on the Beijing campus, and students in the program were to transfer to Cheeloo University 齊魯大學 in Jinan 濟南, Shandong Province. He had never lived far from home and felt that he and his mother were "mutually dependent upon one another for survival,"[130] a very Confucian way of expressing his filial piety toward his mother. While he studied in Beijing, he was able to see his mother at least once a week. If he moved to study in Jinan, he would be able to return home only twice a year. In his first year of university preparatory studies, his mother and sister had already been severely ill, requiring him to take several days off from school to take care of them, and he was concerned that his mother could not survive his departure to study so far away.[131] The summer of 1919 was difficult for Wang as he considered what to do.

By the fall of 1919, Wang heard that Yenching University had officially selected its name. This would be the university that he would naturally enter for undergraduate studies if he were to complete his two-year university preparatory program. However, to do so, now he would have to move to Jinan for at least one year to complete the preparatory program, which he felt he could not do without compromising his mother's health. He came up with an idea that would allow him to remain in Beijing to care for his mother and also provide a way for him to continue his academic career. He decided to request skipping his second year of the university preparatory course and write the examination to qualify him to directly enter the undergraduate program at Yenching University. He wrote the university president to seek permission to write the qualifying examination but received no response. At that time, the president of the university, since February 1919, had been the American missionary John Leighton Stuart.[132] Wang felt rejected and showing little awareness of the audacity of his request, did not expect that such an earnest student as himself would be rejected in this way by an American missionary who was in China to serve the Chinese church.[133] What Wang did not know was that from the time Yenching University began classes in the fall of 1918, the university president Leighton Stuart struggled under a very limited budget.[134] In such a strained environment, Wang's request to allow an unqualified candidate such as himself, who would have to rely on scholarship funds, to skip a year and enter the already crowded university, was quickly dismissed, especially considering that his attendance in his first year of study was spotty due to having to care for his mother and sister.[135] Devastated by the lack of response from Yenching University and the resultant implication that his education was coming to an end, Wang felt that he had no alternative but to leave school.

Describing his mood when he was cut off from formal education, Wang referred to Qu Yuan's 屈原 (339–278 BCE) poem "Encountering Sorrow,"[136] which describes the poet's despair after being unfairly removed from his position as a righteous minister in the king of Chu's court during the Warring States Period in China.[137] Wang makes this allusion to Qu Yuan in a diary entry on August 20, 1919, revealing that at nineteen years of age, Classical Chinese poetry such as the Chu Ci poems had already formed some of his ideas of what can aptly be described as the "spirit of righteousness" in the Chinese tradition.[138] In 1919, Wang, like Qu Yuan, felt very disappointed with the world and uncertain about his future. Two lines from the conclusion to "Encountering Sorrow" must have particularly resonated with how Wang felt at the time: "Enough! There are no true men in the state: no one to understand me. Why should I cleave to the city of my birth?"[139]

Not being fully aware of some of the factors that eliminated his chances for being allowed entry to Yenching University, Wang saw himself as a righteous student who was unfairly rejected by a powerful university president. Wang would later describe this experience as a battle against evil forces in the missionary school.[140] Now back at home on August 22, 1919, he woke and read Romans 14:8 and the next day, Isaiah 54:8 and 10, and those promises from the Christian scriptures comforted him: "But with everlasting kindness I will have compassion on you . . . my unfailing love will not be shaken." Wang found resonance with the rejection of the poet Qu Yuan and comfort provided by the Christian scriptures. Both the Chinese and Christian traditions provided him with intellectual and emotional resources to deal with what had been the most significant disappointment of his life thus far. He then left the role of the student behind, never to return, and also, for a time, the city of his birth. A new opportunity was about to open up for him, this time on the teaching side of the classroom.

It would be helpful to step back from Wang's story for a moment to analyze what had happened on May 4, 1919, to gain a broader perspective on Wang's life. After the death of Yuan Shikai in 1916, various warlords vied for power in several regions of China while Sun Yat-sen's nationalist KMT government, based in Guangzhou, tried to regain power from

Yuan's Beiyang government, which was based in Beijing. In the midst of this political chaos, some important intellectual movements were taking shape. The most important of them for Chinese Christians such as Wang Mingdao was the May Fourth Movement, which is named after the date of the protests of several thousand of Wang Mingdao's fellow Beijing students who gathered at Tiananmen on May 4, 1919. The reason for this student mass gathering was to protest the move during the Paris Peace Conference after the conclusion of World War I to allow Japan to retain the entitlements of Germany in Shandong Province. This complete lack of self-determination for Chinese in their own territory was the reason for the protests and the flashpoint of the May Fourth Movement. Beijing descended into chaos, which prompted Wang's early release for summer vacation in 1919.[141] Some intellectuals thought that the cause of China's inability to control its own territory was due to its traditional Confucian social structure and values. One of the leading intellectuals during the May Fourth Movement, Hu Shi 胡適, wrote in December 1919 that "it has been justly said that the greatest obstacle to progress in China is the deductive habit of mind; that is, the willingness to accept things on authority, to acquiesce in ideas and ideals without questioning whence they are derived and whether they are true or not. A quotation from the Classics is sufficient argument for a national policy, and a spurious saying of Confucius is good enough to justify the existence of any obsolete custom or institution. This habit is the most formidable enemy to innovation and progress."[142] At the time, some Christian leaders became early advocates of the movement,[143] not aware that the fury of Chinese nationalism that had been directed at foreign governments for the Paris Peace Conference and the Treaty of Versailles, which finalized Japan's control of Shandong in 1919, would be directed at Christianity only two years later.[144] It was in the midst of this tumultuous summer that Wang transitioned into adulthood and greater independence.

MARTYR'S FIELD PRESBYTERIAN SCHOOL

In his heart, Wang still harbored a dream to continue his studies, but with that door closed, he had to think about what he was going to do in the meantime. On August 26, 1919, he went to see his older friend who had earlier been a mentor to him at Tsui Wen Academy. His friend encouraged him to attend the Christian education conference that would be taking place in Tong County. There, Wang met another old friend who told him to consider taking a job at an elementary school in Baoding County 保定縣, Hebei Province, about 150 kilometers southwest of Beijing. Reluctantly, Wang decided to accept the job.[145] On September 11, 1919, after a tearful goodbye with his mother, Wang left home for Baoding. This was his first trip of any significant distance away from Beijing. He rode the train early in the morning, and when he arrived at Baoding, he was brought to his new school, Lie Shi Tian, or Martyr's Field Elementary School 烈士田小學, which was administered by the Presbyterian Church of Baoding County. The school was most likely named after the fifteen Protestant missionaries[146] or the thirty-five Presbyterians killed[147] in Baoding during the Boxer Uprising. Martyr's Field had been established as an elementary school in 1902 by the American missionary James Walter Lowrie 路崇德 (1856–1930)[148] under the American Presbyterian Mission. Lowrie had arrived in Beijing in 1883, moved to Baoding in 1894, and after surviving the Boxer Rebellion in Baoding, had gone on to found and oversee the school until 1910.[149] In 1917, with a student body of approximately one hundred students, the middle school was added.[150] In Lowrie's absence, when Wang arrived in 1919, there was a head teacher who administered the school, along with Wang and three other teachers. Wang notes that at the time, there was no principal, but an older American pastor was temporarily filling in.[151] After finding out that Wang had completed one year of university studies, the temporary principal decided to let another teacher instruct the primary level of the elementary school and gave Wang the job of teaching the senior elementary and first year of middle school students, which provided an increased salary. Wang was also to encourage the students in spiritual development. All of these factors led Wang to feel like he had made the right decision to move to Baoding.

Wang decided to model his teaching on the teaching pattern of H. L. Zia that he had learned about through a biography he had read on Zia.[152] After teaching the day's lesson, Wang would preach to the students, but he realized on later reflection that at the time, he had not understood salvation or the "Way of life." Nevertheless, he taught the students to revere God, love people, and to seek moral improvement. Wang's teaching moved several students, and after consulting with them, he decided to begin an evening prayer meeting on November 12. In addition to prayer, he preached on different topics but with what he later described as an unclear understanding of the truth of life. For example, he believed in the resurrection of Jesus, but at the time, he did not know whether Jesus's body had actually physically resurrected. Wang was not yet a Fundamentalist Christian.[153]

Due to the impact he was making on the student's lives, Wang began to see the importance of God's calling on his life to become a Christian preacher 傳道人.[154] He felt that as a politician, he would never be able to change people's hearts to renounce evil and turn to virtue, but witnessing the changes in his students after just a few months of his guidance, as a preacher he could. An important aspect of his calling became clear to him. During his elementary and middle school days, he had been connected to the LMS. In his university days, he had been within the sphere of the MEC. Now he was teaching at a school that was overseen by the Presbyterian Church. In light of this wide range of experiences, it became clear to Wang that the same immorality that was in Chinese society was also in the church. He saw darkness and corruption in all three of the churches he had been and currently was associated with. In a description of immorality that was as Confucian as it was Christian, Wang laid out the wickedness he observed within the church in China: lying and hypocrisy,[155] harming others for personal benefit,[156] using one's strength to bully the weak,[157] flattering the rich while disparaging the poor,[158] mutual deception,[159] and fighting and scheming against each other.[160] Wang became convinced that the church needed a reformation and that the mission to reform it had been given in part to him. This realization enabled him to gradually embrace his future vocation as a preacher. In the late spring of 1920, Wang had fully embraced this calling. By that summer, when he had completed his first academic year as a teacher, he decided to change his birth name, Yongsheng 永盛, to Mingdao 明道 because he was now willing to allow God to use his life "in the midst of a dark and evil world, to testify 證明 to the true Way 真道."[161]

To fulfill this calling, he still hoped to return to his formal academic studies. He planned to study in China for a four-year university degree, followed by a three-year theological degree, and then go to England to complete another three-year theological degree.[162] This plan was formed in Wang's mind through conversations he had had with his former principal at Tsui Wen Academy, Thomas Biggin 金修真.[163] Principal Biggin had told Wang that if the opportunity arose, he would raise money for Wang to go to England to pursue graduate studies. As the principal of Tsui Wen and a representative member of the LMS in the Educational Association of China, Biggin had the power and connections to make good on this plan.[164] After Wang abandoned his plan to become a famous politician, this became his alternative plan. By pursuing advanced education, he could follow God's call on his life by becoming a famous pastor or evangelist.

From the vantage point of hindsight in 1948, Wang set the scene for what happened next at Martyr's Field school by describing the experience that he had gone through as God tested him with strict discipline to encourage others who were experiencing the same kind of testing. He recalled the words of Psalm 66:11–12:

> You brought us into the net;
> you laid burdens on our backs;
> you let people ride over our heads;
> we went through fire and through water;

Wang said that what would eventually happen at the Martyr's Field Presbyterian school was a shameful and painful experience, like lying down on the street and someone running over your head. Wang said it was analogous to Han Xin's 韓信 pain and shame when he had been humiliated.[165] Han Xin (231–196 BCE) had been a military general who had served Liu Bang 劉邦, the first emperor of the Han dynasty, and Han Xin had become known as one of the heroes of that dynasty. However, Liu Bang had feared Han Xin's growing influence and had heard rumors that Liu Bang was planning a rebellion. Liu Bang's wife, Empress Lü 呂后, had Han Xin arrested, tortured, and killed and his entire clan exterminated.[166] Although present-day readers may consider this an exaggerated comparison, once again, it was both Christian and Chinese sources that came to mind when Wang processed a very significant memory. What was it that had made Wang feel such pain and shame?

MOVING TOWARD INDEPENDENCE

On September 8, 1920, Wang returned to Baoding to begin his second year of teaching at the school. Despite the previous academic year's accomplishments, this time he struggled with the work. There were several factors in this: his deteriorating eyesight, concern over his mother and sister's spiritual life, a lack of passion for his work as a teacher, concern about darkness and corruption in the church, and his own feelings of personal spiritual poverty. These all combined to create a pessimistic mood in Wang during the start of the academic year. On November 20, after founding a YMCA group at the school the previous semester, he chaired the school's first YMCA conference. Although he was following in the footsteps of H. L. Zia's YMCA work among young people, he went home that night utterly exhausted.[167]

The next evening on November 21, he had a conversation with a new teacher at the school named Zhang Zian 張子安.[168] This new colleague talked to Wang about sin. Wang became furious at the idea that there was still sin in his life since he had already repented previously and felt he did not need to do so again. His colleague responded that there remains even in Christians hidden sin, especially pride, and that earnest Christians often work hard not to glorify God but themselves. Feeling cut to the heart, Wang saw that his colleague had diagnosed the source and symptoms of his spiritual disease: pride was fueling his desire to work hard to glorify himself. At around ten o'clock that evening, he left his colleague's dormitory residence and went back to his own to pray. He knew that although his outward behavior was blameless and that he considered himself "God's favored one,"[169] he confessed to a number of hidden sins that only he was aware of including hypocrisy, jealousy, and pride.[170] He felt like the Old Testament prophet Isaiah, utterly naked and with no place to hide, standing before a holy God who knows the interior world of a man.[171] This mystical experience of being in the presence of God convinced him that it was only due to the washing away of his sins through Jesus Christ's blood that he was able to stand before a holy God.

This was not a conversion since he had already put his faith in God at fourteen, but it was a deeper mystical encounter that Wang had never experienced before and it awakened him to the spiritual reality that some of the things he had seen as good before were disgusting in the eyes of God.[172] Looking back, this mystical encounter was preparing him to be able to endure the upcoming loss of his dream to continue his studies and become a famous preacher.

His mystical experience also helped him to begin to break with the power of missionary Christianity. Wang's relationship with missionary Christianity in China is complex. As detailed above, he was schooled in LMS and MEC missionary schools and worked as a teacher at the Martyr's Field Presbyterian school. He did not blame foreigners and missionaries for the ills of Chinese society as others would do just a few months later. Even when he was in prison in 1966, he would maintain this position and defend missionary activity in China against what he felt was slander.[173] Moreover, he had positive relationships with several foreign missionaries over the years.[174] Nevertheless, Wang would eventually see the need to sever all formal ties with missionary Christianity and would criticize foreign missionaries when he felt that they did not live up to proper Christian morality. An example from December 1920 illustrates this. Early that month, rumors were circulating in Baoding that some soldiers had mutinied and were in the area plundering goods and that one of their targets was the Presbyterian mission compound on which his school was located.[175] In a panic, several missionaries found firearms and began training some older male students on how to use a gun in case of attack. Wang, "moved by the Holy Spirit," rebuked the missionaries by quoting Jesus's statement that "he who lives by the sword, dies by the sword,"[176] stating that Christians should not kill people. The missionaries did not change their course of action but could not refute Wang's biblical argument.[177] As noted by Thomas Harvey, Wang's pacifist Christian conviction was not in step with American missionary Christianity at the time.[178] The Chinese cultural background of the May Fourth Movement with its anti-foreignism provided Wang with the ability to imagine a church separate from missionary Christianity, while Wang's mystical experience of the holiness of God provided the religious context to imagine a separate community set apart from the immorality he observed in the missionary churches.

The breaking point with missionary Christianity occurred when Wang became convinced that he needed to be rebaptized, this time by immersion. Wang developed a closer relationship with the colleague who had convicted him of inward sin and pride, Zhang Zian, often stopping by his dormitory room to talk. To Wang's surprise, this man had also been baptized by sprinkling in the Presbyterian Church and later became convinced that baptism by immersion was the biblical pattern, and so he was rebaptized. In Wang's long experience in the LMS, MEC, and Presbyterian churches, he had only ever observed baptisms by sprinkling, never by immersion. He immediately went back to his dormitory room and was amazed to discover that he had never noticed that indeed, baptism by immersion in water was the pattern that Jesus and his disciples followed in the New Testament. This biblical argument, combined with the fact that when he was baptized by sprinkling in the LMS church on Easter Sunday 1914, he did not understand the questions being asked of him, after several days of prayer and study, convinced Wang that he needed to be rebaptized, this time by immersion.[179] Due to his views on baptism, Wang's teaching colleague Zhang Zian was expelled from the Martyr's Field Presbyterian school on December 20, 1920, and left Baoding for Beijing. Wang brought him to the train station and greatly admired his willingness to endure this expulsion to keep to his moral principles and biblical convictions. Inspired by his colleague's example, Wang asked him to introduce someone who would be willing to baptize him by immersion. On December 29, Zhang Zian introduced Wang to Zhu Dingchen 朱鼎臣, a former coal dealer who became a preacher in a small Apostolic Faith Mission Church in Beijing.[180] On January 2, 1921, Wang Mingdao told the head teacher, a Mr. Wang, who administrated the school, that he along with several of the students intended to be baptized by immersion. Later that evening, Mr. Wang along with the American interim principal came to Wang Mingdao's dormitory room and told him that they would hate to see him leave, but if he intended to be baptized by immersion, he would be immediately expelled from the school along with any students who joined him. So Wang took a couple of days to think the matter over carefully. Wang concluded that he was like "an ant on a burning hot pan."[181] Both options before him were unappealing. Obeying his conviction to be rebaptized would cause damage to his reputation, the loss of his job and income, and the end of his dream to continue studies. Furthermore, Tsui Wen Academy's principal, Thomas Biggin, had promised Wang financial scholarships to allow him to pursue his university education and theological studies in China and possibly to do graduate theological studies in England. By choosing to be rebaptized, Wang thought that it would be seen as an attack on LMS doctrine by delegitimizing his baptism in the LMS church. Wang would thus be viewed by Biggin as a "traitor," and Biggin would no longer provide scholarship money. Wang calculated that without the scholarship, his family's financial situation was so meager that it would not be enough to provide even one year of university tuition much less the ten years required for him to complete his plan to pursue three degrees.[182] However, not to be rebaptized would violate his moral conviction. As he had done at Tsui Wen Middle School when he criticized the directing teacher according to his internal principle, Wang decided that it would be better to lose everything than to compromise his righteousness. He thought about the possibility of waiting until he returned from England to be rebaptized. On this issue, he concluded that "to obey is better than sacrifice,"[183] and if he did not obey what he thought was the commandment of God, he was not worthy to study theology.[184] This became another internal principle for Wang, that a rebel to God's commandments cannot be a legitimate theologian or a genuine servant of God.

REBAPTISM AND THE BREAK WITH MISSIONARY CHRISTIANITY

On the afternoon of January 4, 1921, the American interim principal came to see Wang for his decision. Wang told him that he planned to get rebaptized, and the principal gave him train fare to leave immediately. Wang said he could not leave right away due to last-minute preparations but promised to leave the next day. That evening, several students came to visit Wang, and he preached to the students the words of Jesus: "Whoever would save his life will lose it, and whoever loses his life for my sake will find it."[185] The next morning, the principal announced Wang's decision and that any students who wanted to follow him in baptism by immersion should leave the school. Five students announced their decision to leave the school and four of them indicated the desire to be baptized by immersion. Wang did not blame the Presbyterian church leaders for expelling him from his teaching role, as this was consistent with their church doctrine. Another factor that motivated the principal to expel Wang and these five students was the fact that Zhu Dingchen, the man who was to baptize Wang, was a preacher from the Apostolic Faith Mission 信心會.[186] This was a group of loosely affiliated preachers that emphasized the gifts of the Holy Spirit and had previously caused a significant uproar among Presbyterian churches in Baoding County, which resulted in a loss of members due to several Presbyterians leaving their churches after becoming convinced of the correctness of Pentecostal theology. Naturally, the principal of Martyr's Field school was wary of the influence of the Apostolic Faith Mission in the school.[187] Although in the future, Wang would occasionally speak at missionary conferences, he would no longer have any official affiliation with missionary Christianity. When he left Martyr's Field Presbyterian school the next afternoon, he was embarking on the path to independent Chinese Christian ministry. The May Fourth context provided the possibility of imagining a world in which foreigners were not the decision-makers for Chinese, while Wang's religious vision of a holy God who demanded obedience from his followers provided the religious vision to motivate the break.

On January 5, at 2:20 p.m., Wang and the five students left the school and stayed the night at a nearby inn. Wang began to fear that he had made the wrong decision. The next day at 1:00 p.m., Zhu Dingchen met with Wang and the five students at Baoding's East Gate to find water to baptize them in. Due to the low temperatures, the river was covered in a thick layer of ice and the only spot they could find that had access to the water was under a bridge where the water gate had not frozen because of the water movement. Zhu Dingchen baptized Wang, and when he came out of the water, his long hair turned into an icicle, and he discovered when he went to take off his inner garment that it had become as hard as a board of wood.[188] The fifth student who left the school but originally did not want to be baptized decided, after seeing the resolution of Wang and the other students, to also be baptized. This student's name was Shi Tianmin 石天民. Shi was one of the students who had developed a close teacher-student relationship with Wang at the school and would go on to become Wang's most trusted coworker at the Christian

Tabernacle.[189] Shi, after he was expelled from the school, eventually became an English teacher while assisting Wang in ministry at the Christian Tabernacle[190] until he was arrested as part of the Wang Mingdao counterrevolutionary clique in 1955.[191]

After the baptisms on January 6, 1921, the newly baptized returned to the inn where they were staying, and Zhu Dingchen led them to "seek the Holy Spirit." Wang stated that Zhu, as a preacher in the Apostolic Faith Mission, was part of the Pentecostal movement 五旬節派.[192] In Wang's opinion, the seeking of the Holy Spirit was the most important teaching of the movement and speaking in "spiritual tongues" was the one and only evidence that a person had received the Holy Spirit. He also indicated that in the early part of the twentieth century, the movement had developed several church groups in China, which by 1948 had mostly become part of the Assemblies of God 神召會.[193] Wang described Zhu as an honest and devout Christian who was thoroughly familiar with the Bible but not very clear on its truths in their entirety and extremely lacking in common sense. For the next three days, Zhu returned to the inn and attempted to lead the group again and again in prayer to seek the Holy Spirit. Wang finally uttered a few sounds on January 9, which Zhu concluded were "spiritual tongues," the evidence that Wang had received the Holy Spirit. At the time, Wang accepted Zhu's conclusion, but in Wang's more mature reflection on the event in 1948, it was his earlier mystical experience on November 21, 1920, where a real spiritual change happened. In Wang's thinking, when he had thoroughly confessed his sin, given up every reservation, completely submitted, and willingly complied to God's commandments, it was then that the Holy Spirit filled him. Wang later concluded that Zhu had been duped by an incorrect teaching on the Holy Spirit.[194] Why did Wang not embrace the Pentecostal movement like other independent Chinese Christian leaders of the time did? For example, another Beijing resident who had been associated with the LMS was Paul Wei (Enbo) 魏保羅 (1876–1919) who embraced Pentecostal practices in 1916 and resultantly founded the independent True Jesus Church 真耶穌教會.[195] Also, Jing Dianying 敬奠瀛 (1890–1957), who, like Wang, had received a traditional education and was associated with the MEC, would also break with missionary Christianity in 1924, but he embraced Pentecostal practices such as speaking in "spiritual tongues" in the independent Jesus Family 耶穌家庭 he had founded.[196] One factor that cooled Wang on Pentecostalism was that after his few days at the inn with the five students and Zhu Dingchen, Wang would return to his home in Beijing and no longer be in the Pentecostal "sectarian furnace" that inspired others to follow the movement's teachings, as will be described below.[197] Another significant factor is that he simply had no taste for the movement. His personality inclined Wang toward a more contemplative interaction with the divine, not ecstatic. Even in his mystical encounter with God on November 21, 1920, Wang uttered no sounds or cried any tears.[198] In China during the early twentieth century, "superstitious" groups, as the adherents to Pentecostalism would surely be considered to be, were despised by the educated, particularly the Confucian literati.[199] Wang Mingdao, with his bent toward learning and his Confucian Christian sensibilities, found no intellectual or emotional satisfaction in the Pentecostal movement. Wang said that during his experience uttering the sounds that Zhu concluded were proof he had received the Holy Spirit, he "felt nothing."[200] He was neither convinced by the movement's theological arguments nor satisfied by its spiritual ecstasies. However, Zhu Dingchen did think that Wang and the five students had received the Holy Spirit, and they went back to the inn believing they were "highly successful" in their departure from school for more spiritual endeavors. On January 10, after five days of intense spiritual pursuits under the direction of Zhu, they finally said goodbye, each taking the train to return to their respective homes on a freezing cold Baoding morning.

FUNDAMENTALIST FORMATION

Completely oblivious to the fact that his mother and sister would be upset with him for leaving gainful employment and leaving with his reputation marred in Baoding, Wang expected his family to congratulate him on his spiritual victory. Nothing could have been further from reality. Upon his return, his mother berated him for throwing everything away to be baptized, and his sister was stunned with despair. Some of the people in his local church thought he had developed a mental disorder while others thought he had been misled by false teaching. His family's reaction was most likely exacerbated by the fact that North China was going through a famine from 1920 to 1921 with twenty million people in the region without food by the summer of 1921.[201] It was through this experience that Wang began to develop his idea about who was a genuine Christian and who was not. His conclusion in 1948 was that those who were willing to sacrifice, even to the point of sacrificing everything for their beliefs, were genuine believers, while those who were not were not true believers.[202] His mother wanted Wang to go back to his former principal, Thomas Biggin, and say that he was wrong in order to secure scholarship money for his university education. However, Wang felt he could not do this, as it would violate his moral principles. This conflict with his mother was especially difficult because despite their differences, he felt she was a caring mother and he tried to be a filial son to her.[203] In this relationship, another aspect of Wang's Confucian Christianity can be clearly seen. Wang says that it was only after he converted to Christianity at age fourteen that he began to strive to show filial piety toward his mother. According to Wang, it was his spiritual connection to Christ that empowered him to fulfill the moral requirements of Confucius to be filial to his mother. Wang sought to fulfill his role as a filial son except when he felt that her will conflicted with his devotion to God.[204] On January 18, he dreamed that his mother banished him from their home. This imagined rejection resulted in Wang being startled awake, and even after he realized it was a dream, he found himself uncontrollably sobbing at the horror of the dream.[205] As detailed earlier, Wang's father abandoned him through suicide before he was born, and his mother's love, having tenderly cared for him several times when he was ill, was a source of deep emotion for Wang. His significant emotional connection to his mother and his desire to show filial piety toward her is an important part of Wang's Chinese Christian story.

It was during this period of deep emotional pain and humiliation that he became convinced of several Christian doctrines such as the second coming of Christ and the resurrection of the dead, which overcame, for a time, his fear of death. From Wang's 1948 perspective, what happened during the suffering he experienced in 1921 was well described by one of his favorite authors, G. H. Knight: "Just as a letter in 'sympathetic' [invisible] ink is illegible till exposed to the heat of the fire, many of God's wonderful messages are never understood till the fire of suffering brings out the message clearly to the eye of faith."[206] It was not the fire of the Holy Spirit but the fire of sufferings in 1921 that made God's invisible "truths of life" real to Wang. The sufferings of this period and the lessons he learned also convinced Wang that he did not need to study theology in a formal academic setting, but rather, what he needed to do the work of God was to spend an extended period in individual Bible study. It was this realization, possibly influenced by Knight's works,[207] that finally convinced him to give up his plan to pursue a university and theological education. This was a conviction that not only Chinese Fundamentalist Christians like Wang Mingdao concluded but is part of the global Christian Fundamentalist tradition that views formal theological education as unnecessary and institutions that do not share similar theological convictions as dangerous.[208] His decision to primarily pursue private study of the Bible allowed him to protect what he saw as fundamental Christian doctrines and ministry decisions from attack, but his individual study was also the source of some of his theological limitations as a thinker who was largely independent in his theological decisions, as will be revealed later in this book.

Wang had an older cousin who found out about his decision to leave his teaching job and to no longer pursue future education and thought this was a sign of a mental disorder.[209] He invited Wang to spend some time with him and his wife in Dayou Village 大有莊 near the Summer Palace northwest of Beijing. Wang accepted his cousin's invitation and found the beautiful mountains, crystal-clear rivers, and evergreen forests of the area to be the ideal spot to actualize his plan to spend time in intense Bible study. On March 16, 1921, he left home and spent his days in Bible study and theological reflection in the idyllic outdoor environment within the shadow of the Summer Palace.[210] He returned home on June 21 and described his time in Dayou Village as his short-term Bible school education.[211]

INDEPENDENT PREACHING

During his time in Dayou Village, Wang Mingdao received a letter from his old friend from Tsui Wen Middle School Chen Zigao expressing his concern about what he had heard about Wang. On June 27, Wang left Beijing to visit Chen in Cang County 滄縣, Hebei Province and dispel the rumors about his mental state. Upon arriving the next day, Chen confided to Wang that he did not believe that he had a mental disorder but rather that Wang had received a special blessing from God. He invited Wang to preach on July 3 at Chen's church in Cang County, which Wang agreed to do. The topic of this first sermon that Wang ever preached in a church was "Repent, For the Kingdom of Heaven Is Near," and on July 5, he returned home.[212] His trip to Cang County was significant. Not only did Wang receive comfort and encouragement from his old friend, but his experience preaching for the first time completely convinced him that he was called to this work.[213] From one perspective, this confirmation of Wang's calling to a Christian religious profession could not have come at a worse time. As Daniel Bays has chronicled, by 1921, China's intellectuals began to see Christianity as an enemy. Christians were not only "superstitious," believing in strange doctrines such as a man rising from the dead and being born of a virgin, but they were also politically dangerous since they were connected to the foreign missionary movement. Bays describes why this was a problem:

> It came to be an article of faith that China's weakness and pitiful condition were not due solely to foreigners' bad intentions or wicked actions, but to a deeply rooted system of socioeconomic relationships that operated worldwide (capitalism), and involved colonial empires which were exploited and kept servile by those countries with more advanced economic and social class systems (imperialism). . . . The alleged true nature of the missionary movement . . . was a case of "cultural imperialism" or "cultural aggression" with foreign missionaries working hand in hand with foreign governments and corporations, to make the Chinese docile and compliant, accepting semi-colonial status.[214]

Seen from this perspective, 1921 was not the ideal time to become a Christian preacher in China. From another perspective, the confirmation of his calling came at the perfect time. Chinese Christians, unwilling to go so far as to abandon religion altogether as some May Fourth proponents would advocate, at least argued that the time had come for the church in China to cast off its foreign cloak and become truly Chinese.[215] In 1921, Wang Mingdao was in the vanguard of that indigenization. After being rejected by Yenching University and Martyr's Field Presbyterian school, new pathways opened up for him as he embraced his calling and imagined new possibilities in the context of the May Fourth Movement. Not only was he thoroughly schooled in the Christian tradition, but he was also thoroughly schooled in the Chinese Confucian tradition. Both were attacked by the May Fourth Movement's proponents, but an opportunity emerged in this environment for independent Chinese Christians with contextualized knowledge of Christian theology, Chinese history, and such ways of thinking as Wang possessed to begin to work independently of missionary Christianity.

Upon mature reflection in 1982, Wang thought that the attack on Christians and Confucius in the 1920s had been linked as an attack against theism and connected an anti-theist strain in China all the way back to Emperor Qin Shihuang.[216] However, despite all opposition at the time, Wang's Confucian Christian preaching would find a following in the early 1920s as he embraced his calling and began an *independent* ministry.

CHAPTER THREE

The Independent Years

1921–1937

With Sun Yat-sen's KMT based in Guangzhou fighting for control over China and with the Beiyang government based in Beijing, different warlords who were either independent or aligned in varying degrees of loyalty on each side continued to battle for control of North China. The social chaos that these battles caused intensified the debate on how China could become a strong nation. An increasing resentment forming in China toward Western nations due to the theory that these nations were guilty of cultural imperialism in the country also contributed to the tension. This idea of cultural imperialism had been steadily gaining adherence among students and intellectuals. In this context, three events took place during 1921 and 1922 that would increase antagonism against Christians in China. The first was the outrage and protest over the English title for the survey of Protestant activity in China—*The Christian Occupation of China*—conducted from 1918 to 1921 and published in 1922, in anticipation for the National Christian Conference in 1922. The second was the anger of students and intellectuals in early 1922 over the report by the Burton Commission on *Christian Education in China*, which sought to expand Christian higher education in China. The third was the news that Tsinghwa University 清華大學 in Beijing was set to host the World Student Christian Federation in April 1922. Although the protests were small in scale, they were signs of much larger anti-Christian and anti-missionary feelings that were brewing in China and smoldering signs of the explosion that was to come in just a few years.[1] Wang's move toward an independent Chinese Christian ministry was formed within this national context.

CHINESE AND FOREIGN CONTACTS

Shortly after his initial preaching experience on August 25, 1921, Wang met with Cheng Ching-yi (Cheng Jingyi) 誠靜怡[2] (1881–1939) at Cheng's home in Beijing. Cheng was a major figure in Chinese Christianity and a pivotal player in the indigenization of Christianity in China.[3] He was ordained through the LMS around 1908 and was an assistant pastor at the LMS church on Rice Market Street 米市街[4] but later went on to establish the Mishi Hutong Church 米市胡同教會, an independent church in East City of Beijing, making him a model for Chinese Christians who, like Wang Mingdao, were moving toward independence from missionary Christianity.[5] Cheng famously commented as one of the few Chinese who attended the 1910 World Missionary Conference in Edinburgh that Chinese Christians desired a united Christian church with no denominational divisions that was not controlled by foreign missionaries but by the Chinese themselves.[6] Cheng was also one of the key leaders who was organizing the National Christian Conference in 1922. Cheng was familiar enough with Wang to later report to the parents of Wang's future wife, Liu Jingwen, when they requested information on Wang that "everything is good, except he is a little stubborn."[7] On August 25, the two men discussed several topics for over five hours with the younger Wang being more interested in talking about salvation and the commandments of God while the elder Cheng was more interested in discussing the corruption of the world and seeking the public's benefit. However, during this meeting, Cheng encouraged Wang on the path toward independence from missionary Christianity and left Wang with much to think about.[8]

On September 19, Wang received an invitation from Chen Zigao to return to Cang County since he had moved so many people with his preaching last July. After a period of prayer and contemplation, Wang accepted the invitation, and on September 30, he left for Cang County. He ended up extending his preaching trip into Yanshan County 鹽山縣 and Xian County 獻縣 for over three months. Wang's itinerant preaching ministry had begun. At the end of January, he got into conflict with

Western missionaries over theological beliefs. He reveals in his diary entry of January 17, 1922, that the conflict was over him baptizing people during his preaching trip in Hebei Province.[9] The conflict prompted him to leave Cang County on January 26, 1922, to return home. After the exhilaration of preaching and baptizing in Hebei, he hoped to find work that would utilize his talents, but instead, he entered a difficult period of waiting, as he was unable to find anything suitable and lived at home with his mother and older sister.

Despite working hard to help with housework, Wang felt like a burden on his mother and sister. His mother wanted him to find a career and felt that he was wasting his talents at home. Wang felt deeply distressed until he read in the book of Exodus that Moses was a lowly shepherd for forty years. He realized through Moses's story that it was through suffering and humbling that some of life's precious lessons are learned.[10] After reading Moses's story, Wang determined to do housework to the best of his ability. Whether it be sweeping, cleaning, cooking, sewing, or washing, he would do it with a Confucian "perfection."[11] His conclusion, informed by both Moses's story and a Confucian work ethic, was that if he were to do the trivial work of housework poorly, he would also do the important work of preaching poorly.[12] From February 1922 to July 1923, Wang spent the majority of his time at home studying the Bible and doing housework as hostility continued to grow against Christians in China.

During the spring and summer of 1922,[13] he began to occasionally attend Zhu Dingcheng's church in Beijing, which was named the Church of God 神的教會. The church did not have a building, but the twenty or so members met in the home of an older Norwegian who was working in China.[14] This Norwegian man would exhort the group to keep the commandments of God, indicating that it was through keeping the commandments, including keeping the Sabbath, that people could receive salvation. He advocated that after believing in Christ, one must seek holiness, leaving every form of sin behind, of which he listed eighty-three forms in detail from the New Testament, in order to receive salvation. Wang initially agreed with the teaching that one must be holy to receive salvation.[15] From his later perspective, however, he realized that in 1922, he had not yet understood the Christian doctrine of justification by faith 因信稱義. The person who explained it to Wang was living in the same housing unit as the older Norwegian, the Swedish missionary

Eric Pilquist 畢勝道 (1857–1925).[16] Pilquist was a Seventh Day Adventist missionary in China whom Wang describes as often preaching the doctrine of salvation by faith 因信得救[17] and who was completely opposed to his Norwegian neighbor's teaching on salvation.[18] Pilquist lived a very simple life, wearing old clothes and eating simple local food, with Wang often coming to his home to listen to his teaching. By the spring of 1923, Wang had become convinced that Pilquist's teaching on salvation was biblically sound.[19] Wang felt fortunate that at this time, he had not yet engaged in a significant preaching ministry as he would have taught one must be holy to receive salvation, but now he had embraced this central Protestant doctrine that faith comes before holiness. In June 1923, he began to translate some English booklets into Chinese for Pilquist, which he continued to do until May 1925; this translation work likely ended due to Pilquist falling ill and later dying in November 1925.[20] An important aspect to notice about Wang's relationship with Pilquist was that Wang was open to instruction from foreign missionaries whom he thought integrated their beliefs with their lives like Eric Pilquist. The factors that would persuade Wang and that he paid the most attention to were the character of the person and the biblical basis of the teaching. Convinced of Pilquist's good character and that the doctrine of salvation by faith was a biblical teaching, he could embrace this foreign missionary's theology, even in the midst of the May Fourth Movement.[21]

BIBLICIST THEOLOGICAL FORMATION

It was during this period largely at home that Wang spent significant time developing his own theology through independent Bible study. On August 6, 1922, Wang's published diary provides the first indication that he did not agree with the doctrine of the Trinity, describing it as an "error."[22] On October 8, we have the first indication that Wang did not agree with the Christian doctrine that Jesus is of the same substance as God, preferring the designation that Jesus is the Son of God.[23] He would later say that the teaching that Jesus is God is "absurd and reckless."[24] The basic principle he developed to guide his theology was that if a teaching was clearly written in the Bible, he would accept it; but if it was not, he would reject it.[25] Also based on this principle, he would eventually come to reject the teaching of keeping the Sabbath as not being for the Gentile churches. Similarly, he would also reject the Pentecostal teaching that tongues were the one true evidence of the infilling of the Holy Spirit. Wang emphasized the importance of personal Bible study, writing that he did not read commentaries on the Bible. He also rejected any church tradition or regulations that he could not find a legitimate basis for in the Bible. However, the final evidence he gives for rejecting the Pentecostal teaching on tongues being the evidence of the infilling of the Holy Spirit was character based. He referred to a young man he knew in 1921–22 who, whenever he would pray, would do so in an extraordinary tongue but who also treated his mother and wife abusively. This young man was so fierce with them that people who observed him would "boil with anger"; at the same time, Wang knew of several Christians who never prayed in spiritual tongues but who lived devout lives.[26] As can be seen, although Wang prioritized the Bible in the formation of his theology, his experience of the moral character of those who held theological positions was also very important in his analysis.

Finally, on July 31, 1923, he left Beijing to accept an invitation from a former student to preach for eight days of special meetings at a church in Zanhuang County 贊皇縣, Hebei Province. During this trip, from Wang's diary entries, he again reveals his disagreement with the doctrine of the Trinity (August 10)[27] and the divinity of Christ (August 11).[28] Later on, these theological positions would have repercussions that would hamper his ability to work with other Chinese Christians. He left on August 14 to visit his former student Shi Tianmin in Tang County 唐縣, Hebei Province but ended up getting sick when he arrived on August 19, returning home on August 25 when the sickness did not improve. He remained at home doing housework and studying the Bible for the remainder of 1923.[29]

CONNECTING WITH OTHER CHINESE CHRISTIAN LEADERS

Feeling quite isolated in his enthusiasm to serve God with his whole devotion, Wang was very encouraged that year to read what seemed like religious opinions that were similar to his own in a journal he was introduced to, *Spiritual Light Magazine* 靈光報.[30] The journal's editor was the Nanjing-based Jia Yuming 賈玉銘 (1880–1964), a Fundamentalist Presbyterian theologian who had been the vice principal of the North China Theological Seminary.[31] Jia had also been deeply influenced by his Confucian education and sought to reconcile his Confucian background with his Christian religion.[32] In 1924, Wang also began to read *Present Witness and Testimony* 復興報 (*Revival Magazine*)[33] and wrote letters to its chief writer and editor, Ni Tuosheng 倪柝聲, also known as Watchman Nee (1903–72), a very significant figure in Chinese Christianity. Nee began to lead small meetings of Christians in 1922 that would eventually develop into the independent Little Flock 小群, which later, when under the leadership of Witness Lee (Li Changshou) 李常受, became known as the Local Church 召會. Impressed with what he read in Nee's magazine, Wang began writing to him on March 2, 1924.[34]

A couple of days later, on March 4, Wang was invited to preach along with thirty other Chinese and missionary speakers at a six-day camp meeting that was being put on for Feng Yuxiang's 馮玉祥 (1882–1948) troops who were stationed in Nanyuan 南苑, south of Beijing.[35] Feng was known as the "Christian General,"[36] a warlord who was aligned at the time with the Beiyang government in Beijing but who would turn to the KMT side in just a few months during the Beijing coup on October 23, 1924.[37] Feng actively promoted the conversion of his soldiers to Christianity, which was the reason Wang and the other speakers were invited to preach.[38] However, Wang was deeply grieved by what he saw at the camp meeting.[39] Not only did he feel that most of the preachers were not deserving of being called servants of Christ, but he also thought that of the more than three thousand soldiers who were signed up to be baptized, a scant few had repented and had actual faith in Christ.[40] On March 11, the scheduled day for the large-scale baptism, Wang left early in disgust so he would not have to see the event.[41] This camp in Nanyuan further convinced Wang that the church in China was morally and spiritually impoverished.

That summer, Wang left Beijing again to do itinerant preaching in various locations. On July 6, he met for the first time Jia Yuming, the editor of *Spiritual Light Magazine* that Wang respected, and the two mutually encouraged each other.[42] The most significant thing that happened during the trip was in early September in De County 德縣 where he was invited to preach in a united Congregationalist and LMS church. There, he heard a preacher whom Wang thought was an "unbeliever" twisting the Bible's teachings and thus in Wang's opinion, causing injury to the faith of the people in the congregation. After a period of intense personal prayer, Wang entered the pulpit in the same church and corrected the "unbelieving" preacher's errors one by one. This caused such an uproar that people verbally attacked him.[43] Wang had privately disagreed with Modernist teachings at least as early as 1922. On January 22, 1922, his diary entry indicated his reflection on a preacher's statements that social reform was a stage along the way to the establishment of the kingdom of heaven, and that Jesus was a social revolutionary, were nonsense.[44] However, it was Wang's refutation of the preacher in De County that was the first time he confronted what he described as "evil forces" within the church publicly and thus marked Wang's public identification as a Fundamentalist Christian. As Kevin Xiyi Yao has pointed out, the key distinguishing mark of a Fundamentalist Christian in China during the 1920s was not doctrinal beliefs, as important as those were, but rather, willingness to publicly battle Modernist teachings.[45]

HOUSE CHURCH BEGINNINGS

When he returned home later in September, a family moved out from his mother's housing unit, which opened up two rooms. Wang had been meeting with an older man in his small room to study the Bible and later a younger person joined the group, but when the rooms in his mother's housing unit became available, he asked his mother if he could begin to use the larger rooms for meetings, to which she agreed. Therefore, on October 4, 1924, he moved into the two rooms, and on October 18, he began a house church meeting with three people. His role as a future spiritual leader of the house church movement began in his home more than three decades before his arrest. Later in December 1924, he started a Wednesday Bible study group.[46] On October 9, Wang received Watchman Nee's *Present Witness and Testimony* magazine and was very impressed with what he read but also ashamed because he felt he was wasting his own time.[47] The prolific writing of Nee, who was three years younger than Wang, no doubt motivated Wang to begin his own writing. So in 1924, Wang also began writing works to publish them for a reading audience. He published four small booklets, *One Very Important Thing*一件極重要的事, *The Voice of Evil in the World* 惡世中的呼聲, *Christians and Idols* 基督徒與偶像, and *The Cross of Christ* 基督的十字架, which he gave away as gifts.[48] With his itinerant preaching ministry having been underway for three years and the beginning of his house church and publishing ministry in 1924, the three major aspects of his work for the next three decades were established. Wang's Christian ministry trajectory was set as the popular opinion in China continued to move in an anti-Christian direction. However, being familiar with Chinese Christian leaders such as Cheng Ching-yi, Jia Yuming, and Watchman Nee, who were pursuing ministry tracks largely independent of foreign missionaries, Wang had growing confidence that a Chinese Christian could thrive in China at the time.

In January 1925, Wang was leading two meetings at his house church, a Bible study on Wednesday and a worship service on Saturday with between two and ten participants. On February 10, a major breakthrough took place in terms of Wang's public ministry. He was invited to preach at a monthly women's meeting in Beijing. An older woman named Zheng Suying 鄭素英, or as Wang addressed her, Mrs. Pan 潘老太太, told Wang that she was moved by his preaching and that she had known his father, Wang Zihou, but had lost contact with his family after the elder Wang's suicide. At this time, Wang believed that many leaders in the churches in Beijing thought that he was mentally unstable due to what happened at Martyr's Field Presbyterian school. Only Mrs. Pan could see the potential in Wang that others failed to see, and Wang was deeply encouraged by Mrs. Pan's confirmation of his calling. Mrs. Pan was well respected among the Christian churches in Beijing and she proceeded to recommend him as a preacher to her large network of connections. From this point on, the attendance at his house church meetings steadily increased. By the beginning of March, twenty new people were attending the meetings. The space he was using at his mother's housing unit had become too cramped, so beginning on March 6, Mrs. Pan invited him to use her home to conduct meetings on Fridays. Then, in April, another older woman who was attending the meetings invited Wang to begin to use her large home to conduct meetings every other Sunday afternoon beginning on April 5 with over seventy people attending. Between the various meetings, Wang was preaching every day, and so on April 24, some people gave Wang a bicycle to save him time in traveling from place to place. By the time he planned a trip to Nanjing for late May, on May 21–22 there were special meetings arranged at Mrs. Pan's home with over a hundred people attending. On May 27, he left for Nanjing.[49] Wang was developing his reputation as a sought-after preacher right at the time that the country was about to see the largest anti-Christian protests since the Boxer Uprising.

THEOLOGICAL CONFLICT AND THE MAY THIRTIETH MOVEMENT

The KMT and the Chinese Communist Party (CCP), who had been working together on a "united front," were using the language of a nationalist revolution to unify the country by getting rid of the regional warlords. Both parties were also utilizing the idea of cultural imperialism to mobilize the population against the Western presence in China, creating a dangerous situation for Christians in the country, especially foreign missionaries. On May 30, 1925, a series of protests against Westerners and warlords took place in several areas of the country and by early 1927 extended to every major city. Chinese Christians like Cheng Ching-yi and Jia Yuming, who were at one time connected to Western denominations, were accused of being the "running dogs" of Western imperialism.[50] As this national crisis was emerging for Christians in China while Wang Mingdao was in Nanjing, a personal crisis erupted for him as well.

On January 2, 1925, Wang had submitted an article titled "The Sound of Joy 大喜之音" for publication in *Spiritual Light Magazine*.[51] After a warm meeting with the editor, Jia Yuming, in July 1924, Wang wanted to go to Nanjing to spend more time with him, so he planned the trip for May 27, 1925. As the May 30 protests were erupting, Wang spent the time getting familiar with Jia and others connected with the magazine. During these conversations, Jia encouraged Wang to think about getting married.[52] Wang was also invited to preach, along with Jia Yuming and the famous evangelist Dora Yu (Yu Cidu) 余慈度 , at a conference for conservative Christian leaders[53] in which Jia was selected to be chairman and Wang secretary.[54] This was a significant recognition of Wang's talents as Jia was the first Chinese with a doctoral degree in theology, and Dora Yu was a well-known evangelist, with most of the other participants older than Wang.[55] However, according to Wang, at a meeting on June 2, while they were discussing the creedal statement of the group, Wang said he was misunderstood and verbally attacked by some of the other participants, with Dora Yu designating Wang a Modernist.[56] What caused this aggressive response to Wang's theology? The disputed issue was Wang's lack of acceptance of the Christian doctrine of the Trinity.[57] Wang thought that there was an inadequate foundation for the doctrine in the Bible. As mentioned above, Wang's position was that if the Bible did not clearly reveal a teaching, he did not feel it was a requirement for belief, a hermeneutical position categorized as biblicism.[58] The problem for Wang with the doctrine is likely that the phrase "Trinity 三一" or "Three persons of one substance 三位一體" does not appear in the Bible, so he believed that Jesus is the Son of God but not God.[59] After a long period of theological debate, on June 4, after Wang tried to talk with Jia Yuming, he was later given a letter from Jia in which he accused Wang of holding a theological position that Jesus was just a "paragon of virtue" or a "perfect person 完人," essentially categorizing him as a Modernist, and that Wang would not be invited to preach at their meetings again. Wang was shocked, hurt, and felt he had been misunderstood. He was also concerned that this would significantly affect his future ministry prospects.[60] He had turned away from missionary Christianity, did not agree with the theology of Modernist Chinese Christians,[61] and now was being shut out by conservative Chinese Christians whom he deeply respected. However, this situation again reveals Wang's internal principle that it would be better to lose everything than to compromise what he thought was right. His later reflection on what happened with Jia Yuming reveals that he was not willing to expound doctrine that was not clear to him from the Bible no matter what the consequences. Another important factor is that he still considered Jia Yuming and Dora Yu to be Christians despite the fact that he disagreed with them on doctrinal issues.[62]

A MEETING OF "GIANTS"

Ying Fuk Tsang thinks that this theological conflict caused Wang to feel uncertainty over his theology, which then led him to turn to Watchman

Nee for guidance. Despite the fact that Nee was three years younger than Wang, due to Nee's conservative theology and prolific writing, Wang looked to Nee as a mentor.[63] On June 5, Wang's diary reveals that he wrote to Nee in hopes of seeing him to discuss what had happened in Nanjing.[64] Since his childhood, Wang had heard stories and poems about the beauty of West Lake in Hangzhou 杭州, Zhejiang Province, so he decided to stay there for a few days on his way to see Nee, who was living in Fuzhou 福州, Fujian Province. While in Hangzhou, Wang toured the legendary West Lake, and through the introduction of another Christian, on June 22, he met his future mother-in-law, Zhang Meiyun 張美雲,[65] and his future father-in-law, Pastor Liu Delin 劉德林, who at the time was a Presbyterian pastor at Hangzhou Tianshuiqiao Church天水橋禮拜堂.[66] On June 26, Pastor Liu invited Wang to preach at his church, which Wang accepted and even stayed for several days in the couple's home. But at this time, Wang did not notice their daughter, Liu Jingwen 劉景文, who would later become his wife of sixty-three years. He planned to continue his journey to see Nee in Fuzhou but became sick along the way. Wang remembered the warm hospitality of his future in-laws and came back to recoup on July 17 and again stayed and preached at Pastor Liu's church for twelve days and left on August 6.[67]

In a fascinating period of Chinese church history, Wang met Nee on August 18, 1925,[68] and the two spent time over the next few days talking about several topics including the Trinity and eternal punishment.[69] On August 20, they went hiking together and in the evening went to a worship service with Nee preaching first and then Wang preaching in Mandarin with Nee translating for Wang into the Min dialect spoken in Fujian Province.[70] On August 21, Wang proofread a manuscript by Nee,[71] and the two set off for Shanghai on August 22 with several visits between the two men over the next few days, including August 26 when the two talked in detail about the Trinity and eternal punishment[72] before Wang left Shanghai on August 28. Wang had an extremely favorable impression of Nee at the time, and after Jia Yuming's rejection in Nanjing, Wang was encouraged by Nee's warmth and acceptance. As Ying Fuk Tsang has observed, Nee also encouraged Wang in his move toward independence from missionary Christianity.[73] In 1925, Wang thought that Nee was both biblical in his theology and devout in his behavior. During this time, Nee may have been able to explain to Wang his teaching on the doctrine of God in a way that did not contain the philosophical Trinitarian language that Jia Yuming and Dora Yu seem to have insisted on. Nee used the phrase "three one 三一" and not "three persons of one substance 三位一體" when describing God.[74] This clearer statement on God, combined with Nee's acceptance of Wang at a vulnerable time and his impression that Nee was a devout Christian, gave Wang great respect for Nee.[75] With both conditions of acceptable theology and devout behavior met, Wang could embrace Nee as a theological mentor despite Nee's younger age. After this first set of meetings with another future "giant" of the Chinese church, Wang traveled back north, preaching at many locations before finally returning to Beijing on September 14 after being away from home for over three months.[76]

A "HALF-OLD, HALF-NEW" COUPLE

In October, Wang resumed leading his house church services in Beijing in three locations for a brief period before returning south, including a trip to Hangzhou for several preaching engagements until the end of 1925. After being originally resistant to the idea of marriage, it was in November that he seriously began to think about finding a spouse.[77] Despite his falling out with Jia Yuming, their conversation in May about Wang being more effective as a married preacher resonated with him. He arrived in Hangzhou on October 31, and after staying with Pastor Liu Delin for the third time, he began to notice the pastor's daughter, Liu Jingwen. On November 5, when another pianist who was to play at a service where Wang was preaching canceled, Liu Jingwen filled in. In Wang's previous trips to her home, he thought of her as a child since she was almost nine years younger than him. However, on this evening, he realized that she was a young woman.[78]

Liu Jingwen was born on March 29, 1909, in Jiangyin County 江陰縣, Jiangsu Province, just as Wang was about to begin his elementary education at Tsui Wen Academy. Her father, Liu Delin (1862–1934), was a respected Presbyterian pastor in Jiangyin County, whose first wife had died, and he later pastored a Presbyterian church in Deqing County 德清縣 in Zhejiang Province. Around 1919, the family moved to Hangzhou for Liu Delin to pastor the church where he invited Wang Mingdao to preach in June 1925.[79] Liu Jingwen's mother, Zhang Meiyun (1880–1974), eighteen years younger than her husband, assisted him in church ministry and oversaw the family, rearing two children from her husband's previous marriage, along with their three sons and the baby, Liu Jingwen, in a happy Christian home.[80] Liu Jingwen studied with a few other students under a teacher who was sent from Hangzhou's Xiongdao School 杭州雄道學校 for her elementary education while the family was still in Deqing County. In 1919, when she was ten, the family moved to Hangzhou, and she attended Mary Vaughan High School 馮氏女校, a missionary school established by the Anglican Church's Church Missionary Society (CMS).[81] While at Mary Vaughan High School, Liu Jingwen studied English and piano and was deeply influenced by a missionary teacher from New Zealand, a Miss Wood, whose example of sacrificial care for her students continued to influence Liu into her senior years.[82] In 1923, she converted to Christianity at the age of fourteen while listening to her father preach.[83] When Wang Mingdao finally noticed Liu Jingwen on November 5, 1925, after staying at her family's home three times and seeing her over twenty times,[84] she was sixteen while Wang was twenty-five. Despite their age difference, which Wang originally thought was too great, the two had several important commonalities. Both had attended missionary schools, both were familiar with the life of a preacher, and both were committed Christians. When Wang was later asked about what kind of marriage he had, old style or new style, he replied, "half-old, half-new."[85] Shi Meiling expands on Wang Mingdao's statement that the couple's marriage was "half-old, half-new," that not only their marriage but "they were also half-old, half-new *people*. They accepted new ways of thinking including [aspects of] Western culture. However, Chinese Confucian culture was still very firmly their framework of thought. Thus, their behavior was basically according to the Bible's teachings, but the way they treated people and conducted themselves in society in many ways was according to a Confucian consciousness in dealing with issues."[86] This way of dealing with issues is evidenced in the way Wang courted Liu Jingwen and how she responded to his interest in her. On November 29, he first approached a third party, an older Christian woman named Aunt Li 李阿姨, who was familiar with Liu Delin and Zhang Meiyun, to broach the subject of his interest in marrying their daughter.[87] After talking with the parents, Aunt Li came back to Wang telling him that they did not promise agreement to the marriage nor did they refuse. They felt the best way forward was to carefully consider the possibility of marriage. When her mother asked Liu Jingwen about marrying Wang Mingdao, the young woman responded, "Whatever God wants, so be it."[88] Wang went back to Beijing, and for the next few months into April 1926, whenever he traveled south for preaching invitations, he would stop in Hangzhou for the couple to become more familiar with each other; however, they were never alone together until after they were married.[89] Wang's greatest concern was how his mother and older sister would react to him marrying a southerner. His mother wanted him to marry a woman from Beijing and, due to her experiences renting to southerners, felt that people from outside of the capital were inferior.[90] She also had a mindset that once her son was married, his affection for his mother and sister would be replaced by his affection for his wife.[91] On May 12, 1926, Wang talked to his mother and sister about marrying Liu Jingwen. He had decided previously that to show filial respect 孝敬 to his mother for all of her sacrifices for him, that if she objected to the marriage, then he would end his relationship with Liu Jingwen. To his delight, his mother and sister agreed to the marriage, and Wang saw their approval as a sign from God.[92] In July 1926, with his mind on marriage, Wang wrote his book titled *Jesus's New Bride* 基督的新娘.[93] He again went south on preaching appointments, and on November 24, he and Liu Jingwen were engaged.[94] Wang Mingdao's conduct in courting Liu Jingwen is another evidence of his Confucian Christian consciousness.

INDEPENDENT PUBLISHING AND THE NORTHERN EXPEDITION

Wang continued to visit Liu Jingwen when his preaching tours took him south and they wrote letters to each other. However, 1927 was an eventful year in another aspect of Wang's life as well. With Jia Yuming no longer accepting his articles for *Spiritual Light Magazine*[95] and motivated by Watchman Nee's prolific literary production, in the spring of 1927, Wang began publishing his own journal, *The Spiritual Food Quarterly* 靈食季刊. This journal, which he published quarterly until the summer issue of 1955 for a total of 114 volumes, would be the major literary production of Wang's life. The fact that Wang did not stop publishing during those nearly three decades provides historians with extraordinary insight into the content of indigenous Chinese Christianity during the Republic of China and early People's Republic of China periods.[96] On the first page of the first issue was printed the publisher's declaration, which included the purpose of the new journal: "Purpose: To declare God's voice to this evil generation, to alarm the rebellious masses and awaken the sleeping church; to testify to the essential points of the Bible, to lead the lost sheep, to strengthen believers' faith, to explain the way to victory and the essentials of becoming holy, to guide believers into completeness, and to prepare a clean new bride for Christ. To obtain spiritual food from the treasure house (the Bible) given to us by God and share it with everyone in God's house (the Church)."[97] Moreover, since the purpose was to communicate the main teachings of the Bible, news on current affairs and advertisements would not be included in the journal. The first issue contained a translation into Chinese of Martin Luther's prayer at the Diet of Worms, articles on the cross of Christ, the resurrected Christ, true and false piety, Lot's failure, as well as a translated Bible song, a section on informal thoughts, and news from the editor. The two articles on Christ's death and resurrection were Wang's thoughts on the doctrines from a Fundamentalist perspective as opposed to a Modernist one, affirming that Jesus physically died and came back to life. As can be surmised from Wang's purpose statement, the journal was meant "to testify to the essential points of the Bible" from a Fundamentalist perspective, which included countering Modernist Christian teachings on several theological topics. In the next few years, a stream of articles would be published in the journal to uphold Wang's Fundamentalist perspective on several Christian doctrines.

The inclusion of Martin Luther's prayer at the Diet of Worms is interesting. Wang translated it noting that Luther wrote this prayer before his trial, in which he was accused of heresy due to his opposition to the Roman Catholic Church, and was in extreme danger.[98] Wang always admired those like Luther who, for conscience's sake, were willing to stand for what they thought was right no matter the cost. Wang published Luther's prayer in March–April 1927, in the midst of the first phase of the Northern Expedition 北伐 in China. Wang resonated with Luther's path toward independence in the midst of conflict both inside and outside of the church. Not only was there conflict between Modernists and Fundamentalists like Wang in the Chinese church, but there was also conflict in Chinese society as the Northern Expedition was underway. The purpose of the KMT's expedition was to unify China after the fragmentation that took place following the establishment of the Republic of China in 1911. After Sun Yat-sen died on March 12, 1925, Chiang Kai-shek 蔣介石 (蔣中正) eventually took control of the KMT on June 5, 1926, and beginning in July 1926 led an upward sweep from Guangzhou to unify control of China under the KMT. He initially worked in a united front with the CCP to wrestle control of various regions of China out of the hands of warlords and the Beiyang government. As the expedition moved north, with the May Thirtieth Movement's ideology of cultural imperialism still being held against Christians, especially foreign ones and those connected to them through missionary agencies, Christian churches were damaged and several Christians were killed. Most foreign missionaries left the interior and fled to Shanghai with over two thousand returning to their home countries.[99] In many ways, it seemed like an unfortunate time to be a Christian preacher in China,[100] but for an independent Chinese Christian, the situation provided a unique opportunity. Chinese Christians were looking for a way to be both Chinese *and* Christian. People like Wang Mingdao, who were providing a path that was independent of foreign missionary agencies yet still committed to the Christian faith, were able to find a following. The first phase of the Northern Expedition ended in August 1927 after Chiang attempted to purge the Communists from within the KMT. As the Northern Expedition paused, in the summer of 1927, Wang was back in Beijing conducting his house church meetings in his and Mrs. Pan's homes for short periods, publishing his journal every three months, and back on the road for itinerant preaching meetings.[101] His ministry was flourishing as people responded to his preaching and writing as he forged the path toward independent Chinese Christianity. In January 1928, the second stage of the Northern Expedition began. By May 1928, the KMT had effectively taken control of Beijing with Wang busy in the city focused on ministry work.[102] On May 27, 1928, during the final battles in Beijing, he wrote in *The Spiritual Food Quarterly* that recent ministry work in the city was exceptionally good.[103] He had resolved earlier to not be concerned with political battles but rather to focus on the cross of Jesus and to leave the world behind. Therefore, he kept busy with his preaching and writing in the midst of the conflict.[104] This was certainly a theological decision but may also have been influenced by Wang's observation of the lack of effective government in Beijing during his life thus far.[105]

FAMILY COMPLEXITIES

By December 1928, China was reunified under Chiang's KMT government based in Nanjing.[106] This created a more stable social environment in China, which allowed Wang to expand his ministry throughout the country over the next decade. The most significant event of 1928 for Wang personally was that he got married. On August 8, he and Liu Jingwen were married at her father's church in Hangzhou with her father officiating.[107] Liu Jingwen's older brother Liu Chongen 劉崇恩 got married to his fiancée first, and then her father wittily said to the surprised guests assembled, "Please wait. There is another couple" to be married, which was Wang Mingdao and Liu Jingwen.[108] Wang's former student and now friend Shi Tianmin attended the wedding, but his mother and sister did not. His mother-in-law asked Wang before he left with her daughter for their new home in Beijing, "Don't all people used by God have to go through refinement?" to which Wang replied, "Yes." His mother-in-law responded, "A girl like Jingwen has never had such refinement. What about her?"[109] This statement should have been a warning to Wang Mingdao, but just as with his lack of understanding of his mother's reaction to his leaving his teaching job in Baoding, he did not anticipate her negative reaction to his marrying Liu Jingwen.

When the newly married couple returned to his mother's home in Beijing on September 18 to live in her housing unit, Wang Mingdao and Liu Jingwen were surprised by his mother and sister's cold welcome. They arrived at 6:30 p.m., around dinnertime, and were told by Wang's mother, "We have already eaten. You prepare yourselves food for the two of you to eat." Since his mother and sister did not oppose the marriage to Liu Jingwen when he previously talked to them about it, Wang expected that there would be a warm welcome including a sumptuous meal to welcome the new couple. Dejected, he went out to the street to buy some food and cooked dinner for himself and his new wife. He described his feelings at the time as having fallen into a thick fog. Early the next morning, his sister made a commotion in the yard, which he felt was an indirect outburst of anger directed at Wang and Liu Jingwen. Not clear about why they were being treated like this, Wang and Liu Jingwen wept in their room.[110] Upon reflection, possibly of several years since Wang wrote this section of his autobiography in 1950, he realized that Liu Jingwen would never be accepted as part of his mother's family, which created a problem for his Confucian Christian ethics that would never be fully resolved until his mother died.

The significant relationship trauma that Wang's mother, Li Wenyi, (1865–1947), had experienced may, in part, explain her coldness toward Wang's wife. When she was thirty-five, her husband, as detailed previously, had committed suicide, leaving her to take care of Wang's older sister, Wang Enrong, and the unborn Wang Mingdao. As the landlord of a lower socioeconomic–class housing unit on Sweet Rain Lane (Ganyu Hutong) in Eastern Beijing, Li Wenyi personally observed the abuse that family members inflicted on one another including daughters-in-law mistreating their mothers-in-law. Li Wenyi's mother and younger sister also lived in the housing unit with them, and her relationship with her younger sister by three years was particularly painful for her. Li Wenyi's younger sister used her for whatever material profit she could and rejected her older sister when there was no more left to be gained from her. Wang Mingdao saw this relationship as convincing his mother that if her sister would do this to her, there was no one she could trust except for her two children. Wang later recalled that when he was a child, his mother said to him and his older sister that when Wang Mingdao got married, there would be an outsider in their home.[111] He later realized that when he brought Liu Jingwen home from Hangzhou, he had brought an outsider into his mother's home who would never be trusted by his mother and sister. Furthermore, due to his union with his wife, even Wang Mingdao became an outsider to his sister and mother.[112] The pain from this perceived loss of her son resulted in the cold reception given to the newly married couple and ongoing hostility that Li Wenyi showed to them. Even into her later years after Wang's older sister died, Li Wenyi increasingly distrusted Liu Jingwen for fear that her daughter-in-law, as she had seen in other relationships, intended to do her harm.[113] Also, Li Wenyi believed that "when a son takes a wife, he no longer wants a mother." All of these feelings combined with the fact that Liu Jingwen, as a southerner from Hangzhou, did not understand northern Beijing social customs and habits, as well as the fact that she did not speak the Beijing dialect in 1928, made both Wang and Liu Jingwen feel that they could not do anything right and that there was nothing they could do to please Wang's mother and sister.[114]

This interfamily conflict created an enormous problem for Wang and is further evidence of his Confucian Christian sensibilities. As a twenty-eight-year-old man, he now had to decide whether his primary loyalty was to his mother or to his wife. Wang's reading as a child and adolescent would undoubtedly have made him familiar with the message of books like *The Classic of Filial Piety* 孝經 and *The Twenty-Four Filial Exemplars* 二十四孝, which taught him to express filial piety toward his mother. This teaching was in harmony with the admonition from the Christian scriptures to honor one's mother and father[115] and resulted in Wang originally saying that he would rather sacrifice his wife than his mother.[116] However, upon further reflection influenced by the Christian admonition that a husband should leave his father and mother and be united with his wife,[117] he realized that this way of thinking was not correct. Wang came up with a compromise. He decided he would love his mother *and* his wife. He would not give up his mother for his wife or give up his wife for his mother.[118] As noted by Gloria Tseng, "In his deep affection for his widowed mother and older sister, despite the many ways they made his marriage and family life difficult, Wang revealed himself to be a Confucian. . . . However, in the way that he learned to treat his wife with respect and understanding, despite the many personality differences between them, Wang also exhibited values and virtues not expected in traditional China."[119] These "values and virtues" were Christian ones that propelled Wang to be united with Liu Jingwen. However, his love for his mother would not allow him to leave her for his wife. Therefore, the compromise for Wang was to love both of them and leave neither of them, which is another practical expression of Wang Mingdao's Confucian Christianity.

In 1929, Wang Mingdao accepted more preaching invitations from locations farther away from Beijing as his reputation grew from the distribution of his quarterly journal. He was so busy, in fact, that on July 11, 1929, while he was preaching in Shou County 壽縣, Anhui Province, his only child was born at Douw (Daoji) Hospital 道濟醫院 in Beijing.[120] Apparently alone, Liu Jingwen delivered her son, Wang Tianduo, and left the hospital unable to pay the hospital fees.[121] Wang had little to say about his son in his autobiography[122] except that he was loved by his grandmother and aunt,[123] he appreciated the fact that Tianduo would not pass on information about his mother and father (Wang Mingdao and Liu Jingwen) to his grandmother and aunt (Wang's mother and sister),[124] and that, as a lover of books, he was upset with Liu Jingwen for letting Tianduo play with his world atlas, which the young boy ripped.[125] His mother loved him and had high expectations for her son.[126] Although she would rarely criticize him, Tianduo said that she was strict with him when he did something wrong.[127] While in university, due to the influence of new ideologies in China after the CCP victory, Tianduo began to have doubts about the Christian faith.[128] He was deeply loved by his father and he in turn loved and respected him. According to Stephen Wang (Wang Changxin) 王長新, nothing hurt Wang Mingdao more than Tianduo's unbelief.[129] Wang Tianduo graduated from Beijing Agricultural University 北京農業大學 in 1951.[130] Following his paternal grandfather Wang Zihou's path into the natural sciences, after graduation Tianduo worked in quantitative analysis and mathematical simulation of plant population photosynthesis, yield formation process, and water use efficiency of plants for decades. Later, he became a researcher at the Shanghai Institutes for Biological Sciences 上海生命科學研究院, which is a part of the Chinese Academy of Sciences 中國科學院.[131] This job provided him with the dormitory that housed Wang Mingdao and Liu Jingwen in their twilight years and where they conducted their Shanghai house church meetings beginning in the spring of 1984.[132]

FRUSTRATED RELATIONSHIPS

In January 1930, Wang Mingdao took his wife and young son to Hangzhou to visit Liu Jingwen's family. Wang noted that the previous year had been exhausting and that he felt the need to spend time with his wife's family and rest.[133] In late February, while in Shanghai, he met Zhang Yijing 張亦鏡 (1871–1931), who was the long-serving editor of *True Light Magazine* 真光雜誌. Zhang used the magazine to defend the Christian faith during the May Fourth Movement among Chinese intellectuals through his articles.[134] In his writings, he attempted to align Confucian and Christian teachings.[135] This seemed to have appealed to Wang, and he noted that Zhang had made a special contribution to Chinese Christian literature. Later, Wang was pleased to receive Zhang's letter after Zhang had read a 1929 issue of Wang's *The Spiritual Food Quarterly*, which resulted in the two beginning a correspondence. To Wang's regret, this would be the one and only time they would meet. It was especially unfortunate for Wang because after his rejection by Jia Yuming, he was also now being given the cold shoulder by Watchman Nee. Wang must have been hopeful that he had finally found a reliable mentor in Zhang Yijing and was disappointed that this was their only meeting as Zhang died on December 9, 1931.[136] The date is uncertain, but it seems that Wang went to visit Nee in June 1929 in Shanghai, and after briefly meeting Nee at the door, for some unknown reason Nee walked away and Wang was brushed away by a maid. Wang was confused and deeply hurt by Nee's rejection.[137] Shortly after meeting Zhang Yijing, he went to visit Watchman Nee again in Shanghai on March 3, 1930, and the two discussed church unity.[138] Since Wang had some misgivings about Nee's ecclesiology with his insistence that all indigenous churches should unite with his Little Flock and after the cold brush-off Nee had given Wang previously, it is possible that this is where the divergence between the two men began.[139]

Due to the busyness of his expanding family, frequent preaching trips, and publishing work on *The Spiritual Food Quarterly*, along with the fact that Mrs. Pan had moved and both her new home and his home were not large enough for the increasing number of people who attended, the Beijing house church Wang led had not met since the fall of 1927. He decided in the summer of 1930 to begin meeting in the yard of his housing unit to accommodate the attendees. They met nine times before he again went away on preaching trips. When he arrived home, on October 1, he met with Arie Kok 葛嘉 (1883–1951), who had heard that Wang's home was too cramped for the number of attendees, and so Mr. Kok offered his rented home for the church to meet in.[140] Kok was a diplomat from the Netherlands,[141] eventually becoming the chancellor of the Dutch legation.[142] Since Wang had known him for several months and was confident that the two men's religious beliefs were consistent, he accepted Kok's offer to use his residence.[143] Kok was formerly a Pentecostal missionary who arrived in China in 1911 but left the Pentecostal Mission Union in May 1919, more interested in spreading Christianity among the Chinese than Pentecostalism. Due to his familiarity with China, including the Chinese language, Kok was quickly employed by the Dutch diplomatic office in Beijing. He was interested in developing a network of Fundamentalist Christians in China, already having developed a meeting in his home for Western Christians, and so Kok and Wang were able to mutually advance each other's goals.[144] Kok was also convinced that the Chinese were the best evangelists to their own people and was looking for ways to partner with Chinese Christian leaders like Wang Mingdao.[145] The church met twice in Kok's home on October 12 and 19 with around 150 attendees before Wang left Beijing again for preaching appointments.[146] Even with the anti-foreign atmosphere in China after the May Fourth and May Thirtieth Movements, Wang was still willing to work with foreigners whom he thought had proper theological beliefs and corresponding behavior. In November, Wang added a Wednesday Bible study group in addition to his Sunday worship service at Kok's house. When Wang left Beijing, which he regularly did to preach in various Chinese provinces, other trusted leaders from the house church led the meetings. He entrusted the work of preaching in Beijing mainly to Shi Tianmin.[147]

THE VALUE OF THE PHYSICAL WORLD

Wang described what happened in April 1931 as a serious test of his family, which once again shows his conflict between being a dutiful son and a loving husband. Liu Jingwen became very ill with pneumonia, which created a complicated misunderstanding with his sister and mother who accused Liu Jingwen of being lazy and wanting a vacation. The conflict in choosing between his wife and his mother and sister caused Wang enormous stress. With Liu Jingwen's health dangerously deteriorating, on June 6, upon the invitation from one of the families of the churches where Wang was preaching, he finally brought her to Huang County 黄縣, Shandong Province to recover for several months, and then they went to her parents' home in Hangzhou on November 28 where she remained until December 1932.[148] While in Shandong Province on July 14, Wang took the opportunity to visit Qufu 曲阜, the hometown of Confucius. While in Qufu, he visited the Temple of Confucius 孔廟 and the Confucius family mausoleum 孔林 and noted that the stone pillars of the Dacheng Hall 大成殿 were of extremely high artistic value.[149] Wang returned to Beijing in January 1932 and while at home, led house church meetings but continued to accept invitations to preach in various locations before returning home to Beijing. That summer, he did a significant amount of historical tourism between preaching appointments. On May 11, he visited the ruins of Yellow Crane Tower 黃鶴樓 in Wuhan City 武漢, Hubei Province, a favored place of Tang dynasty poets such as Cui Hao 崔顥 and Li Bai 李白.[150] On May 12, while crossing the Miluo River 汨羅江 on his way to a preaching engagement, Wang again thought of one of his heroes, Qu Yuan.[151] The river was thought to be where Qu Yuan committed suicide in 278 BCE, shortly after he wrote the poem "Embracing Sands 懷沙" in which the poet protests the corruption of his time and reiterates his upstanding character.[152]

After Wang crossed the Miluo River, he arrived in Changsha 長沙, Hunan Province, and from May 12 to 30, 1932, he stayed with Marcus Cheng (Chen Chonggui) 陳崇桂 (1884–1963) who had invited Wang to preach in several churches in the city.[153] Cheng was a prominent Chinese Christian who had been teaching theology at the Hunan Bible Institute 湖南聖經學校 since 1929 and who edited the magazine *Evangelism* 佈道雜誌. Cheng was also a Fundamentalist Christian who took seriously both his publishing work and his faith and who wanted to see the Chinese church led by the Chinese.[154] Wang respected Cheng and later remarked that he was a true believer and a skilled preacher.[155] However, shortly after he left Changsha, Wang read an article Chen published in *Evangelism* that troubled him. It was a speech by Chiang Kai-shek given to the students at the Hunan Bible Institute titled "The Principles of Jesus concerning National Salvation."[156] In the speech, Chiang, who on October 23, 1930, was baptized as a Methodist in Shanghai, presents his thought that the way that Jesus saves people is the same way to save China—namely, that through universal love, sacrifice, and regardless of personal danger and difficulty is the way to achieve national salvation. Chiang encouraged Christian students who heard his speech to exhibit the character of Jesus to influence the students of China and to use the principles of Jesus to save the country and the people.[157] Wang concluded after reading Chiang's speech that Chiang's gospel was not the gospel of the Bible but rather the gospel of the Modernists or as Wang referred to them, the "unbelievers 不信派." He was also disappointed that Marcus Cheng had published what Wang felt was a political article in a religious magazine.[158] Wang thought that Chiang did not join the church because he truly believed in Christ but rather because he knew that the United States was the richest and most powerful country in the world and the largest country among Christian nations and because Chiang needed American help to establish long-term political control over China.[159] Wang's negative assessment of Chiang Kai-shek's speech illustrates that Wang was willing to critique anyone who did not meet his theological or moral standards, regardless of political affiliation.[160]

In late June, Wang visited what had been known as one of the four ancient towns of Qing dynasty China, Zhuxian 朱仙鎮 in Henan Province. He was disappointed that the town was in such a dilapidated state, but when he saw the still-standing Yue Temple 嶽廟, dedicated to the Song dynasty general Yue Fei 岳飛 (1103–42 CE), famous for his loyalty[161] and one of Wang's heroes,[162] he noted that the architecture was magnificent.[163] Lian Xi has commented that Wang did not think that the indigenization of Christianity required buildings that were built in a Chinese style.[164] In fact, Wang thought that the effort to build churches in a Chinese style was a form of secularization since he believed that the real issues in indigenizing Christianity in China were theological. He did see value in having contextualized knowledge of local customs and social mores.[165] However, Wang saw the effort to make Christian architecture in Chinese style as a superficial issue and a distraction from where Christian leaders should focus, which was on preaching the essential points of the Bible. Wang believed that the true issues in the indigenization of Christianity in China were theological.[166] However, overemphasizing this point can misrepresent Wang as seeing no value in the physical world. Although Wang certainly valued the spiritual world more than the physical world, as can be seen from his appreciation of Confucius's ancestral home, the Yellow Crane Tower, and the architecture of Yue Temple, Wang did see value in physical places that inspired people to follow the moral example of men like Confucius, Qu Yuan, and Yue Fei. In this sense, the physical world was subservient to the spiritual world but was important as it drew one closer to have a "spirit of righteousness" like these Chinese heroes of his possessed.[167]

FRIENDSHIPS

In September 1932, his friend from Tsui Wen Academy Chen Zigao, who had given Wang his first preaching opportunity, died, leaving Wang deeply grieved that he had lost his close and loyal friend.[168] After a brief two-day visit in Hangzhou on September 24 with his wife and son whom he had not seen in nine months, at the end of the month he traveled to Hong Kong and in October went to Macau to preach and teach, which were the only places outside of China that Wang ever traveled in his life.[169] This lack of foreign experience and financial connections would become a point of pride for him later when he was attacked for being "an errand boy of foreign powers."[170] Gloria Tseng, after studying a collection of twelve sermons that Wang preached during this period while he was in Guangzhou, concluded that "Wang's sermons and writings are marked by their plainness and common sense. His exegesis comes slightly closer to biblical studies than to theology, but study of the Bible as an academic discipline is not what preoccupies him. Instead, he focuses on the integrity of the Christian's personal life and the church's moral witness to a corrupt society."[171] Wang, in both his writing and his speaking, focused on the combination of correct religious beliefs with corresponding moral behavior in a way that was helpful to his audience. He also appears to have been a very insightful and penetrating writer and preacher who was able to find interesting topics to elaborate on from seemingly uninteresting subjects. While in Hong Kong on November 11, he wrote an article titled, "The Gospel in Genesis 5" in which he was able to take the dry family lineage of Adam and write an interesting article on the gospel.[172]

While Wang was in Guangdong Province, John Sung (Song Shangjie) 宋尚節 (1901–44), came to Beijing on October 11 and remained in the city for thirty-two days, leading revival services for the first ten days at a Presbyterian church and for the next three weeks at Asbury Methodist Church 亞斯立堂. Asbury Methodist had a capacity of 1,200 people and was filled twice a day with those who came to hear Sung preach.[173] According to Wang, ministry work in Beijing experienced a new development, as many people were converted and many Christians were revived in their faith due to Sung's preaching. Sung had grown up in a Christian family and attended missionary schools in Putian 莆田, Fujian Province until he went to study in the United States, eventually earning a PhD in chemistry from Ohio State University before studying at Union Theological Seminary in New York. While at Union, Sung seems to have gone through both extreme religious experiences and a mental-emotional breakdown.[174] In 1927, he returned to China and worked as an evangelist with a vehemently Fundamentalist theology. Sung's preaching drew huge crowds in China, and he was a powerful preacher as evidenced by Daniel Bays's statement that "he must be considered probably the single most powerful figure in Chinese revivalism in the mid-1930s."[175] Wang wrote that Sung encouraged people to attend Wang Mingdao's house church in Beijing.[176] Before Sung became well known, the two had briefly met in January 1931 when Sung came to visit Wang's church.[177] At that time, the church was still meeting in Arie Kok's home, and Wang and Sung only exchanged a few words at the end of the service, but Sung was able to listen to Wang's preaching on the topic of "The Loyal Servant."[178] In 1932, while Wang was in Shandong Province, he heard stories about Sung's fanciful interpretations of scripture and dramatic performances onstage. Wang was appalled that Sung was apparently distorting the meaning of the Bible and originally had a negative impression of him. However, after hearing about Sung's revivals in China in which multitudes of people were converted and revived in their faith as well as Sung's denunciations of evil in society and the church, Wang's impression of Sung changed. The evidence Wang saw in his own church in Beijing in early 1933 confirmed in his mind that Sung was a servant of God. That Sung recommended Wang's church to people after hearing him preach is evidence that he also mutually respected Wang Mingdao. Although the two did not frequently meet, this was a significant friendship that lasted until Sung died in 1944.[179]

THE CHRISTIAN TABERNACLE

In the spring of 1933, with the extra people added to their meetings due to Sung's recommendation, Wang's house church needed to find a larger location to accommodate the increased number of attendees. On February 19, the house church moved to a social hall on 5 Longfu Temple Street 隆福寺街, and since the social hall was no longer a church within a house, the church needed to pay a usage fee. Therefore, Wang had an offering box installed to cover this fee.[180] It was in 1933 when the church began to move out of homes that Wang considered the beginning of the Beijing Christian Tabernacle 北京基督徒會堂.[181] On April 23, they moved again to 23 Chaomian Lane 炒麵胡同 to a location that could accommodate around two hundred people inside and one hundred outside; they remained there for the next four years. With the meetings filling up with around three hundred attendees, Wang decided to add two more meeting times to a total of four meetings per week.[182] On June 10, Wang baptized six people from his church, the first baptisms of the Christian Tabernacle, in a river outside of the Summer Palace.[183] With around three hundred people attending the four meetings of the church, only six people being baptized was a relatively small number. However, Wang was extremely selective about whom he would baptize. After his own experience of giving up both his teaching job in Baoding and his dream of pursuing overseas education in England to be baptized by immersion, Wang felt that baptism was extremely important and he was only willing to administer baptism to those he felt had both proper religious beliefs and a life that had been morally transformed by those beliefs.[184] His reticence to baptize people is further evidence of Wang's emphasis on the combination of proper thought and behavior, this time in his Christian ministry to others. From July 30 to August 13, he began what became an annual tradition in Beijing to hold summer services for ten to fifteen days each summer.[185] His desire to conduct these services illustrates the influence of Christian revivalism on Wang Mingdao.[186]

During the Chinese New Year holidays of 1934, Wang added another annual tradition to his ministry, which was to use the vacation, the most important in Chinese society with most people returning to their family homes, to hold an annual revival meeting for about a week. Since the weather in Beijing during February could be brutally cold, Wang encouraged a policy that those with thicker clothing sit outside, while those with thinner clothing sit inside where there were some heating stoves. In August, the church held the second series of summer revival meeting services, but on August 8, heavy rain soaked those sitting outside. At this point, due to the weather challenges with both cold in the winter and rain in the summer, Wang began to contemplate finding another place to meet. He felt that God had given him the idea to purchase a plot of land to build a church.[187]

Also in August 1934, Wang faced another challenge with his family. His father-in-law, Liu Delin, was diagnosed with stomach cancer and was receiving treatment in Shanghai, but Wang's mother and sister objected to Wang and Liu Jingwen going to care for him, claiming that they were desiring a vacation, which caused such enormous stress on both Liu Jingwen and Wang that Wang even contemplated suicide. When Liu Jingwen's brother informed them that Liu Delin's situation was critical, Wang's mother, fearful that her son might do something drastic like her husband had in 1900, finally permitted the couple to leave. They arrived in Shanghai on August 17 with Wang preaching at a Baptist summer camp in Shanghai from August 20 to 30. On August 25, with Liu Delin's case appearing terminal, the family escorted him back to Hangzhou. Wang had scheduled another ten-day preaching assignment in the city, so he remained in Shanghai. Liu Delin died on September 4, but Wang, feeling great love for his father-in-law, yet knowing that he would approve, reluctantly remained in Shanghai due to his ministry commitment and did not attend his father-in-law's funeral or burial. Wang was confident that Liu Delin would have most certainly said to him, "Only be concerned with preaching. Don't be concerned about my funeral affairs." In Wang's thinking, he felt it was better to be utterly loyal to God than to do one's filial duty to his father-in-law. Here again, the Confucian Christian tension is evident in Wang's thinking and family relationships. Wang finally arrived in Hangzhou on September 11, and while visiting his father-in-law's grave, he thought about Liu Delin's love and kindness toward him and could not help but weep.[188]

On September 16 while in Hangzhou, Wang met with a former attendee of his Beijing church, Luan Hongbin 欒宏斌, whom Wang had baptized but who had later left Beijing and was now serving as a coworker in the Hangzhou location of Watchman Nee's Little Flock.[189] Luan invited Wang to cooperate with Nee's Little Flock as Watchman Nee had been trying to convince Chinese to leave Christian churches in China that were part of Western denominations 宗派.[190] Despite his own independence from missionary Christianity, Wang countered that these churches had also made a contribution to Chinese Christianity. When Wang tactfully declined the invitation due to not being convinced by Nee's ecclesiology, it marked the formal separation of Wang and Nee.[191] Wang spent the rest of the year traveling south to lead preaching meetings into Guangdong and Guangxi Provinces.

CONFUCIUS AND QIN SHIHUANG

The year 1935 was again full of preaching engagements for Wang, who was away from Beijing for eight months. In April, he was preaching in Xian 西安, Shaanxi Province, and during a few days of break time, he saw the tomb of Emperor Qin Shihuang. The terra-cotta warriors were not discovered until 1974, and when Wang visited in 1935, the tomb complex was completely covered with not even a sign to indicate the presence of Qin Shihuang, whom he describes as "the one who swallowed up the six states, the unifier of China,[192] noble enough to be the Son of Heaven, and rich enough to possess the whole world."[193] Wang, familiar with the emperor's story since a child, concluded that people should come to realize that the glory of the rich and powerful would all come to the same end.[194] In his 1982 "Rehabilitation Request Manuscript," Wang would recall this trip and contrast it with his 1931 visit to the tomb of Confucius in Qufu. In Wang's thought, Qin Shihuang and Confucius were contrasting characters in Chinese history.[195] From Wang's perspective, Qin Shihuang, who burned the Confucian books to secure his control over the Confucian literati and buried alive those who constructed his tomb,[196] disappeared into such obscurity that not even a wooden sign for his tomb could be seen. Wang, using the categories established by Mencius, said that Qin Shihuang was one who "subdued men by force."[197] In contrast, Confucius, when he realized that the King of Lu 魯君 was practicing immorality with female musicians and that no court was being held, which thus left undone the king's responsibilities to the people of Lu, Confucius left his service to teach others the way of virtue[198] and has cultivated millions of disciples over two thousand years. Again, using Mencius's categories, Wang wrote that Confucius was one who "subdues men by virtue."[199]

During this visit to Qin Shihuang's tomb in 1935, Wang was deeply moved by the contrast of these two legendary figures.

MAKING FRIENDS AND ENEMIES

While Wang was away in April, John Sung preached at his church in Beijing.[200] Since Wang was extremely careful about whom he would allow to preach at his church, only ever inviting someone whom he was confident in both their theology and moral character, it shows the confidence he had in Sung.[201] Liu Jingwen wrote to her husband telling him that Sung preached an excellent sermon at their church.[202] While he was in Xian, Wang wrote an article that he would later publish in the summer issue of *The Spiritual Food Quarterly* titled "The Evils of the Modern YMCA 現代基督教青年會的罪惡."[203] Wang later reflected that it was this article which named the YMCA that began his conflict with the YMCA leaders who would become the future leaders of the TSPM. Wang used the idiom "to hate me to the bone" to describe the reaction that YMCA leaders had to him after writing this article.[204] Y. T. Wu 吴耀宗 (Wu Yaozong) (1893–1979) had served as the director general of the Shanghai YMCA, and Liu Liangmo 劉良模 (1909–88) was the executive secretary of the Lanzhou 蘭州, Gansu Province YMCA. In "The Sin of the Modern YMCA," without naming them, Wang accused men like Wu and Liu of "hanging up a sheep's head but selling dog meat"—in other words, doing work in the name of Christ that had nothing to do with Christianity. Wang said that the YMCA leaders were focused on arranging social activities like watching movies and ice-skating and participating in educational and hygiene movements while teaching "new theology" and preaching the "social gospel," which in Wang's opinion was veiled atheism.[205] In 1919, in the wake of the May Fourth Movement's disparagement of religion, when Wang read the journal articles provided in YMCA reading rooms and after he had recounted his own experience of nearly abandoning his faith in God, Wang went on to state that most of the people involved in YMCA service were people without faith:

> It is not surprising that the YMCA is corrupt to such a degree, because most of the people involved in YMCA service have no faith.

> The officers of the YMCA when they hear what I said would certainly argue: "How can you say that we have no faith? We are Christians and we believe in Christ, but we are not as superstitious as you are, so stupid and outdated like you are driving backwards." Alright, alright. To sincerely believe in the Bible and in Christ's salvation is superstition, folly, outdated, and backwards. The officials of the YMCA have admitted that they have no faith. What other evidence do I need to cite? I dare not say that all the officials of the YMCA have no faith. There may be believers who are very pious and love the Lord among the officials of the YMCA. But there are not many. There are more than forty locations where there are YMCAs in China. I have visited at least two-thirds of these places. I am neither blind nor deaf, are there reasons why I cannot see or hear? Don't tell me what I observed, in terms of their own speech, attitude and work, it is enough to prove that most of them have no faith.[206]

Along with Wang's alarm over what he perceived among YMCA leaders as the lack of belief in the Bible and the neglect of the need for personal salvation, he also lamented that the YMCA was no longer producing literature as they had when H. L. Zia was with the YMCA, literature that helped young people in both their religious beliefs and their moral conduct. Wang concluded that if Zia was alive, he would no longer be welcome in the YMCA.[207] According to Wang, YMCA leaders like Wu and Liu who hated him to the bone after reading this article in 1935, would, after 1951, control the church in China through the TSPM. The division in the contemporary Chinese church between registered and unregistered factions can be traced back to these earlier divisions in the first half of the twentieth century between Modernists and Fundamentalists.[208]

In the spring of 1936, Wang read Zhang Ziping's 張資平 novel *God's Children* 上帝的兒女們 (1933). Zhang, an important writer of the May Fourth period, wrote this work describing church life, religious emotions, and the Bible. Wang felt that Zhang had made irresponsible remarks and maligned the gospel in *God's Children*.[209] Wang also read T. C. Chao's *Life of Jesus* 耶穌傳, which was a creative and highly influential biography of Jesus from a Chinese perspective.[210] Since Chao added details that were not present in the gospel narratives of Jesus's life and he was also seeking to remove any elements from Christianity that could be perceived as superstitious to make the religion more acceptable to modern Chinese, Wang thought that the *Life of Jesus* was full of fabrications and dangerous.[211] These two critiques reveal that Wang, despite his own efforts to promote vernacular and modern literature like Zhang Ziping and articulate Christianity to people with a Confucian background like Chao, sought to present the Christian faith from a Fundamentalist Christian theological perspective and rejected attempts at what he thought were compromising the theological integrity of the Christian message by saying things about Jesus that Wang did not find in the Bible.

As the Nanjing decade drew to a close in 1937, the expansion and development of the KMT government centered in Nanjing was matched by the expansion and development of Chinese Christianity in many parts of China.[212] Wang Mingdao in Beijing had established his reputation as an outstanding *independent* Chinese Christian writer and preacher with many Chinese Christians being drawn to his confident Fundamentalist theology that was backed up by a devout lifestyle. These both would be put to the test as Wang entered his years of conflict beginning with the Second Sino-Japanese War.

CHAPTER FOUR

The Conflict Years

1937–1955

The Second Sino-Japanese War significantly curtailed Wang Mingdao's travels, resulting in him spending more time in Beijing. As Timothy Brook has observed, since the only places that the Japanese military respected as places of refuge at the beginning of the war were Christian churches and mission compounds,[1] this likely had an impact on the number of people that swelled the services that Wang Mingdao led in Beijing. With the construction of his new church, the stage was set for the establishment of a Chinese Christian legend as he entered his years of conflict.

MINISTERING DURING THE SECOND SINO-JAPANESE WAR

After adequate funds had been donated for the new church building,[2] during the spring of 1937, the name of the church Wang Mingdao led was officially registered with the Beijing city government as the Christian Tabernacle 基督徒會堂. On March 21, an inscription tablet was hung on Chaomian Lane with the five characters of the church name inscribed on it. In May, the church leaders purchased property at 42 Shijia Lane 史家胡同 to build a new building.[3] With the purchase of the property settled, Wang went south again, and while conducting a preaching tour all the way to Guangdong Province, he became ill and returned to Beijing to recuperate on August 27 and spent a number of weeks in bed. By October, several people were scheduled to be baptized by Wang, but he was still very weak with severe pain in his legs. Since the new building had not been constructed with the planned baptismal tank, a pragmatic addition due to his own rebaptism experience in icy waters, Wang decided to risk the possibility of his sickness worsening by baptizing the people in the river water, which by October had become quite cold. On October 17, to his delight, not only did he not get sick when he baptized the seven people, but the pain completely stopped, which confirmed to him that God still performed miracles.[4]

In the first half of 1937, Wang was away from home again preaching in various locations throughout the country, but after the Marco Polo Bridge incident 蘆溝橋事變 on July 7, 1937, his travels temporarily came to a halt. This conflict between the Chinese and the Japanese imperial army began the Second Sino-Japanese War. Wang saw intense fighting in the suburbs of Beijing with the Japanese winning the battle for Beijing and the Chinese army retreating.[5] Despite this political reality, the Christian Tabernacle opened on August 1 for the first service with around five hundred people attending the meeting; this was the start of eighteen days of services at the church.[6] While these services were taking place on Shijia Lane, the Japanese army began their occupation of the city on August 8. With all of the chaos outside in the city, the Christian Tabernacle provided a place of security and comfort inside for those residents of Beijing who met there.[7] The original design was a large basic structure with no pictures and no cross since, according to Wang, the cross was a symbol of the Roman Catholic Church.[8] Wang and the leaders of the Christian Tabernacle seem to have put a lot of thought into the "simple, clean, and dignified" appearance of the church in keeping with the simplicity of Fundamentalist Christian architecture of the time.[9]

The simplicity of the design of Wang's church was not matched by simplicity in relationship with other churches, though. Watchman Nee in his 1937 book *Rethinking the Work* 工作的再思 had advocated for a policy of one city, one church.[10] Wang had already rejected joining with Nee in 1934, as described previously, but in 1938, one of Wang's ministry assistants, Yang Runmin 楊潤民, considered leaving the Christian Tabernacle after reading Nee's article "The Assembly Life 聚會生活" and his book *The Open Door* 敞開的門.[11] Fundamentalist churches like Wang's Christian Tabernacle were beginning to lose members who were transferring into Nee's Little Flock. In 1939,[12] Wang went to visit Nee in Shanghai to find out from the man himself if Nee had instructed his followers to encourage members of other churches to leave to join Little Flock. They talked for nearly three hours with Nee denying that he encouraged his followers to pull members away from other Fundamentalist churches; other than that statement, Nee was largely silent. Wang concluded that Nee was lying to him and was "beyond cure" and that his situation was "hopeless." The two men never met again.[13]

With the Japanese army occupying Beijing beginning in the summer of 1937 and fearing that the atrocities that had taken place during the Nanjing massacre 南京大屠殺 from December 1937 to January 1938 might continue in other locations,[14] Wang thought that the Christians who read his journal needed some comforting words to encourage their faith in the midst of their distress. He turned to the works of the man who, besides Wang, constitutes the largest amount of content in *The Spiritual Food Quarterly*, George H. Knight (1835–1917).[15] Knight had been a Scottish Free Church minister, and Wang was so impressed by Knight's works that he translated four of Knight's books from English into Chinese in serial form in *The Spiritual Food Quarterly* beginning in the spring of 1928 in nearly every issue until the winter of 1943. In the summer of 1938, Wang began to translate Knight's book *In the Cloudy and Dark Day: God's Message of Peace to the Weary, the Sorrow-Laden, the Troubled, and the Tired* 在密雲黑暗的日子, an appropriate title to choose to translate to encourage his readers in the midst of their suffering.[16]

However, while Wang utilized this foreign source of theological comfort and guidance during the Second Sino-Japanese War, he also began to make more frequent quotations of classical and ancient Chinese sources in *The Spiritual Food Quarterly*. In the early years of the war from 1938 to 1940, Wang quoted from *The School Sayings of Confucius* 孔子家語,[17] *The Analects*,[18] *The Enlarged Writings of Worthies* 增廣賢文,[19] and the Yuan dynasty history book *Nancun Chuogenglu* 南村輟耕錄[20] to elucidate his thought in a way that would be familiar to Chinese readers. In addition to the Bible, which is the overwhelming source of his articles, and the many translated works from Western Christians, Wang apparently thought that his readers also needed to hear from the sources that have nourished the minds and morals of the Chinese for thousands of years. Wang utilized these Chinese references by supplementing the Christian scriptures with these classical and ancient Chinese sources to instruct Chinese Christians on how to live morally upright lives in the midst of difficulty in a way that was appropriate for the Chinese context. As mentioned previously, Wang felt that building churches with classical Chinese architecture or singing hymns with Buddhist tunes was secularism because he thought that the real issue in contextualizing the Christian message in China was to indigenize the Christian gospel in a way that was appropriate for people who had been shaped by a Chinese Confucian worldview.[21]

For example, in an important article where he discusses who is fit for service as a Christian preacher, Wang refers to the personal morality extolled in *Mencius*:

> People who are afraid and cowardly cannot work for God. Those who are afraid of insults, slander, offending people, loss, suffering, and danger, are best to go home. Only a preacher who is able "to be above the power of riches and honors to make dissipated, of poverty and mean condition to make swerve from principle, and of power and force to make bend"[22] can be a powerful worker in the hands of God. To be a good worker for God, in addition to reading the Bible with your heart, you must also read people with your heart. Many people who work for God have faith, love, and enthusiasm. But because they do not understand people, they are deceived, fooled, and used by others, corrupting God's work, and corrupting God's congregation. Reading people is something that the workers of God cannot ignore. God's workers must not sin.[23]

Along with inner Confucian integrity that Mencius will describe in the next verse that is not quoted by Wang, Wang blends the need for practical ministry skills such as devout Bible reading and a shrewd understanding of people as the characteristics that constitute a great man.

In an article written in 1941, Wang made public in *The Spiritual Food Quarterly* his disagreement with Watchman Nee and his ecclesiology.[24] With Wang concluding in 1939 that Nee was lying to him and that Christians, including some from the Christian Tabernacle, were being influenced to leave their churches in favor of Nee's Little Flock, Wang went on the offensive to defend the validity of the name Christian Tabernacle, which had been criticized by Nee.[25] In this article, as Wang argues his perspective on the meaning of the word "church," he coincidently provides some insight into his thinking about Chinese thought. In his discussion of the word "saint," Wang states that all Chinese consider the ancient Chinese sage rulers Yao 堯, Shun 舜, Yu 禹, Tang 湯, King Wen 文, King Wu 武, the Duke of Zhou 周公, Confucius 孔子, and Mencius 孟子 to be saints 聖人 but in a way that is different from how Christians use the term.[26] The term can also be translated as "sage" and is better understood in this Chinese sense as the English word "sage," a revered figure of the past who has great wisdom and is worthy of study and emulation, as opposed to the Protestant Christian sense of the word, one who believes in Jesus, which is better translated as "saint" in English. Nevertheless, Wang reveals here that he sees this collection of legendary Chinese figures as being universally revered in China and a basis of common Chinese historical memory.

ZHANG XUN AND "THE CHURCH'S SUIYANG WARRIORS"

The period of Japanese occupation was challenging for Wang Mingdao, but 1942 brought a particularly difficult test for him: with the Japanese having taken control of Beijing and having closed most churches, a letter was sent to him from Japanese authorities, which he received on December 17, 1941. The letter informed him that his church must become a part of the Beijing chapter of the League for the Promotion of Church Union in North China 北京基督教維持會, a group founded by the Japanese military. Wang wrote that in asking God to liberate him from the demand to join the league, he felt like Israel asking God for deliverance in Egypt.[27] Later, he was informed that the group's name had changed to the North China Christian Union Group 華北基督教聯合促進會 and that he must join.[28] He saw this group as a tool of Japanese political control over the Chinese church.[29] Wang was told that if he did not join, the Christian Tabernacle would be permanently closed.[30] After traveling for some time, he returned to Beijing, and on April 30, 1942, he received another letter from the North China Christian Union Group indicating that the purpose of the group was to promote three areas of independence from foreign control of the church in China: self-governance, self-support, and self-propagation.[31] These goals had long been cherished ideals of and for the Chinese church to become an indigenous church and came to be known as the three selfs. Wang wrote a response letter indicating that his church was, and always had been, a three-self church in this sense and thus continued his opposition to joining the group.[32] Wang was very concerned about the consequences of not joining the union as it was quite possible that he would be imprisoned or even killed because of his resistance. However, Wang had watched in December 1939 with admiration Wu Peifu's 吳佩孚 (1874–1939) funeral procession.[33] Wu, a warlord who subscribed to a Confucian ethic, had refused to become a leader in the puppet government of the Japanese in China despite being offered government positions. Wu's resistance to the Japanese had become so legendary that the American weekly magazine the *Saturday Evening Post* wrote an article in 1939 that centered the Japanese effort to recruit Chinese to their side around wooing to no avail Wu to capitulate to the Japanese.[34]

Wang heard that Wu had previously put a coffin in his home signaling his willingness to die to resist Japanese control over China, and Wang saw in the funeral procession how even the Japanese respected Wu's integrity.[35] In 1942, Wang was grieved that Chinese Christian leaders were accepting leadership positions in the North China Christian Union. For example, the Congregationalist Church pastor Wang Zizhong 王梓仲 (1895–?) took the role of secretary-general 總幹事, and the Methodist bishop Z. T. Kuang (Jiang Changchuan) 江長川 (1884–1958) took the role of chairman 主席 of the North China Christian Union Group. Wang saw them as collaborators with the Japanese, and he personally continued to refuse to participate in the union.[36] Following Wu Peifu's model of determination unto death, Wang kept a coffin inside his home as well.[37]

As Thomas Harvey notes, Wang was "a master story-teller who was able to cleverly weave current circumstance into the ancient text,"[38] but Harvey focuses only on Wang's use of the Bible as an ancient text, which had significance for Wang's interpretation of current events. Harvey does not mention Wang's use of ancient Chinese Confucian texts to provide moral exemplars for current situations. An example of this Confucian influence is described in Wang's autobiography, *The Last Fifty Years*, which was completely edited out of the English translation by Arthur Reynolds. One fascinating part of Wang's story of resistance to the Japanese was how Wang rallied himself and his coworkers to fight in what he perceived to be both a political and spiritual battle. His resistance to joining the Japanese-controlled union brought to his mind the Tang dynasty history of the An Lushan Rebellion 安祿山作亂, which began in 755 CE.[39] The rebellion formally began when General An Lushan led a revolt against the Tang dynasty by declaring himself the emperor of Northern China and, in doing so, establishing the upstart Yan dynasty. While resisting joining the union controlled by the Japanese, Wang thought of General Zhang Xun 張巡 (709–757 CE) who demonstrated loyalty to the Tang dynasty by protecting Yongqiu and Suiyang, which were rich and prosperous areas during that time and had fallen under attack during the rebellion. Zhang Xun knew that if Suiyang was to fall to the enemy, the region south of the Yangtze River would likely fall under the control of the rebels. Even though Zhang Xun died in the end, the Yongqiu and Suiyang battles weakened the enemy to the point that the Tang dynasty was able to resist the Yan army. Instrumental to the battle was Zhang Xun's unflinching resistance to his enemy in the Battle of Suiyang, which became the turning point of the war.[40] By expounding this story to his coworkers at the Christian Tabernacle, Wang encouraged them to be the church's "Suiyang Warriors 睢陽勇士" who were loyal unto death. Wang told his church members that Satan was the instrument behind the Japanese-controlled North China Christian Union that was so ravaging the churches in North China. He exhorted his people that no matter what the future held, they should be willing to sacrifice themselves to protect this "clean land" of the Christian Tabernacle just like Zhang Xun, Nan Jiyun 南霽雲, and Lei Wanchun 雷萬春 had done during the Tang dynasty.[41] By referring to both biblical and Chinese narratives, Wang developed what Carsten Vala calls "religious leadership capital" to influence his church members to follow his lead in resisting the Japanese influence.[42]

After finally agreeing to meet with a Japanese official, a Mr. Takeda 武田熙, on November 11, 1942, yet remaining firm in his convictions, incredibly, Wang was excused from having to participate in the North China Christian Union Group. After hiring a spy in the Christian Tabernacle to closely observe Wang, Takeda apparently felt that he would never turn Wang.[43] Takeda was adequately impressed with Wang's character and personal fortitude but was unwilling to make a martyr out of him. Wang felt that this was a major spiritual victory[44] and interpreted this political opposition between his church and the Japanese military as a spiritual battle between God and Satan. However, what reveals the particularly Chinese nature of the story is how he called on exemplars from Chinese history to rally the members of his church to not capitulate to the Japanese.[45] It is through this matrix of biblical and Chinese history and heroes that influenced Wang's thought that we see that Wang was an indigenous Chinese Christian theologian and not the "American-style fundamentalist" he is sometimes characterized as.[46]

It is very curious as to why Reynolds's English translation of Wang Mingdao's autobiography titled *A Stone Made Smooth* does not mention any of Wang's inspiration drawn from Zhang Xun and the Sui Yang warriors during the An Lushan Rebellion. Arthur Reynolds, who translated several of Wang's works into English, mentioned that Wang's conflict with the Japanese "throws considerable light on our brother's character."[47] It is strange, then, that Reynolds, who has done non-Chinese readers a considerable service by translating Wang's autobiography into English, completely edits out this Chinese history-driven inspiration. It may simply have been an editing decision, but it is also possible that Reynolds thought that the story was too enmeshed in Chinese history and characters for readers of English to understand and benefit from. Also, in 1981, when the English version was published, interest in the indigenization of Chinese theology was not as strong as it is currently.

One wonders, then, how Wang had become familiar with Zhang Xun's story. Wen Tianxiang 文天祥 (1236–1283), another of Wang Mingdao's heroes, as will be seen in the next chapter, also admired Zhang Xun's character, as recorded in Wen Tianxiang's *Song of Righteousness* 正氣歌. Wang had drawn great inspiration from Wen's song,[48] but it is more likely that his source for the story of Zhang Xun during the An Lushan Rebellion was *The Old Book of Tang* 舊唐書, as Wang's recollection of the story bears significant similarities with the Tang history book.[49] This recounting of the An Lushan Rebellion by Wang provides evidence that during the 1940s, Wang's thought was deeply enmeshed in the heroic characters of Chinese history and he drew inspiration from them to fashion a uniquely Confucian Christian theology.

THE DEATH OF A FRIEND

With his successful resistance to participating in the North China Christian Union Group, Wang's popularity in China soared, and since his church was the only one to remain independent from the Japanese-controlled union in Beijing, he became the "preeminent popular preacher in the country" after the death of John Sung in 1944.[50] After a number of years where Wang did not see Sung, they reconnected in 1940. These last years of John Sung's life were filled with intense pain due to suffering from tubercular fistula and until nearly the end of his life refusing medical help and advice to rest. Sung reasoned that since he had seen so many people physically healed through his own ministry, to seek medical treatment would be contrary to God's healing power.[51] It was Liu Jingwen's biblical quotation and Wang Mingdao's admonition on March 20, 1940, telling Sung, "It is not those who are healthy who need a physician, but those who are sick," that finally convinced Sung to receive medical treatment for his condition with Wang visiting him several times in the hospital.[52] However, after surgery, Sung began leading revival meetings again throughout Southeast Asia, and his condition gradually worsened. The two men would meet several times in the next four years but only for brief periods.[53] They met for the last time on June 16, 1944, when Wang visited Sung in Beijing while he was in the hospital recovering from another surgery. Sung went to recover from this surgery in Xiangshan 香山, about thirty kilometers from Beijing. When Wang rode his bicycle to visit him in Xiangshan on August 18, he arrived in the afternoon to hear the sad news that Sung had died that morning.[54] Like Sung, Wang Mingdao was a very distinguished Fundamentalist preacher and he was also a personal friend of Sung's, two reasons why Wang was the natural choice to preach the funeral sermon on August 22. This touching memorial, the content of which was recorded in the fall 1944 issue of *The Spiritual Food Quarterly*, reveals the warm friendship that these two men shared.[55] Wang, never one to gloss over a person's weaknesses, noted that Sung was headstrong and lacked knowledge on how to conduct himself in society, which caused people to be offended by his lack of manners. Wang said that in one of his visits to Sung at the Peking Union Medical College Hospital 北京協和醫院, he advised Sung to read his book *Conduct in Society Common Sense for Believers*.[56] Sung responded with a childlike smile, indicating that Wang was embarrassing him, but Wang also responded with a warm smile, and the two looked at each other for a long time. Finally, Sung nodded, indicating his promise to read the book. Wang never asked him if he read it but noticed in his next visit with Sung a significant improvement in his manners toward other people. Sung looked at Wang and said, "conduct in society common sense," indicating that he had taken his friend's advice and read the book. Wang deeply respected Sung's openness to correction, courage, honesty, and integrity. However, what Wang loved most about Sung was that he was not false, but "what he felt in his heart, he said with his mouth."[57] In the 1980s, when Wang was interviewed on church leaders in China, he quoted Confucius and said, "At first, my way with men was to hear their words, and give them credit for their conduct. Now my way is to hear their words, and look at their conduct."[58] Ying Fuk Tsang notes that Wang's respect for John Sung was ultimately due to Wang's admiration for Sung's moral character, which drew the men together, while Wang's lack of respect for Watchman Nee's moral character drove Wang and Nee apart.[59] In this, Ying sees the influence of Confucianism's priority on morality as shaping Wang's relationships with these two men who have been so influential in Chinese Christianity.[60]

MOTHER'S DEATH AND THE CHINESE CIVIL WAR

After the defeat of Japan in World War II and the Japanese departure from China in 1945, the country plunged into a period of civil war with Chiang Kai-shek's Nationalists (KMT) seeking to eradicate Mao Zedong's Communists. The CCP eventually gained the upper hand and defeated the Nationalists, establishing the People's Republic of China in 1949. During this civil war period, although Wang's reputation as the premier Fundamentalist Christian preacher in China was firmly established, with seven hundred to eight hundred people attending worship services at the Christian Tabernacle by 1948,[61] he also experienced some personal suffering.[62] He became severely ill in 1945,[63] his sister, Wang Enrong, died on September 1, 1946, from illness,[64] and his mother died on October 18, 1947.[65] He published a memorial for her, which brings out some neglected nuances of his Confucian Christian character.[66] While not glossing over the facts that he felt his mother had a terrible temper and was quite stubborn, he also emphasized her tender, sacrificial care for him many times when he was sick, sometimes spending day and night tending to his needs. Stressing his own filial character, Wang lamentingly quotes the Han dynasty book *The Han Shi Waizhuan* 韓詩外傳:[67] "The trees long for peace, but the wind will never cease." He quoted this metaphor, in a somewhat exaggerative manner, to lament that when a man finally wants to show his mother filial piety, she has died. Showing both his Christian religious outlook and his Confucian sense of propriety, Wang rejected all Chinese rituals in his mother's funeral that he thought were superstitious. Wang used the opportunity not only to illustrate his own filial piety but also to admonish other Christians in China who followed what he felt were superstitious religious practices.[68] For example, he rejected the practice of changing his mother's clothes shortly before she died, and also, although it was customary to do so, he did not move her to a flat board in her last moments since he felt this was cruel.[69] Flaunting common auspicious practices, Wang wore black to the funeral and purposely buried his mother on the fourth day after she died.

> It was four days from the death of my mother until the funeral. I made this arrangement deliberately. Because according to general custom, an odd number of days from death to funeral is always selected for the funeral day. At least three days, or five days, seven days, nine days, with the days always being an odd number of days. In their view, if you select an even number of days, two people in the family will die. Many Christians have been influenced by this custom, definitely arranging the funeral on an odd numbered day. To the point that even if the fourth is the most suitable day, they would delay by one day. They say that they don't believe in these things that don't conform to the truth, but they do not dare take this risk, for fear that a person will really die. I must take the lead in smashing these superstitions, so I arranged it like this.[70]

What is interesting about Wang's preparations for his mother's funeral is that the rejection of what he viewed as "superstitious" Chinese religious practices were also rejected by many Confucian literati for centuries.[71] Again, these uniquely Chinese details about his mother's death were entirely edited out by Arthur Reynolds in his English translation of Wang's autobiography.[72]

With his Confucian Christian theology, Wang continued to practically guide the growing number of people who were reading his articles or hearing him preach at the Christian Tabernacle. In the fall of 1948, he wrote an article in which he extolled the humble contributions of rickshaw drivers and shoemakers and any job that contributes to society by being beneficial to humankind. Wang pointed to the humility of Jesus to learn carpentry skills[73] and Confucius to acquire abilities in many low-level matters, describing Confucius as "China's sage" to encourage his readers and listeners to make practical contributions to society in China.[74] Wang made this interesting pairing between Christ and Confucius not in an isolated environment apart from people but rather among them as a church leader in the midst of a civil war. By December 1948, Wang reported that the fighting between the Communists and the Nationalists had reached the Beijing suburbs, with Fundamentalist Christians flocking to the Christian Tabernacle to seek stability and comfort.[75] Wang's narrative of events in his autobiography *The Last Fifty Years* stops in 1948 since the writing began then and was completed in 1950. The Nationalists were defeated in 1949, and departed for Taiwan, which ended the period of the Republic of China on the mainland. Chairman Mao Zedong 毛澤東 made the proclamation of the establishment of the People's Republic of China on October 1, 1949, from Tiananmen Square, about a forty-minute walk from Wang's Christian Tabernacle on 42 Shijia Lane. As Thomas Harvey has observed, Wang was not committed to any political party as some Western missionaries have purported and did not support the KMT Nationalists or the CCP.[76] In fact, since Wang observed that the People's Liberation Army had shown good discipline during the Chinese civil war, he was initially optimistic about China's future. His main concern was that the CCP would restrict religious freedoms in China after observing what had happened in Russia following the victory of the Bolsheviks in 1917. However, after being allowed to freely move about and preach in various locations in 1949 and 1950, he thought that Christians in China would be able to go about their religious pursuits without any hindrance.[77]

CONFLICT WITH THE TSPM

The first half of the 1950s is where a significant amount of academic research has already been focused on the study of Wang Mingdao.[78] To not replicate the research previously accomplished by other scholars, only a brief outline of this period is provided to bring out the social context as well as some of the more neglected nuances of the story. Wang notes that "a strange thing" began to happen in the spring of 1950. As the organization's leader, Y. T. Wu led a group of Chinese Christian leaders on a tour of some of the major cities in China promoting the Three Self Reform Movement (TSRM) 三自革新運, calling on the churches in China to rid themselves of imperialism and connections with foreign organizations.[79] Many Christians in China were eager to see the Chinese church become independent from foreign control and fully develop into an indigenous church and freely joined with the movement.[80] Since the TSRM was connected with the new CCP government, with Wu's delegation meeting several times with Prime Minister Zhou Enlai 周恩來 in Beijing, other Christians who were not as concerned with imperialism but feared opposing the new government also joined with the TSRM.[81] Wu and other delegate leaders created a document that became known as the "Christian Manifesto 基督教宣言." This document called on Christians in China to acknowledge the record of imperialism in China and resolve to remove its residual influence in the church.[82] Wang Mingdao refused to sign it. Although he had resolved to be independent from Western missionary agencies since his rebaptism in 1921 and refused to cooperate with the Japanese-controlled North China Christian Union Group in 1942, he did not think that the TSRM was truly interested in the development of an indigenous Chinese church that was self-sustaining, self-propagating, and self-governing. Rather, he saw the TSRM as a tool for Modernists, whom he described as "unbelievers," to control and eventually destroy the church. Wang was familiar with the writings of Y. T. Wu, having read his 1945 article "Where Is God 上帝在那裡?"[83] as well as his 1949 book, *Darkness and Light* 黑暗與光明,[84] and Wang concluded that Wu was an atheist lurking inside the church who was trying to destroy it from the inside.[85]

On November 20, 1951, Wang read Watchman Nee's article "How I Turned Around 我是怎麼轉過來的," which was Nee's explanation for why he led his independent Little Flock into participation in the TSRM, attended its meetings, and accepted its leadership.[86] Wang commented that "what the congregation [Little Flock] is doing is totally different from what they are saying. Originally, they were against all other churches, saying that, whatever their organization and name, they were all sects and that sects are sinful: therefore everyone must leave their sects. That's why anyone who attended their meetings was required to leave their own church immediately. But today Mr Ni has totally changed his position. Now he can sit in meetings alongside priests and even non-believers."[87] Wang, already dubious about Nee's character, became convinced that the reason that Nee participated in the TSRM was an effort at self-preservation. A former member of the Christian Tabernacle, Yan Jialei 閻迦勒, who had left to join Little Flock after becoming convinced of Nee's ecclesiology, later revealed personal testimony about Nee's dealings to his old friend Wang Mingdao. On April 10, 1952, Nee had been arrested by the Public Security Bureau. On October 20 and again on October 30, 1952, Yan confided to Wang that since Little Flock owned large swaths of land in Fujian, Nee, before he was arrested, was concerned that during the CCP land reform efforts, Little Flock's property would be split up and taken away. So he made a request to the government to retain their land by having tens of thousands of Little Flock members from all over China sign a petition to keep their land.[88] Nee later realized that to do this was extremely dangerous as significant numbers of landlords began to be murdered during the Chinese Land Reform Movement 土地改革運動.[89] To stave off disaster, he took the signature list and sent it to Y. T. Wu, who was the chairman of the TSRM, fictitiously indicating that it was a list of Little Flock believers who supported the TSRM.[90] After Yan's testimony, Wang concluded that Nee was jailed not for opposing the TSRM, nor for his Christian faith as some have argued,[91] but rather because of his lying and cheating.[92] Because of this, although Wang disagreed with Nee's ecclesiology, it was ultimately Wang's view of Nee's moral character that troubled him the most.

The independent Chinese churches, who would have reason to argue that they already self-governing, self-supporting, and self-propagating and therefore independent of foreign connections and imperialistic influence, were nevertheless targeted to come under the control of the TSRM. With John Sung dead and Watchman Nee imprisoned, Wang was the most significant independent Chinese Christian to remain outside of the TSRM.[93] Just as Mr. Takeda had done during the Second Sino-Japanese War, spies were dispatched to the Christian Tabernacle to try to catch Wang saying or doing something that could provide a basis for future denouncements against him.[94] However, with Wang's reputation for resisting the Japanese and his well-known personal integrity, it was difficult to entrap him. The TSRM changed its name in 1954 to the Three Self Patriotic Movement (TSPM) due to concerns that some Christians had over the idea of "reforming" Christianity. Wang would later comment that when Empress Wu Zetian 武則天 (624–705) changed her name to Wu Zhao 武曌, she was still known as Wu Zetian, just as when Y. T. Wu changed the name of the Three Self Reform Movement to the Three Self Patriotic Movement, it did not change the fact that the movement was intended to "reform" Christianity in China just as before.[95]

At first, a soft approach of persuasion was attempted by the TSPM leaders to coax Wang Mingdao into joining. While the July 22–August 6 National Christian Conference was being held in Beijing, he received four visitors at the Christian Tabernacle who were delegates from the Beijing TSPM, including the chairman, Wang Zizhong, who had previously cooperated with the Japanese-controlled North China Christian Union Group, but Wang Mingdao refused to meet with them.[96] A few days later, he received another five visitors including Z. T. Kuang, who had become vice chairman of the TSPM. Wang would later ask, due to Wang Zizhong and Z. T. Kuang's previous participation in the Japanese-controlled union, "Were they patriots?"[97] However, another person included in the second group of five was Marcus Cheng whom Wang knew and respected from his visit with Cheng in 1932; Wang was disappointed that Cheng had joined the TSPM and concluded that he was a fallen prophet.[98] Again, Wang refused to meet with them.[99] Instead, they talked with Liu Jingwen who told the five visitors that it would be better not to see Wang because he does not worry about saving face and that "things will become heated, and you will all be embarrassed." A rumor surfaced that "even Wang Mingdao's wife knows his temper. You can tell how hard it is to deal with him."[100] Wang responded in the winter issue of *The Spiritual Food Quarterly* that he had written a book on social etiquette, *Conduct in Society Common Sense for Believers*, but that he was willing to be rude when it came to dealing with "false prophets."[101]

After the failure of the soft approach, the leaders of the TSPM attempted a hard approach to silence Wang with an unsuccessful denouncement campaign and a war of words erupting in the TSPM's *Tianfeng* and Wang's *The Spiritual Food Quarterly,* culminating on Wang's side with his article "We Are for the Faith 我們是為了信仰!" completed on June 9, 1955.[102] These developments in Wang's life were in line with larger developments in China as intellectuals who were not convinced to support the CCP began to be silenced to mobilize the population for a unified effort to achieve the CCP economic program.[103] Wang described in this article that the five main points of theological divergence between the Modernist and Fundamentalist Christians in China were their respective views of the Bible,[104] the Virgin birth incarnation of Jesus Christ,[105] the atonement,[106] the resurrection of Jesus Christ,[107] and the Second Coming of Christ.[108] Wang had been writing about these areas of disagreement between the two groups in *The Spiritual Food Quarterly* since the late 1920s. He concluded that Modernists did not believe in these teachings in the same way that Fundamentalists did and so he could not unite with these "unbelievers" and would therefore not join the TSPM. One month later, on July 7, 1955, Wang Mingdao taught on Lü Zuqian's 呂祖謙 (1137–1181) *Mr. Donglai's Extensive Deliberations* 東萊博議. Lü was a Southern Song dynasty Confucian author who explored how morality affected the political and natural world.[109] As he had when under duress to join the Japanese North China Christian Union in 1942,[110] Wang again found Lü to provide helpful Confucian insight on how to negotiate the extremely stressful conflict with the TSPM concluding based on this ancient work, after a years-long war of words with the leaders of the TSPM movement, that "one should not write anything lightly."[111] One month later, on August 7, 1955, Wang was arrested.

Wang Mingdao established a ministry that was independent from missionary Christianity and during his years of conflict became by 1944 the most famous Fundamentalist Christian in China. During these years, his theology was mainly influenced by his study of the Bible,[112] but he was also influenced by a host of Chinese Confucian authors who guided his moral thinking and gave shape to his practical Confucian Christian theology, with Wang going so far as to call Confucius "China's sage" in 1948. However, after August 7, 1955, Wang was to begin a nearly decade-long fall from his Confucian Christian moral ideals as he entered his prison years.

CHAPTER FIVE

The Prison Years

1955–1980

There are two main primary sources for the events of Wang Mingdao's life for the prison period 1955–80. The first is the set of interviews of Wang Mingdao and Liu Jingwen that were conducted by Stephen Wang from 1989 to 1990 and published as *Another Forty Years* in 1997, which was later translated into English as *The Long Road to Freedom: The Story of Wang Mingdao* in 2002. The other is Wang Mingdao's "Rehabilitation Request Manuscript" published as *Wang Mingdao's Last Confession,* which he wrote between 1982 and 1983 and was published in 2012 by Ying Fuk Tsang as the editor, with currently only the original Chinese version available.[1] In recounting this narrative, the key historical events will be highlighted to more fully bring out the nuances of Wang Mingdao's Confucian Christian thought and to provide a more complete social context than is currently available.

FIRST ARREST

On August 7, 1955, Wang was reading letters at his desk after the evening prayer meeting. At around midnight, Liu Jingwen heard some sounds on the roof and went to investigate. Wang was shocked when someone behind him shouted, "Don't move!" When he turned around and saw a police officer pointing a gun at him, he was so terror stricken that his legs gave out and he collapsed on the bed. Not only were Wang and Liu

Jingwen arrested that night, but so was his former student and coworker Shi Tianmin as well as Stephen Wang, who would later conduct the interviews that comprised *The Long Road to Freedom*,[2] along with dozens of others who were arrested as part of the "Wang Mingdao counter-revolutionary clique," a group of Christians from various locations considered loyal to Wang who also resisted participation in the TSPM. Wang reported that the interrogator told him that "opposing the Three Self is a crime."[3] Previous to this statement, Wang did not realize the political connection between the CCP and the TSPM. The news of his arrest was significant and politically connected enough that on September 19, 1955, the assistant mayor of Beijing who also functioned as the Chief of the Public Security Bureau, Feng Jiping 馮基平, mentioned in a report at the third session of the National People's Congress in Beijing the arrest of Wang Mingdao and the uncovering and capture of his "clique."[4] The terror of his arrest, the realization that he had set himself up against the CCP government through his opposition to the TSPM, and the beatings he received from the other prisoners[5] resulted in Wang abandoning his Confucian Christian convictions about telling the truth: he began lying in order to survive. The internal principle that Wang had cultivated for decades—that it would be better to lose everything than to compromise his righteousness—was met with something even more basic to his being: the fear of death that Wang had dreaded since childhood had not yet been eradicated, despite his great admiration for biblical and Confucian martyrs. In January 1956, after five months in the Weed Haze Lane (Caolanzi Hutong) Detention Center 草嵐子胡同看守所,[6] he submitted a report that he had given up his faith,[7] but even this was a lie, an attempt to say what his interrogators wanted to hear to lessen his suffering, while still secretly believing in the existence of God.[8]

When spring 1956 arrived, under duress, Wang had already confessed to over a dozen crimes with the only one that he would later not say was false was that he had opposed the TSPM.[9] On September 14, after promising to join the TSPM, Wang was allowed to see his wife, who had herself been held in the same detention center although they had not been able to see each other.[10] She was deeply distressed by Wang's mental state believing that he would never be able to go through with his promise to join the TSPM.[11] On September 28, two officers led Wang to write a confession, or "self-examination," that was edited and re-edited several times. He would later repudiate the confession as "a pack of lies."[12] He was released from the detention center the next day on September 29, 1956, after having been in prison for 429 days. The director of the Religious Affairs Bureau told Wang Mingdao to be at Wang Zizhong's home, the chairman of the Beijing TSPM whom he had refused to meet with in the summer of 1954, at 2:00 p.m. to discuss next steps.[13] Wang Mingdao was also told that Western newspapers had been reporting that he and Liu Jingwen had been arrested and that with his release, these rumors would stop.[14] Wang Zizhong told him to go to the Beijing YMCA the next day to read his confession publicly. Stephen Wang notes that this was particularly humiliating for Wang Mingdao after having written his article "The Evils of the Modern YMCA" in 1935.[15] On September 30, Wang Zizhong brought Marcus Cheng, the man Wang formerly respected until he joined the TSPM, to escort Wang Mingdao to the YMCA to read his confession before the hundred-plus assembled listeners. Cheng had earlier written an article published in the TSPM's journal, *Tianfeng*, critical of Wang Mingdao after his arrest.[16] Wang's confession was published the next month in *Tianfeng*.[17] Liu Jingwen was released the day Wang read his confession.[18] Prior to this, Wang had firmly established his reputation as a respected Confucian Christian; however, now with his humiliation complete through both forms, oral and written, he would seek to protest his indignation through the only recourse left available to him, suicide, as a way to maintain his dignity.

SUICIDAL PROTEST

To some Western observers, to commit suicide could be seen as evidence of a guilty conscience for wrongdoing. However, in Chinese history, there is a long tradition of committing suicide as a form of righteous protest for the wrong that has been committed against a person.[19] Qu Yuan, who was one of Wang Mingdao's heroes, exemplified this kind of suicide when he drowned himself in the Milou River after being unjustly banished by his king.[20] Wang had memorized and would later quote Qu Yuan's poem describing the injustice committed against him, which also aptly described the sorrow in Wang's own heart:[21]

> The world is turbulent and impure:
> They call a cicada's wing heavy and a ton weight light;
> The brazen bell is smashed and discarded; the earthen crock is thunderously sounded.
> The slanderer proudly struts; the wise man lurks unknown.[22]

Coupled with Qu Yuan's model of suicide by drowning, Wang was filled with despair over his future. He had promised while in prison to attend TSPM meetings and to preach upon release and he feared returning to prison if he failed to keep his promises.[23] He lost his sense of self-respect after what he perceived as his moral failure for lying while in prison. Just as his father had sunk into a suicidal despair when he looked out at a sea of Boxers on June 22, 1900, Wang Mingdao determined to take his own life as he looked out at his future. Wang crafted a plan to take Liu Jingwen back to her mother's home in Hangzhou after which he planned to slip off to the legendary West Lake and drown himself. It seems that if not for his wife's awareness of her husband's character that he would rather die than be dishonored, Wang's life would have ended in 1956.[24] Liu Jingwen stayed close by his side every moment since she feared that he would follow his father's precedent and commit suicide.[25] Wang's plan was finally quashed when the Public Security Bureau told them that they could not leave Beijing. However, his mental state was still unstable. When T. C. Chao, the famous theologian whom Wang had written was an "unbeliever" after reading Chao's book *Life of Jesus*, came to visit him, presumably to encourage him to attend the TSPM since he himself was a participant, Chao determined that Wang was so unwell that he advised him to rest in bed.[26] On April 8, 1958, after concluding that he could preach no longer, Wang Mingdao and Liu Jingwen moved out of the Christian Tabernacle and back into their family home on Sweet Rain Lane.[27]

SECOND ARREST

When Wang dissolved all connections with the Christian Tabernacle by moving out and resigning from the board of the church, his rearrest was certain. Since he would not preach and did not attend any TSPM meetings after reading his confession, he had not fulfilled the conditions of his release. On April 29, 1958, just as the country began the Great Leap Forward 大躍進, Wang was rearrested along with Liu Jingwen. This rearrest convinced Wang Mingdao that the TSPM was a covert government organization, a conviction he held to the end of his life since in Wang's mind, he was not a counterrevolutionary due to his lack of political participation and because his only "crime" was not participating in the TSPM.[28] In late 1959, Wang Mingdao and Liu Jingwen were transferred from the Weed Haze Lane Detention Center to the Gongdelin Detention Center 功德林看守所, which was located north of the Beijing city wall near the Virtue Victory Gate 德勝門.[29] Shortly thereafter in February 1960, they were transferred again, this time to the Zixin Road Detention Center 自新路看守所 in the south of Beijing, which was connected to the Beijing Prison 北京監獄.[30] They remained there for five or six years. Stephen Wang believes the reason for their long stay at the Zixin Road Detention Center, not yet receiving their prison sentences, was that the government continued to hope that they would join the TSPM.[31] Although they saw each other occasionally, Wang Mingdao and Liu Jingwen were not permitted to speak to each other. On July 18, 1963, Wang was sentenced to lifelong imprisonment with all political rights permanently revoked for counterrevolutionary crime. Liu Jingwen was sentenced to fifteen years of imprisonment (April 29, 1958–April 28, 1973), with her political rights revoked for five years after release, also for counterrevolutionary crime. Their family property on 29 Sweet Rain Lane, the twelve rooms that had been purchased by Wang's mother, Li Wenyi, in the East City section of Beijing and that was now her son's property, was confiscated by the government. Wang Mingdao appealed his sentence, and two months later, his appeal was rejected with the final sentence upholding the original sentence.[32]

WANG "STOOD BACK UP"

By the fall of 1963, Wang Mingdao's worst-case scenario had been realized. He had to face the reality that he would spend the rest of his life in prison. In the midst of intense anger over what he felt was an unjust sentence and deep shame over his moral failure of lying since being arrested, a scripture passage he had memorized when he was twenty-one after he was released from his teaching position in Baoding came to his mind. It was from the Old Testament prophetic book Micah 7:7–8:

> But as for me, I watch in hope for the Lord, I wait for God my Savior; my God will hear me. Do not gloat over me, my enemy! Though I have fallen, I will rise. Though I sit in darkness, the Lord will be my light. Because I have sinned against Him, I will bear the Lord's wrath, until He pleads my case and establishes my right. He will bring me out into the light; I will see His righteousness.

He concluded that the government's sentence of life imprisonment and the loss of his home was God's punishment for having lied upon his arrest and throughout the last eight years by saying he would join the TSPM if released.[33] He resolved at this time to tell the truth and no longer lie. Over the next few months while at the Zixin Detention Center, he wrote hundreds of pages refuting his previous confession in which he indicated that it was full of lies that he had written due to fear of being shot.[34] After retracting his confession, he began compiling a list of "suggestions" for the government that he wrote after being allowed to read the *People's Daily* newspaper.[35] These suggestions were the first signs that we see in Wang's adult life of an engagement with politics, and it is also in line with what Confucian literati had felt was their responsibility for centuries in China: to serve China, regardless of the consequences, "in order to correct mistakes and reform the government."[36] After he finished writing his suggestions, he was told that he was required to do some light work, and he began to polish the edges of plastic shoes after they had been machine pressed. After a few days of this work, he refused by stating that forced labor was the work that criminals are required to do, but "I am not a criminal. I did not commit any crime."[37] Due to his refusal to work, he was placed in solitary confinement for four months. During that period of isolation, he recalled the words of Confucius in *The Analects* 15.15: "Judge oneself harshly but others kindly; in that way you will keep yourself far from complaints." The next day, he asked for paper to write a letter of apology to the prison official he had spoken to harshly when he refused to work.[38] As was evidenced earlier in his life, both the Bible and the Confucian classics were on his mind during his imprisonment.

At some point in 1965, Wang was transferred to a larger prison, the precise name unrecorded, where the famous playwright Lao She 老舍 (Shu Qingchun 舒慶春, 1899–1966) was also imprisoned. He was familiar with Wang Mingdao after visiting the Christian Tabernacle to hear him preach in the early 1950s.[39] Lao She, one year older than Wang Mingdao, grew up very close to Wang's home in Beijing and became a significant name in twentieth-century Chinese literature. He and Wang shared some history as well. Beginning in 1921, Lao She had attended the LMS's Gangwashi Church 缸瓦市教會, the church affiliated with Tsui Wen Academy where Wang had gone to school, with Lao She eventually becoming the head of administration of the Tsui Wen Primary School.[40] Later during the Cultural Revolution, after being condemned as a counterrevolutionary, publicly beaten and humiliated, Lao She would drown himself in Beijing's Taiping Lake 太平湖 on August 24, 1966, revealing that the pressure Wang was under that forced him to contemplate suicide was not unique during this period.[41] By January 1965, although Wang felt that he had "fully recovered my life before I was in prison," by now resolving to tell the truth no matter the consequences after his nearly decade-long failure to do so, he was about to face perhaps the most difficult period of his life as the pressures of the Cultural Revolution that destroyed Lao She extended to the Chinese prison system.[42]

DATONG MINING CAMP AND THE CULTURAL REVOLUTION

In 1966,[43] when the government realized that Wang would never be convinced to join the TSPM, he was transferred to the Datong Mining Camp 大同勞改煤礦 in Datong, Shanxi Province, 264 kilometers west of Beijing, just as the Cultural Revolution 文化大革命 was beginning.[44] Most prisoners at the Datong Mining Camp were required to work in the coal mines, but since Wang Mingdao was sixty-six years old and increasingly deaf, the prison authorities did not make him do so.[45] Datong's enormous coal reserves were mined during the Cultural Revolution in part by convicts like Wang Mingdao's fellow prisoners who were required to reform through labor in the coal mines. Prisoners may have been funneled to Datong (Tatung) to increase production levels, which had dropped off in 1967.[46] As early as the 1920s, it was difficult to find laborers for Shanxi's coal mines with conditions being described as "so bad that no one except criminals or desperadoes would risk working in the mines, a situation which resulted in a shortage of labor."[47] Wang was not required to participate in a political study group due to his increasing deafness but was allowed to study by reading the newspapers, mainly the *People's Daily*, a government-controlled newspaper, which provided him with information on the political changes that were taking place at the time. Although there were many reasons why Mao Zedong had launched the Cultural Revolution in May 1966, one of them was to consolidate his grip on power over the CCP.[48] The changing political fortunes of Liu Shaoqi 劉少奇, the first vice chairman of the CCP from 1959 to 1966 and Mao's chosen successor, Peng Dehuai 彭德懷, defense minister of China from 1954 to 1959, Lu Dingyi 陸定一, minister of the Propaganda Department of the CCP Central Committee, Luo Ruiqing 羅瑞卿, minister of Public Security of the People's Republic of China, and Wu Han 吳晗, a historian, writer, and vice mayor of Beijing beginning in 1949, all once exalted by the CCP but now vilified in the *People's Daily*,[49] convinced Wang that the CCP was untrustworthy.[50] Had he simply pondered these political changes in his heart, he would not have undergone such a bitter struggle. Instead, angered over what he felt was his own experience of injustice, concerned about the fate of the country under dishonest leadership, and now regaining confidence to act on his conviction that it would be better to lose everything than to once again forfeit his righteousness, Wang quoted Confucius's dialogue on politics from *The Analects* 2.22 to the prison officials to level a critique against the CCP: "When a man is not trusted there is no way of knowing what he can do. It is like a vehicle with faulty wheels. How can you make a journey with it?"[51] Looking back to this period in his "Rehabilitation Request Manuscript" written in 1982, Wang saw himself as a Chinese knight fighting injustice with a sword, but the weapons he wielded were his mouth and pen through speaking and writing.[52] This decision to defend ousted political figures during the Cultural Revolution would cost him dearly.

At some point in 1968,[53] Mr. Xin 辛幹事, a prison administrator at the Datong Mining Camp in charge of Wang Mingdao, had Wang handcuffed for five months at all times and accusation meetings were organized against him at the camp as a consequence of defending Liu and the other fallen politicians. Wang, unable to see the complexity of the motivations for the Cultural Revolution from his vantage point, saw the conflict in purely religious terms.[54] During one accusation meeting, he referred to the beheading of the China Inland Mission missionaries John and Betty Stam, executed by Communists in 1934 as proof that the CCP was anti-theist and anti-Christianity.[55] Xin turned up the pressure and organized a group of nine prisoners in Datong to physically and psychologically torture Wang to reform him in line with CCP thinking at the time. In the spring of 1968, Wang was subjected to physical torture for the first time.[56] Wang was no longer willing to lie, but the five months of torment were so terrible that Wang begged Xin to have the government kill him. Wang quotes Xin as saying that the government would not kill Wang but was confident that it would be able to "reform 改造" him, which Wang interpreted as a desire to eradicate his belief in God.[57] Although Wang did not lie, the trauma of what happened in Datong in the spring of 1968 effectively silenced him for the rest of his imprisonment there. The group organized by Xin to break Wang down consisted mainly of people who were imprisoned for collaborating with the Japanese but also a Methodist pastor from Beijing named Zhan Rugeng 詹汝耕 who did not physically harm Wang but was the group's mouthpiece.[58] While at Datong, Wang received a letter from a Christian woman in Hamburg, Germany, who wrote in English inquiring about Wang Mingdao and Liu Jingwen's well-being. Although he was not permitted to respond, this does indicate that Wang's story was continuing to circulate overseas while he was in prison.[59] Wang's suffering in labor camps during the Cultural Revolution was not unique. Millions of Chinese, often labeled as "counterrevolutionaries" like Wang, were imprisoned in labor camps during this time.[60] What is unique is how he processed what had happened to him with a Confucian Christian perspective on history. As he remembered his failures and sufferings, it was a "process of interpretation and meaning-creation"[61] within a worldview that had been formed years before. However, in the next few years, he would be given the time as well as significant Chinese intellectual resources to add new nuances to his historical narrative.

YINYING LABOR CAMP: WANG'S CONFUCIAN RENAISSANCE

At some point between April 1968 and the spring of 1970,[62] Wang Mingdao and Zhan Rugeng, along with many other prisoners, were transferred from Datong to the Yinying Labor Camp 蔭營勞改 in Yinying 蔭營鎮, Shanxi Province.[63] In 1971, the director of the prison informed the prisoners that corporal punishment would henceforth be strictly forbidden.[64] After a period of observation to see if this was in fact true, Wang began to return to his writing.[65] Between 1973 and 1975, his son, Wang Tianduo, visited him three times in Yinying[66] and over these years provided his father with a treasure trove of over five hundred books and periodicals, many of which were Chinese classics.[67] Starting in the spring of 1973, Wang spent the majority of the day reading the newspaper and pouring over these books, which included a ten-volume *Records of the Grand Historian* 史記 and a three-volume *Records of the Three Kingdoms* 三國志.[68] As a lover of historical books,[69] he was able to read through these histories to review an enormous period of Chinese history and given unprecedented time to contemplate the lessons that the historians like Sima Qian 司馬遷 (145–86 BCE) wanted to impart to their readers. He was also given a collection of the writings of Xunzi 荀子 (310–235 BCE), a Confucian philosopher who lived during the Warring States Period. It seems that Wang had read the histories before but had only read Xunzi upon coming to Yinying.[70] Wang quoted Xunzi extensively in his "Rehabilitation Request Manuscript" and said that of all the books he was given at Yinying, he enjoyed Xunzi the most and read through the volume several times.[71] What seems to have intrigued Wang is that he found in Xunzi's writings the reconciliation between a conflict in the two philosophical systems that shaped his thought. In his "Rehabilitation Request Manuscript," Wang wrote, "In the past, I only knew that there was a man in ancient times named Xunkuang [Xunzi], and I also knew that his teaching was completely opposite to Mencius. Mencius said 'human nature is good [性善],' but Xunzi said 'human nature is evil [性惡].' However, I had never read Xunzi's writings."[72]

Wang's Christian theology included the belief that due to the fall of humankind into sin, human nature is evil.[73] Mencius, as the interpreter of Confucius in the *Four Books*, argued that human nature is good,[74] creating a conflict between the two systems of thought. However, during his reading of Xunzi while at Yinying, Wang had found an alternative interpretation of Confucius that human nature was indeed evil,[75] thus reconciling for him the difference on this important point between Christianity and Confucianism.[76] The reconciliation on the nature of humankind for Wang should not be underestimated. Wang's experience of humanity, from the time he observed human nature as a child in his mother's housing complex in Beijing,[77] to working with people at the Christian Tabernacle,[78] to his experiences in prison, all confirmed for him the teaching that human nature is by nature evil. Xunzi, as an alternative interpreter of Confucius to Mencius, had a perspective on human nature that provided for Wang a way to harmonize his Confucian education with his experiences in life and Christian theology.

WEN TIANXIANG AND THE "SPIRIT OF RIGHTEOUSNESS"

While in Yinying, Wang also contemplated the life of the Southern Song dynasty poet and politician Wen Tianxiang 文天祥 (1236–1283). Wang does not refer to Wen in *The Spiritual Food Quarterly*, nor does he mention reading his works in his published diary. However, he does indicate that he had memorized several of Wen's poems long before his prison years.[79] It seems that Wang's time at Yinying, having been in prison for many years due to a cause he felt was not just, gave him an even greater appreciation for Wen Tianxiang and an even deeper resonance with his historiographic poetry. When the Mongols led by Kublai Khan 忽必烈 or 元世祖 (1215–1294), grandson of Genghis Khan, attacked the Song dynasty, Wen Tianxiang accepted the role of prime minister 丞相 from Emperor Duanzong 宋端宗 and commanded the Song troops of resistance against the Mongol invaders. He was captured in 1278 but refused to serve the upstart Yuan dynasty 元朝 (1279–1368), despite Kublai Khan's offer to make him a high official in the new dynasty. Instead, Wen wrote his historiographic poetry such as the "Song of the Spirit of Righteousness 正氣歌" and "Eight Words of Praise 八句贊" while in prison to express his loyalty to the Song dynasty. He was detained in the Yuan empire's capital, Dadu 大都, which is modern Beijing, for four years and was finally executed.[80] The song is a recapitulation of some of the glories of Confucian Chinese history, and Wang Mingdao memorized every word of the "Song of the Spirit of Righteousness":[81]

> In the world there is the spirit of righteousness, taking many forms, bestowed on the ever-changing things.
> Below they are the rivers and the mountains; above they are the sun and stars.
> With people it is called the spirit of honor and fearlessness, so vast it fills the universe.
> When the empire is tranquil one pours forth harmony in the splendid court.
> When times are extreme true fidelity is seen, and goes down in history case after case.
> During the State of Qi it is the official historian's bamboo slats; during the State of Jin it is Dong Hu's pen.
> During the Qin dynasty, it is Zhang Liang's hammer; during the Han dynasty, it is Su Wu's ambassadorial staff.
>
> It is General Yan's head; it is imperial attendant Ji's blood.
> It is Zhang's teeth at Sui Yang;[82] it is Yan's tongue at Chang Shan.
> Or it is the Eastern Liao hat, the incorruptibly purer than ice and snow.
> Or it is the Memorials to Embark on the Campaign—the courage and fierce loyalty make gods and spirits weep.
> Or it is the oar during the river crossing—the fervency swallows up the barbarians.
> Or it is the court tablet striking the villain, breaking the rebel rogue's head.
> What is permeated by this spirit lives on forever revered.
> It links up the cosmos, so how can life and death compare in importance?
> The corners of the earth depend on it to stand; the pillars of heaven depend on it to maintain their honor.
> The three relationships really do determine one's life; moral righteousness is the root.[83]

In Wen Tianxiang's "Song," Wang had found a retelling of the history of China with an explanation that it is moral righteousness, described as a "spirit of righteousness," as seen in the lives of Chinese exemplars who are loyal, trustworthy, and sincere, that holds up both society and heaven itself.

Furthermore, Wang seems to have seen himself as a modern Wen Tianxiang discovering several points of similarity in the two men's experiences and finding encouragement in Wen's steadfastness while in prison: Wang wrote that just like Kublai Khan sent people to persuade him to join the Yuan dynasty, Y. T. Wu sent people to persuade him to join the TSPM. Just as Wen Tianxiang did not surrender to the Mongolians, so Wang did not surrender to the atheists. Wen Tianxiang served the Song emperor, and Wang served the God of heaven.[84]

While at Yinying, Wang contemplated another of Wen Tianxiang's poems, titled "Eight Words of Praise," in which Wen expresses that human moral development is achieved through contemplating the sages of the past and putting their teachings into practice:[85]

Confucius teaches benevolence,
Mencius teaches righteousness,
As long as morality and justice are pursued to the utmost,
Then the desired benevolence will naturally be achieved to the utmost.
What do we learn from the works of sages?
Now that I have learned benevolence and righteousness,
From now on,
There is nearly nothing to be ashamed of.[86]

Wang, inspired by the ideas in the "Eight Words of Praise," wrote his own Christianized version of Wen's Confucian poem while in prison:

The Prophets teach benevolence,
The Apostles teach righteousness,
Appointed to preach,
They gave the most weight to steadfastness.
Read and re-read the Bible,
Thoroughly know the truth,

Be faithful and unyielding,
Of indomitable spirit.[87]

Wang saw himself as a patriot in the line of Zhang Xun, Wen Tianxiang, and other Chinese worthies.[88] His years in Yinying allowed him the time to rethink Chinese history, with the help of Wen Tianxiang's poetry and Xunzi's philosophy, to see God at work through morally upright Chinese who possessed a "spirit of righteousness."

CRITICIZE LIN BIAO, CRITICIZE CONFUCIUS MOVEMENT

The spring of 1974 brought these peaceful days of contemplation in the Yinying Labor Camp to a halt when the impact of the Criticize Lin Biao, Criticize Confucius Movement 批林批孔運動 was felt in the prison.[89] The movement, which began in the fall of 1973 and lasted until the end of the Cultural Revolution in 1976, was used by Mao Zedong to explain how Lin Biao 林彪, the leader of the People's Liberation Army and another of Mao's designated successors, went from being a CCP political hero to a villain. Mao, who was losing credibility after Lin's mysterious death on September 13, 1971,[90] with the support of the Gang of Four 四人幫,[91] organized a mass campaign to explain how Lin Biao had pretended to put on an extreme left-leaning Communist ideology, which he used to disguise his "right essence," thus making him a counterrevolutionary reactionary.[92] At the same time, another mass campaign was focused on criticizing Confucius and the values he represented with the former "sage of China" now labeled as a reactionary who was against the progressive movement of social development.[93] With the attack on Confucius, CCP ideology picked up themes of the earlier May Fourth Movement attack on Confucius but pushed them much further and with different nuances. Confucius was attacked, but now Qin Shihuang, long viewed as a violent tyrant, was lifted up for praise as a unifier of the country whose burning of the Confucian books and slaughtering of Confucian scholars was necessary to establish the landlord class.[94] Wang read many of the articles attacking Confucius in the *People's Daily* and wrote responses while at Yinying that defended Confucius.[95] When prison officials asked Wang in 1975 about the story of Confucius while he was prime minister of the State of Lu 魯國 executing Shao Zhengmao 少正卯, an act that was criticized in the 1970s as further establishing a dictatorship of the slave-owning class,[96] Wang responded with a thorough knowledge of the classics that apparently surprised the prison officials. Wang argued that it was not due to brutality on Confucius's part that he executed Shao but that it was because of the immorality of Shao Zhengmao and to establish social order in Lu.[97] he maintained that Confucius should not be criticized, making the statement that "Jesus is my Savior and Confucius is my teacher" and reiterated that Confucius was "the national saint of China," a statement that he had made in writing twenty-seven years earlier.[98] His suffering in Datong and Yinying did not efface his Confucian Christian commitment despite the fact that the official opinion in China had changed from viewing Confucius no longer as a sage but as a hypocrite.[99]

Wang was also aware of some of the developments and changes among Neo-Confucian scholars through his reading in Yinying. Wang had read some of the Neo-Confucian scholars at least as early as those from 1937 and he mentioned that he had a good impression of Feng Youlan 馮友蘭 (1895–1990) before the Second Sino-Japanese War. Feng had developed a name for himself as a distinguished Neo-Confucian scholar, and Wang may have read Feng's most famous work, *A History of Chinese Philosophy* 中國哲學史,[100] in which Feng sought to develop a Neo-Confucian philosophy that could provide philosophical resources for a modern Chinese context. However, after the Communist victory in 1949, Feng began to reinterpret Confucian philosophy through the perspective of Marxist thought. In the later years of the Cultural Revolution, Feng even denounced Confucius.[101] Wang Tianduo had sent Wang Mingdao a copy of Feng's 1973 publication, *On Confucius* 論孔丘, which reflects Feng's change of perspective on the sage.[102] After reading the book, Wang concluded that Feng was shameless in his turning on Confucius.[103]

In an article Wang likely read in the January 4, 1974, *People's Daily*, the conflict in both ancient and modern China was laid out as one of class struggle:

> The two incidents of Confucius killing Shao Zhengmao and Qin Shihuang's "burning books and burying Confucian scholars" during the struggle between the two lines of Confucianism and Legalism in the Spring and Autumn and Warring States tell us that in a class

> based society, the struggle in the ideological field is a reflection of class struggle. It is irreconcilable, and one side always overwhelms the other. Of course, Confucius killing Shao Zhengmao and "burning books and burying Confucian scholars" are dictatorships of two different classes. The former is the dictatorship of the reactionary slave-owning class over the emerging landlord class, and the latter is the dictatorship of the landlord class that has just gained power over the slave-owning class that is engaged in counter-revolutionary restoration. According to Marxist views on class and class struggle, we should praise and affirm Qin Shihuang's "burning books and burying Confucian scholars," and we should condemn and criticize Confucius for killing Shao Zhengmao.[104]

Wang viewed the conflict in China through a different lens: he believed that it was not Marxist class struggle that gave rise to conflict in both ancient and modern China but that the battle was between theists and atheists. No longer fearful of being tortured as he was in Datong,[105] Wang later reflected that he felt like Confucius in Yinying, assured in the midst of danger that he had been given a divine mission:

> I believed what Confucius believed at the time: "While Heaven does not let the cause of truth perish, what can the people of Kuang do to me?"[106] I was sentenced to life imprisonment, that is, "I will never go out of prison while alive." However, I believed that authority is in the hands of God. My life is completely under God's control. I believe that the authority of God is greater than the authority of anyone in the world. It is this faith that allows me to write materials and testify in a prison set up by those who oppose God, so I say if a person wants to oppose God, it is tantamount to striking a stone with an egg [attempting the impossible] and courting disaster.[107]

Wang believed that Confucius, due to his references to heaven 天 and God 上帝, was a theist. Wang had concluded that Daoism was "absurd"[108] and that Buddhism had introduced idolatry into China during the reign of Emperor Ming 漢明帝 (28–75) of the Eastern Han dynasty, but previous to this, China's scholars were theists.[109] In Wang's opinion, Confucius, as the national saint of China, showed the Chinese people the way to follow

God before the way was made more fully known by Jesus Christ through the preaching of Christian missionaries.[110] Other Chinese Christians, like T. C. Chao,[111] also believed this, but what is unique about Wang's Confucian Christianity is that he did not embrace Modernist theology like Chao and many other Confucian Christians did but rather held to a Fundamentalist Christian theology that he blended with a thoroughly Confucian worldview and maintained his religious faith until the end of his life.[112]

RELEASE FROM PRISON

Following a wave of significant events, Mao Zedong's death on September 9, 1976, Deng Xiaoping's 鄧小平 (1904–97) emergence as paramount leader 最高領導人 in December 1978, and the establishment of Sino-American diplomatic relations in January 1979, "counterrevolutionaries" like Wang Mingdao began to be released. News of Wang's release was reported in *Time* magazine on September 10, 1979, which shows that the wheels for Wang's release were set in motion and this news was eagerly shared with the United States.[113] Some have argued that it was due to foreign pressure that political prisoners like Wang Mingdao were released.[114] Indeed, Wang Mingdao's story was featured in the 1978 Amnesty International Report *Political Imprisonment in the People's Republic of China*.[115] In May 1978, Amnesty International staff had written to Deng Xiaoping, China's paramount leader, to request information on Wang's release and rehabilitation.[116] It has even been rumored that in January 1979, when Deng Xiaoping visited the United States to discuss with President Jimmy Carter the normalization of diplomatic relations between China and the United States, the release of Wang Mingdao from prison was one of the topics of discussion between the two world leaders. It is alleged that Carter asked Deng about Wang's prison status to which Deng promised Carter that Wang Mingdao's situation would be resolved that year.[117] Yet in addition to foreign pressure, there was also a more determinative internal Chinese desire to correct and heal some of the excesses of the Mao era and to refocus the country's efforts away from ideological campaigns and to economic development, which prompted the release of those prisoners.[118] Nevertheless, it would not be so easy to make Wang go away quietly, the man who felt he had been wrongly imprisoned for twenty-three years and whose mind had been fed for the past decade on stories of men like Zhang Xun and Wen Tianxiang who held true to their convictions in the face of death.

Y. T. Wu had died on September 17, 1979, and Wang read in the September 25 edition of the *People's Daily* that a memorial service would be held for Wu in Shanghai.[119] In response to this, Wang wrote a document he titled "A Thorough Exposure and a Bold Challenge 一個徹底的大暴露和一個大膽的挑戰" in which he described his battle with the TSPM and his perspective on what the TSPM really was.[120] On November 11, 1979, Wang was given permission to leave Yinying Labor Camp and return home. He initially agreed to leave and asked the prison officials that his document "A Thorough Exposure and a Bold Challenge" be sent to the State Council of Beijing 北京國務院, possibly in preparation for his future request for rehabilitation.[121] However, Wang refused to sign a paper from the High Court of Shanxi Province as part of the release procedure since it said that he was a counterrevolutionary. He refused to admit that he was a counterrevolutionary or that he was a criminal; he said that he would not leave the prison. Having dealt with Wang for nearly a decade, the prison officials realized that he was serious. On December 29, they concocted a plan to have him stay in a "three-room" domicile located outside of the prison compound where he was told to write his objection and await a court official from Beijing to discuss his objections. Wang, believing they were sincere, agreed to this arrangement. It was a clever trick by the prison officials since no one would ever come from Beijing.[122] During his stay in the three rooms, Wang believes that Mr. Xin, the same man who organized the group of nine individuals to torment Wang while in Datong Mining Camp, looked in the domicile and nodded at Wang, who later interpreted the nod as a mark of respect from his enemy who admired Wang's fortitude. It was also a mark of victory for Wang because Mr. Xin had told him while at Datong that the government was confident that it was able to "reform" him, which Wang interpreted to mean that the government desired him to abandon his faith in God. Now on his way out of prison, Wang felt he had been victorious in maintaining his faith. If Wang was correct that indeed this was Mr. Xin, uncertain due to his deteriorated eyesight, it seems that Xin was also transferred with the prisoners to

Yinying in 1968.[123] Wang's perception of the event does reveal his process of interpretation and meaning creation. It should always be kept in mind that Wang's autobiographical writings are biased sources that are often the only source available to describe a particular event[124] since, as stated by Kao Chen-yang, "the study of Christianity during the Cultural Revolution is notoriously constrained by the lack of written documentation."[125] However, although some of the details may have been exaggerated, after his moral renewal in 1963, Wang appears to have been fastidious about telling the truth as he perceived it. The Confucian biographies he had read while in prison were written to teach the great moral lessons of the past.[126] Wang wanted to teach the readers of his autobiographical writings the great moral lessons of his life as well. Despite the respect Wang perceived he had received from Mr. Xin, Wang's glaucoma was by now so bad that he could not prepare his own food, and he was unable to use the squat-style toilet that was in the three rooms, so Wang conceded that he could not remain there. On January 1, 1980, Wang wrote to his son to come pick him up to bring him to his home in Shanghai.[127] With this decision, the prison era ended and a new one began.

Wang's prison years reveal not only the impact of previous Confucian Christian education and formation but also new developments in his thought due to his imprisonment and the larger political context. He had memorized significant passages from the Chinese classics as a student at Tsui Wen Academy.[128] From 1921 to 1955, he memorized large portions of the Bible and settled on a Fundamentalist Christian theology as a preacher and author. Building on this Confucian Christian background, it was the period in Yinying that allowed him time to review the scope of Chinese classical history, with a new interpretation of Confucius in Xunzi, and inspiration from the life of Wen Tianxiang. These factors combined to help Wang make meaning out of what had happened in China during his lifetime. It was this intellectual formation that would shape Wang's next stage in Shanghai as a spiritual father to the unregistered house church movement.

CHAPTER SIX

The Spiritual Father Years

1980–1991

With Deng Xiaoping's policies of Reform and Opening 改革開放 to the outside world, a hopeful new era had begun in China. The beginning of the 1980s was also a hopeful time for Wang Mingdao. After nearly twenty-three years in prison, he was a free man. On January 7, 1980, his son, Wang Tianduo, brought one of Wang Mingdao's dearest friends, Zeng Pingdao, to pick him up from Yinying Labor Camp. While Wang and Zeng waited a day for Wang to receive the appropriate release forms, they spent the day catching up, praying, reading the Bible, and reciting poetry. Wang recited Wen Tianxiang's "Song of the Spirit of Righteousness" from memory "without missing a word."[1]

A SPIRITUAL FATHER ON PINGJIANG ROAD

On January 10, 1980,[2] Wang arrived in Shanghai at his son's home at 13 Pingjiang Road 平江路 and lived in a small room with his wife, Liu Jingwen, from whom he had been separated since April 29, 1958. Imprisoned for the past two decades with his only knowledge of the world outside of the Datong and Yinying Labor Camps provided by the government-controlled *People's Daily*, Wang was shocked that not only was he not forgotten, but he had become the "spiritual leader" of much of the unregistered house church movement in China.[3] Wang's model of suffering for his faith inspired many unregistered Chinese Christians who heard his story to follow his example. Without his knowledge while he was in prison, Wang's writings had been republished in Hong Kong[4] and Taiwan,[5] and he was surprised to find out that his story continued to circulate overseas through organizations such as Amnesty International and the publications of former China missionaries such as Leslie Lyall and David Adeney who had become "China watchers." What Wang found most moving was the fact that many other Christians in China had also suffered as he did in prison and they also did not give up their faith. Many of them were implicated with him in the Wang Mingdao counterrevolutionary clique in the 1950s, but of the ones who came to see him, not only did they not hate him, but they respected him even more for having maintained his faith while in prison.[6] This creates an interesting question: since Wang was imprisoned and his writings were banned, how did he become such an influential figure to Christians in post-Mao China? It seems that his story was passed on by word of mouth among Chinese Protestant Christians,[7] and his theology was promulgated through unregistered house church training sessions that flourished when government control of religion was relaxed after the Cultural Revolution in 1976, such as the ones conducted by Jonathan Chao (Zhao Tianen) 趙天恩 of China Ministries International.[8] Wang's conservative theology and high personal integrity were particularly relevant to the Chinese house church context.[9] Thus, this made Wang's "fundamentalist theological perspective the framework for pastoral training in the house churches."[10] As word of his release spread, Wang Mingdao and Liu Jingwen received a stream of visitors from all over China and overseas.[11] Perhaps recognizing the hagiographic light that these visitors were putting him in,[12] Wang was careful to recount his period of personal moral failure beginning with his arrest on August 8, 1955 until the fall of 1963, the period that Wang considered to be when he was unable to live out his Confucian Christian convictions due to fear. He would often quote Proverbs 28:13 to these visitors: "He who conceals his sins does not prosper, but whosoever confesses them and renounces them finds mercy."[13]

FACING CRITICISM

While he lived on Pingjiang Road in Shanghai, Ng Lee-Ming 吳利明, a professor of religion at Chung Chi College 崇基學院, Chinese University of Hong Kong,[14] wrote *Christianity and Social Changes in China* 基督教與中國社會變遷 in which he included Wang Mingdao as one of the significant theologians who had influenced Chinese Christian theology.[15] Wang was aware of his inclusion in the book.[16] Ng conceded that of all the theologians he covers in his book, Wang Mingdao is probably the most respected by the average Chinese Christian believer, but that does not mean that he is a good theologian.[17] In Ng's conclusion on Wang's theology, Ng states that

> Wang Mingdao's messages undoubtedly have attracted and helped many people in the midst of suffering difficulty. This help can give life, in the midst of disappointment, hope. However, to those who are not seeking to escape the world, but rather want to positively change the world, Wang Mingdao's message is completely meaningless. In his hope for the next life he hides an unexplained criticism of the world including human culture and social organizations. So even though Wang's message provides help to those in the midst of turmoil, to those who are courageously going out to face reality, his message does not find a sympathetic response. Of course, we cannot because of this conclude that Wang's message has no meaning. However, we cannot help but doubt the value of religious beliefs that only create meaning for people who are disheartened and have lost hope.[18]

Wang most likely read Ng's critique of the "meaninglessness" of his theology for those who are positively trying to change the world. Another critique of Wang that he was made aware of during his time on Pingjiang Road was by Zhang Zhiyi 張執一, the deputy minister of the United Front Work Department of the CCP Central Committee 中共中央統戰部副部長. In 1981, at the Third National Christianity Conference 基督教全國會議, he criticized Wang Mingdao by name and said, "There are also a few people like Wang Mingdao who are pawns of foreign reactionary forces."[19] Wang later gave a tongue-in-cheek response, thanking Zhang for his promotion to a "pawn of foreign reactionary forces" from a lowly "running dog of American imperialism."[20] With these two critiques in mind, that he was a pawn of foreigners and that his theology was useless for modern Chinese Christians trying to change the world in a positive direction, Wang would begin writing his final major manuscript.

REQUEST FOR REHABILITATION

Wang's greatest desire upon his release from prison was the rehabilitation of his reputation, or political rehabilitation 平反.[21] This kind of rehabilitation involves the restoration to a positive public reputation along with the restoration of legal rights of a person who has fallen into disgrace.[22] To accomplish this goal, Wang began to write a request to Jiang Hua 江華 (1907–99), the president of the Supreme People's Court of China 中國最高人民法院院長 to have his case reevaluated. Jiang Hua had presided over a large number of court reversals of counterrevolutionary convictions resulting in rehabilitation during his tenure from 1975 to 1983.[23] Jiang Hua wrote a report titled "On the Work of the Supreme People's Court," which chronicles the changes in perspective of the court since February 1978 and the subsequent work to review and redress unjust, false, and wrong cases.[24] Noticing this change, Wang wrote his "Rehabilitation Request Manuscript" from 1982 to 1983, meaning that he began writing it while living on Pingjiang Road in Shanghai.[25] Wang saw that there was an openness in Chinese society following Deng Xiaoping's Reform and Opening that had not been present since the Hundred Flowers Campaign in 1957. Wang read in the *People's Daily* on June 14, 1980, an article titled "The Chinese Communist Party Members Must Tell the Truth 共產黨員要說實話," which besides indicating through the article's title that the CCP members had *not* been telling the truth, Wang argued that the CCP members had not been telling the truth since the late 1950s.[26] He also read an article on December 31, 1981, which was a speech from 1945 by Chen Yun 陳雲, second in power only to Deng Xiaoping in the Reform and Opening era, titled "Speak the Truth, Don't Talk about Saving Face 只講真理, 不要講面子." Wang saw in these articles a correction in the direction of the CCP toward telling the truth.[27]

Wang had also seen from the case of Hu Feng 胡風 (1902–85) that previous judgments were being reviewed by the courts. Hu Feng was a writer and art theorist who was purged in 1955 along with those connected to him, known as the Hu Feng counterrevolutionary clique, and charged like Wang as a counterrevolutionary. Hu's charges were reviewed by the Supreme People's Court who concluded in July 1980 that Hu Feng's was a misjudged case with an incorrect verdict. Hu Feng was subsequently rehabilitated, along with many who were connected to the Hu Feng counterrevolutionary clique, following this verdict.[28] Ying Fuk Tsang's research shows that in reassessing Hu Feng's case, "the Central Committee of the Communist Party of China admitted that at the time the judgement 'confused two types of contradictions of different natures and designated some comrades with erroneous remarks and sectarian activities as counter-revolutionaries.' It was decided that 'everyone who was determined to be a Hu Feng counter-revolutionary would be corrected and their reputation restored.'"[29] The rehabilitation of Hu Feng and those connected with him made Wang Mingdao think about his own legal status and that of those implicated with him in the Wang Mingdao counterrevolutionary clique.[30]

Wang's motivation in writing his request was to restore both his own personal reputation and legal status in the eyes of all people. He was already esteemed by Christians in China and around the world,[31] but as can be seen from his refusal to sign his release documents in Yinying, he despised being officially known as a criminal when he held that the only "crime" he committed was opposing the TSPM, which he did not believe was in fact a crime. He viewed his opposition to the TSPM as a religious issue and not a political one. If he were to achieve rehabilitation, it would mean that his suffering, like that of Wen Tianxiang, would be viewed by *all* Chinese as righteous suffering. Another important reason it seems he pursued rehabilitation is that if he were successful, those who were implicated with him in the Wang Mingdao counterrevolutionary clique would also be rehabilitated. He felt a responsibility for those people who were imprisoned in connection to him and who had suffered varying degrees of loss due to their personal loyalty to him.[32] Several of these people had been young university students at the time of their arrest in 1955.[33] With all of these thoughts in mind, Wang began the arduous task of writing his request for rehabilitation. Since the manuscript is not one document and by the time of its writing, Wang was an octogenarian, the following argument is pieced together from different parts of the *Last Confession*.[34]

WANG MINGDAO'S LAST CONFESSION

With advanced glaucoma so severe that he could no longer read,[35] he began his "Rehabilitation Request Manuscript" by writing a preface from memory that included over one hundred quotes from ancient Chinese sources. Showing a familiarity with the classics of China that no "pawn of foreign reactionary forces" would have had interest in, he wrote that he wanted to begin his request to Jiang Hua with some of the "precious teachings of the ancients of China" and thus firmly located his thought in the ancient Chinese Confucian tradition.[36] Quoting the *Five Classics*, the *Analects*, *Mencius*, *The Great Learning*, *The Doctrine of the Mean*, *Xunzi*, Sima Qian, Yue Fei, Wen Tianxiang, Lü Zuqian, Du Mu, Bai Juyi, *The Book of Han*, *The Old Book of Tang*, and others, Wang laid out his moral and religious vision as displayed through his selections of quotes from a wide variety of sources. In the end, he brought the preface to a Christian turn with the last quotes being of the Qing dynasty's Kangxi emperor, Aisin Gioro Xuanye 清聖祖愛新覺羅玄燁 (1661–1722). The Kangxi emperor was "one of the most admired rulers in China's history."[37] He, in turn, was an admirer of the Jesuits and in 1692, issued an edict of toleration of Roman Catholicism.[38] Emperor Kangxi wrote several poems on the Christian religion including Wang's final quote in the preface, which was Emperor Kangxi's "Poem on the Death of Christ":

> When the work on the Cross was finished, blood formed a creek;
> Grace from the west flowed a thousand yards deep.
> He stepped onto the midnight road, to subject Himself to four trials;
> Before the rooster crowed twice, thrice by His disciple was He betrayed.
> Five hundred lashes tore every inch of His skin;

> Two thieves hung on His either side, six feet high.
> Sadness greater than any had ever known;
> Seven utterings, one completed task, ten thousand spirits weep.[39]

Through the editorial selections of his memory, Wang directed the quotes to show that the moral vision extolled in the Chinese Confucian tradition was brought to a climax in the Christian God, and particularly in the death of Jesus Christ, as displayed in the great Chinese emperor Kangxi's poetry. In the conclusion to his preface, he explained his moral and religious vision. Wang believed that honesty and personal moral integrity are the keys to changing the world in a positive direction. By the 1980s, he had lived through countless ideological movements and campaigns and thought that telling the truth was crucial for moral improvement and the development of a just society.

He found these lessons in the *Four Books* during his days at Tsui Wen Academy but had not understood them until he became a Christian in 1914:

> The quotations of the sages of our country quoted above, except for Xunzi, which I have read in prison in Shanxi Province, have been familiar to me for decades. These good words cover all aspects of life: from thought to speech to behavior, from individual to society, from family to country, from small things to big things, from a trickle of water to a giant current, everything is mentioned. The *Four Books* was the first text I read after I entered elementary school. At that time, it was just recitation from memory. Although it was recitation, I did not understand the meaning. After I was fourteen years old (1914) as a Christian, I began to understand many of these lessons. Since then, I have paid special attention to absorbing all the words about behaving with integrity from the ancient texts and other books from history. Confucius, my first teacher, said, "It is all over! I have not seen one who loves virtue as he loves beauty!"[40] No matter what book I read, I have paid attention to the words related to "moral conduct," so I can recite words about morality well, and I can remember them. I even noticed this when reading English. I can even now still recite two sentences from an English reading book I read: "Always

> speak the truth. To speak the truth is brave, lying is cowardly." From then on I decided to be a brave person, "To speak the truth," to be an honest person.[41]

Relatedly, personal immorality and social decay was on the minds of Chinese in the early 1980s. Wang noticed that in February 1981, the CCP proposed a policy of emphasis on the "Five Stresses and Four Beauties 五講四美" to facilitate, among other things, moral development after the destruction of the Cultural Revolution.[42] The Five Stresses refer to decorum, manners, hygiene, discipline, and morality while the Four Beauties refer to the beauty of the mind, language, behavior, and environment.[43]

The solution Wang advanced in the "Rehabilitation Request Manuscript" for the ills of personal immorality and social decay was theism, lived out through upright personal morality, especially among leaders. The foundational tenet of this solution was to tell the truth, which would have a resultant positive effect on Chinese society. He quoted *The Great Learning* to Jiang Hua to show the ancient Chinese foundation for this pattern of individual to social moral renewal:

> *The Great Learning* said: "Their thoughts being sincere, their hearts were then rectified. Their hearts being rectified, their persons were cultivated. Their persons being cultivated, their families were regulated. Their families being regulated, their states were rightly governed. Their states being rightly governed, the whole kingdom was made tranquil and happy. From the Son of Heaven [Wang adds:] (including the emperor, president, chairman, and all other heads of state) down to the mass of the people, all must consider the cultivation of the person the root of everything besides."[44]

After his twenty-three years in prison, Wang seemed to be more convinced than ever that it was through personal moral cultivation and renewal that the broader society would benefit. Leaders were especially important in Wang's thinking. Turning again to *The Great Learning*, Wang argued that the personal moral choices of leaders have far-reaching societal consequences: "On this account, the ruler must himself be possessed of the good qualities, and then he may require them in the people. He must not have the bad qualities in himself, and then he may require that they shall not be in the people."[45] Also, Wang quoted Mencius's statement that "when the prince has no principles by which he examines his administration, his ministers have no laws by which they keep themselves in the discharge of their duties."[46] Wang indicates that the state is in danger when such unprincipled behavior is exhibited by its leaders. Wang's two major problems with the CCP leadership, particularly until the downfall of the Gang of Four,[47] were the lack of honesty among CCP leaders and their promulgation of atheism. Wang reveals in the "Rehabilitation Request Manuscript" that what he believes is at the root of immorality in China is atheism or materialism.[48] After making several quotes from Chinese classics, which advance his belief that ancient Chinese Confucians were theists,[49] Wang argues that atheism removes the ideological constraints on immorality, or as Wang said, "Once people are instilled with atheistic thoughts, they are not afraid of doing anything" since they no longer fear repercussions in an afterlife. To prove his point, he quotes Mao Zedong who said, "A thorough materialist is fearless."[50] In Wang's opinion, atheism or materialism had been the ideological foundation for the past twenty years of catastrophe, which had culminated in the Cultural Revolution.[51]

CONFUCIANISM AND CHRISTIANITY

In stark contrast to Mao Zedong, Confucius was not an atheist but a theist. Wang believed that the "sage of China" revealed the Way, or Dao 道, of God in China before it was made more fully known in Jesus Christ: "In the East (China) God preached this 'Dao' through Confucius. . . . In the West, God preached this 'Dao' through Moses and the prophets in the Old Testament era. By the 30s CE, Jesus Christ had fully revealed the 'Dao.'"[52] Wang saw Confucius as being the Chinese representative of God who taught the Way of God to people before Christian missionaries had brought Jesus's message to China. Jesus's message to love God and love people were consistent with Confucius's message to revere heaven and love people. Therefore, Wang thought that the attacks on Confucius and Christianity in the 1920s and the 1960s came from the same atheistic source.[53] Wang believed the CCP reasoned that unless Confucian thought was dislodged from Chinese thought, atheism would never be established as the ideology of the Chinese people.[54] Picking up on themes he had read about in the *People's Daily* in 1974 while in the Yinying Labor Camp, Wang believed that the atheistic attack on theism in China went all the way back to Qin Shihuang's burning of the Confucian books and burying Confucian scholars. He saw this mirrored in attacks in the 1920s and 1960s on Confucian scholars and Chinese Christians, particularly by the CCP. Wang does not directly make the connection between Mao Zedong and Qin Shihuang as was made in the 1970s for Mao's persecution of intellectuals, but the comparison is right below the surface in the *Last Confession*. Mao himself stated in 1958, referring to Qin Shihuang, that "he buried only 460 scholars alive; we have buried forty-six thousand scholars alive. . . . You [intellectuals] revile us for being Qin Shi Huangs. You are wrong. We have surpassed Qin Shi Huang a hundredfold."[55]

However, Wang noted that it was not the Confucian literati who brought down the Qin Empire; it was two "illiterates"—Xiang Yu 項羽 (232–202 BCE) and Liu Bang 劉邦 (256–195 BCE) who ended the Qin Empire with Liu Bang establishing the Han dynasty.[56] Wang's point is that just as it was not the theistic Confucians who ended the Qin Empire, Christians in modern China are not attempting to overturn the CCP's regime in modern China and therefore should no longer be persecuted since they are law-abiding citizens. Wang argued that one significant aspect of this ongoing persecution was the fact that his legal case, and the cases of those who were implicated in his "clique," had not yet been rectified.[57]

Wang asserted that the attempts to paint him as being unpatriotic are groundless. Rather, he argues that the officers of the TSPM were in fact the ones who were unpatriotic. Wang states that Y. T. Wu was silent while the Gang of Four "ran rampant," only to come out after they were defeated, criticize them, and lay the blame for the persecution of the church at their feet while in prison Wang suffered for his defense of people unjustly charged.[58] He also argues that Z. T. Kuang and Wang Zizhong both accepted roles in the Japanese-controlled North China Christian Union Group and later became leaders in the TSPM, while he resisted the Japanese at the peril of his life.[59] He refers to the *North China Christian Union Group Memorial Book* 華北中華基督教團成立周年紀念冊 published in 1943 as providing evidence of their cooperation with the Japanese during the Second Sino-Japanese War.[60] The reason he does not use the word "patriotic" reveals something about what Wang sees as sources of authority for his thought:

> I never mention the word "patriotic" in my sermons and writings, because the term is not mentioned in the Bible, the *Four Books*, nor in the writings of ancient Chinese sages. They only talk about "love." *The Analects* say: "Fan Chi asked about benevolence. The Master said, 'It is to love all men.' He asked about knowledge. The Master said, 'It is to know all men.'"[61] The Bible makes it clearer. In the Law and Prophets of the Old Testament, in the Gospels and Epistles of the New Testament, it is difficult to calculate how many places speak of "love." What is a "nation"? Is it not composed of people? If there are no "people" on a large area of land, can this land be called a "nation"? Can you "love" people and not "love" the nation? What I said and the articles I wrote contributed and benefited others. How can they say that I am not patriotic?[62]

To Wang, patriotism was the practical love of the people in a nation. His defense of those he felt were falsely maligned such as Liu Shaoqi and Peng Dehuai, defense that cost Wang dearly in Datong,[63] and his resistance to oppression as shown by his unwillingness to cooperate with the Japanese were evidence of his practical patriotism. In the end, though, the reason why he does not use the word "patriotism 愛國," literally, "love for the nation" in Chinese, is that in his study of the sources of authority for his thought, the Bible, the *Four Books*, and the ancient Chinese sages, he did not find the term. More will be said about the sources of authority for Wang in the next chapter of this book.

Since Wang saw Confucianism and Christianity as being consistent in their religious messages revealed in the *Four Books* and the Bible, respectively, he could sincerely write to Jiang Hua that "I am a disciple of Christ, and I am also a disciple of Confucius."[64] By describing himself in this way and laboring to show the consistency between the two traditions, Wang attempted to convey to Jiang Hua that Christianity is not a foreign religion but a Chinese one. Wang's belief that positive social change would happen through cumulative personal moral action and that social decay could be reversed through theistic belief was not new.

He had advanced these ideas throughout his ministry as a Christian preacher before his arrest.[65] What *was* new was how he articulated that moral action and theism were foundational to positive social change not only in modern China but throughout the Chinese past reaching all the way back to Confucius. He also traced destructive elements at work in Chinese society all the way back to the anti-theistic purges of Qin Shihuang. Wang attempts to convince Jiang Hua that he has been maligned by those he considers to be atheists within the TSPM, chief of them being Y. T. Wu. This slander of Wang's character is in line with those good Chinese who possessed a "spirit of righteousness," who have been maligned for millennia by those who pretend to be patriotic but are, in fact, opportunists. Therefore, Wang recommends the advice of Confucius to Jiang Hua: "At first, my way with men was to hear their words, and give them credit for their conduct. Now my way is to hear their words, and look at their conduct."[66] In this way, he makes his request for Jiang Hua to look at his conduct and to reevaluate his legal case.

There is no conclusion to the "Rehabilitation Request Manuscript" since it was never completed, but it is important to note that in 1982–83, at the time when Wang was writing it, according to the large-print headlines in the newspapers that he could still make out and from the radio broadcasts that he listened to, Wang believed that the CCP government authorities were doing their best to get back on track.[67] Wang would have been aware of the fact that on July 1, 1981, at the sixth plenum of the CCP, the blame for the Cultural Revolution was placed on Mao Zedong.[68] Change was certainly in the air in the early 1980s in China. However, Wang never sent out the "Rehabilitation Request Manuscript" for several reasons, foremost because Liu Jingwen strongly opposed the request for rehabilitation, thinking that it would bring negative consequences on them and result in his greatest failure.[69] Wang's deteriorating eyesight also hindered his ability to complete the project, and it seems that the sheer scope of the work, attempting to prove his points through references to an enormous array of classical allusions, was too much for Wang's octogenarian abilities to complete.[70] In 2000, the request for rehabilitation was sent by Wang Mingdao and Liu Jingwen's son, Wang Tianduo, to the Supreme People's Court of China after his parents' deaths, but the request was rejected.[71] Regardless of the outcome, the "Rehabilitation Request Manuscript" provides the most thorough evidence of the integration of Confucian and Christian ideas in Wang's thought. However, the Confucian Christian character of Wang's theology is largely neglected in discussions of his role as a spiritual father to the house church movement.

HOUSE CHURCH MEETINGS RESUME ON WUKANG ROAD

In the fall of 1983, the Wangs moved into a third-floor apartment provided by Wang Tianduo's workplace with the Shanghai Institutes for Biological Sciences 上海生命科學研究院 at 69 Wukang Road 武康路 in Shanghai; he offered it to his parents to live in.[72] Since their previous dwelling place at 13 Pingjiang Road had included only one room, the two bedrooms and one sitting room on Wukang Road was a significant upgrade. They also required more help with this new living arrangement, and so Chang Kuan-Ing 章冠英 also lived with them, the man who had been assisting Wang Mingdao as a live-in helper since Wang's eye operation to correct his glaucoma performed in September 1982.[73] In addition to comfort, the extra space on Wukang Road also opened up the possibility for Wang Mingdao and Liu Jingwen to once again conduct house church gatherings from within their Shanghai home. Starting in the spring of 1984, the Wangs began to hold a meeting every Sunday morning where forty to fifty people crowded into their apartment.[74] Liu Jingwen would frequently lead singing from the piano, and Wang Mingdao would speak in the early years and in the later years would read his articles, which he would comment on. These unregistered house church meetings were open to the public and were unhindered by the government or the TSPM.[75] Some of these sermons and interviews given at Wukang Road were recorded and are still available on YouTube.[76]

In these later sermons and conversations, the interplay between Confucian and Christian ideas is clearly evident in Wang's thought. He quoted Mencius to encourage himself and others not to yield when under pressure.[77] He taught from Matthew to show that the ability to forgive others, a lesson he learned while in prison, was rooted in God's forgiveness of him.[78] He referred to the lives of Jesus and Confucius to show that the most powerful authority in the world was moral authority.[79] Wang also revealed part of the 1 percent of disagreement he had with

Confucius's teachings, having earlier stated to Jiang Hua that Confucius's "lessons are as important to me as the Bible. I respect Confucius, and I accept 99 percent of his lessons."[80] Wang postulated that Jesus's declaration to "love your enemies" is superior to Confucius's teaching to "return kindness with kindness, and injury with injury." Wang concluded that God wants people to repay injury, of which he has suffered much, with kindness.[81] However, Wang was back to extolling the wisdom of Confucius again just a few days later when he quoted the sage in a sermon saying, "When a prince's personal conduct is correct, his government is effective without the issuing of orders. If his personal conduct is not correct, he may issue orders, but they will not be followed."[82] Wang saw this as being harmonious with Paul's advice to Timothy to guard his conduct and teaching, the same advice his mother-in-law had given to him when he married Liu Jingwen in 1928.[83] In a recollection of his own story, Wang revealed the universal recognition of the need for spiritual renewal by referring to the statement of the Old Testament prophet Jeremiah that "the heart is deceitful above all things and beyond cure. Who can understand it?"[84] as well as the lines from a poem written by the Tang dynasty poet Bai Juyi that "heaven can be guessed at, earth can be measured, it is only a person's heart that cannot be defended."[85] These references show that Wang was working with both biblical and Chinese sources to communicate to his visitors his theology that God was at work in both traditions to reveal the divine will to humankind.

WEI ZHENG: A MODEL OFFICIAL

In one of the more interesting stories that Wang referred to in at least three of his Wukang Road sermons, he told the story of Emperor Tang Taizong (Li Shimin) 唐太宗李世民 (599–649) whom Wang respected for modeling humility by accepting the advice and correction of his chancellor Wei Zheng 魏徵 (580–643).[86] Wang mentions in a sermon on the proper conduct of officials that back in the 1940s, he purchased a four-volume book in Beijing's Dongan Market 東安市場 on statecraft that had been written during the Tang dynasty, *Essentials about Politics from the Zhengguan Reign* 貞觀政要 (Zhengguan Zhengyao), which may be the source of the lessons he taught about Tang Taizong and Wei Zheng.[87] The *Essentials* is a compendium written by the historian Wu Jing 吳兢 during the Tang dynasty in which Emperor Tang Taizong requests advice from his officials including Wei Zheng. The humility shown by the emperor in requesting advice depicted him as having the virtue and talent to successfully govern the dynasty.[88] Wang recounts how Wei Zheng told Tang Taizong that he had lost the faith of the people, and after the emperor demanded the reasons why his people no longer trusted him, which Wei Zheng recounted, the emperor resolved to regain the faith of the people. Wang was impressed with Wei Zheng's courageous honesty in conveying to the emperor that the time he spent keeping eagles and catching rabbits would be better spent attending to the affairs of the empire. Wang also noted that once when the emperor had plans to go to Nanshan 南山 for a vacation, he delayed his trip. When Wei Zheng noticed his baggage was all prepared, he asked him why he had not yet left, to which the emperor responded that he feared Wei Zheng's rebuke.[89]

This Confucian official rebuking his emperor apparently impressed other Chinese as well as Wang. In the same sermon, Wang says that Lu Dingyi (1906–96), the politician ousted by Mao whom Wang had defended while in Datong but who had now been rehabilitated by Deng Xiaoping, "had worked day and night to publish his *Biography of Wei Zheng* 魏徵傳 because he hoped that the highest authorities of the CCP would accept the words of loyal officials" who were like Wei Zheng.[90] Unfortunately for Lu, Mao Zedong was no Tang Taizong.[91] In another sermon, Wang referred to Tang Taizong and Wei Zheng to show the importance of leaders admitting mistakes and accepting correction.[92] In a third sermon, Wang connected the stories of Naaman and Elisha in the Old Testament with Emperor Tang Taizong and Wei Zheng to articulate that a truly humble person listens to the advice of people of lower status.[93] Wang's main point in using these stories in his sermons was to show the historical precedent that Emperor Tang Taizong's success was based on his willingness to accept critique and because he had an honest official in Wei Zheng who was willing to tell him the truth.[94] As noted by Howard J. Wechsler, "a pantheon of worthies famed for admonishing their sovereigns without regard for their personal safety had been created in China that served to inspire later remonstrators like Wei Cheng."[95] Wang Mingdao saw himself in this line of "worthies," possessing a "spirit of righteousness," whose critique was something crucial in China in the 1980s after what had happened in the previous two decades in the country.[96] It is clear throughout his mature theology that Wang had significantly integrated Confucian and Christian history and thought. As Wang had told Jiang Hua, "For more than two thousand years, the lessons of Confucius have guided countless scholars on the path of how to conduct oneself properly."[97] In the last years of his life, Wang saw it as his responsibility to build on Confucius's *ancient* foundation of following the Way, by showing his house church attendees and visitors how to live like a Christian and follow the Way in *modern* China.

MEETING BILLY GRAHAM

As well as providing a larger space for Wang to do his writing, the extra space on Wukang Road also furnished a more conducive place for hosting the nearly constant flow of visitors the Wangs received.[98] During these visits, Wang continued to insist that the only reason he was imprisoned was due to his resistance to the TSPM. Even when the most famous Protestant clergyman in the world, Billy Graham (1918–2018), wanted to visit Wang in 1988, with notes of introduction from former president Richard Nixon and future president George H. W. Bush, which opened up incredible opportunities for Graham in China,[99] Wang rejected Graham's request to visit him because Graham had been invited to come to China by K. H. Ting 丁光訓 (Ding Guangxun) (1915–2012).[100] Ding was one of the people whom Wang had described as an "unbeliever" in his 1955 article "We Are for the Faith!"[101] and had become the president of the China Christian Council (CCC) 中國基督教協會 (established 1980) as well as the TSPM after it was reestablished in 1980. Billy Graham's wife, Ruth Bell Graham (1920–2007), who had grown up the daughter of missionaries in China, had visited the Wangs previously in 1980 and was welcomed by them since she was not connected in any way with the TSPM.[102] A previous interview of Wang in 1983 by Werner Bürklin, who grew up in China and later became the director of Billy Graham's Conferences for Itinerant Evangelists, more fully explains Wang's perspective on Graham. Wang told Bürklin that "he [Billy Graham] is a great evangelist, but I don't agree with his posture toward our government. . . . I hear that Billy Graham wants to visit me. But I am not ready to receive him. He plays along with those who hold power in our country. Those people are enemies of our Lord. . . . I don't agree with his preaching in churches under the control of the Three-Self Patriotic Movement."[103] Just as Wang rejected Jia Yuming and Marcus Cheng when they joined the TSPM in the 1950s, similarly, Billy Graham's visit to China under the auspices of the CCC and TSPM made him persona non grata in the Wang residence.

Graham desired to go to China to experience his wife's past and to evangelize the Chinese; he did not want to offend either the TSPM or the unregistered house church leaders or take sides on the issues that separated them.[104] Although Wang respected Graham as a gifted evangelist, he thought Graham's perspective on the Chinese church was naive and wanted no contact with anyone connected with the TSPM.[105] Nevertheless, Graham would not be denied, and on the morning of April 23, 1988, he showed up at 69 Wukang Road. Despite the fact that the Wangs had said no three times previously to the visit, since Graham had not brought anyone from the TSPM with him, he and his wife and Philip Teng (Teng Jinhui) 滕近輝 (1922–2013), who acted as their translator,[106] were allowed in by the Wangs' helper Chang Kuan-Ing.[107] Wang Mingdao was asleep in a metal chair with his head lying on the kitchen table when the Grahams arrived. When Wang woke up, Billy Graham asked him if he had a word from the Lord for him. Wang was silent for some time. He finally quoted Revelation 2:10: "Be faithful, even to the point of death, and I will give you the crown of life." Their conversation lasted only a half hour and was entirely focused on "the Bible and spiritual things" and they did not discuss the conflict between the TSPM and the unregistered house churches.[108] In an interview of the Wangs a few months later in December 1988 by Timothy (Siang Hui) Tow 杜祥輝 (1920–2009), they were asked about how the Grahams' visit to China was being seen by some as a bridge-building trip between the TSPM and the unregistered house churches.[109] Wang Mingdao and Liu Jingwen reiterated that they had not wanted Billy Graham to come and that it had resulted in their being "greatly inconvenienced in this matter."[110] Wang Mingdao was not feeling well and was nearly deaf, so Liu Jingwen was the main speaker during the interview.[111] Although Liu Jingwen said that Graham "is working for the Lord," after observing the

Grahams' visit to China to both churches that are registered with the government through the TSPM and unregistered house churches, Graham and some Christians in the country believed that there was greater unity in the Chinese church than in fact there was. Liu Jingwen, at the close of the interview, recommended that Graham should read "We Are for the Faith!" to better understand the issues involved in the division between the registered and unregistered churches.[112] Although it should be noted that Tow asked leading questions in his interview, it is clear that Billy Graham had hoped for a unity in the Chinese church beyond what Wang Mingdao and Liu Jingwen thought possible, unless the issues that Wang had brought up in "We Are for the Faith!" were first reconciled. As noted earlier, Deng Xiaoping's reforms had brought about a greater degree of openness to China, so now with Billy Graham visiting, many thought that perhaps the TSPM and the unregistered house churches could be reconciled by resolving some of the disagreements that had kept the Chinese church divided. This was before the Tiananmen Square protests.

TIANANMEN

On April 15, 1989, Hu Yaobang 胡耀邦 (1915–89), a pro-reform former general secretary of the CCP, died. On April 17, revealing a growing desire among students for change, thousands of university students throughout Beijing met at Tiananmen Square 天安門廣場 to mourn Hu and call for government reform, better university conditions, and greater democratic involvement in decision-making. The next day, students began to occupy the square. Eventually, thousands of citizens of Beijing joined the Tiananmen Square protests, and other protests began throughout the country. By May 17, the protesters exceeded one million in Tiananmen. On May 20, martial law was declared by the CCP leadership and the People's Liberation Army (PLA) was brought in to clear the square, but they could not remove the throngs of protesters acting in concert to avoid dispersion. However, on June 3, in the late hours of the evening and going into the early hours of June 4, the Twenty-Seventh Army of the PLA struck with brutal force to crush the protests. Throughout the day on June 4, throughout Beijing, the PLA killed students and others they thought were protesters. Deng Xiaoping later thanked the PLA for clearing the square.[113] This became known as the Tiananmen Square massacre 天安門大屠殺, or as it is known in China, the June Fourth incident 六四事件. Following the event, the CCP began a concerted campaign to blame the demonstrations, which had been headline news around the world, on "counter-revolutionaries and 'hooligans.'"[114] Stephen Wang believes that this political context created the conditions for Wang Weifan 汪維藩 (1927–2015) to write his article in September 1989, "Wu Yaozong and Wang Mingdao" in *Tianfeng*, after decades of silence on Wang Mingdao.[115]

Wang Weifan was another person Wang had lumped in as an "unbeliever" in "We Are for the Faith!"[116] Wang Weifan had responded critically to Wang Mingdao's article with "Is It for Faith?" in July 1955 in *Tianfeng*.[117] Wang Weifan had graduated from Nanjing (Jinling) Union Theological Seminary 金陵協和神學院 in 1955 and had suffered criticism during the Cultural Revolution, but after the relaxation of religious control in 1980, he became a professor of the New Testament at Jinling Seminary where K. H. Ting had been named president.[118] After the Tiananmen event, Stephen Wang believes that the political conditions at the seminary, an institution controlled by the TSPM, prompted Wang Weifan to write another article after more than four decades of silence on Wang Mingdao. In this article, Wang Weifan compares Wang Mingdao with Y. T. Wu, who had died in 1979.[119] The political context of post-Tiananmen, with the CCP attempting to unify the country by blaming the demonstrations and massacre on counterrevolutionaries, brought Wang Mingdao back into focus in the Chinese church. The fact that he was chosen as Y. T. Wu's counterpart in Wang Weifan's article shows the importance of Wang Mingdao as a figurehead of the unregistered house church movement. In the article, Wang Weifan makes the case that Y. T. Wu displayed great patience toward Wang Mingdao in trying to bring him into the TSPM. Wang Weifan also states that during the Japanese occupation of Beijing, Wang Mingdao did not resist the Japanese and later opposed new China and the TSPM, and preferred the KMT government to the CCP.[120] Wang Weifan also argues that although articles in *Tianfeng* during the 1950s referred to Wang as a "reactionary," they did not call him a "counterrevolutionary" and therefore did not allege that he was a counterrevolutionary criminal. Wang Weifan alleges that the idea that Wang Mingdao was arrested due to his opposition to the TSPM "is in total disagreement with the facts."[121] However, Wang Weifan never indicates, if it was not for opposition to the TSPM, the reason why Wang Mingdao was imprisoned for twenty-three years. Again, inadvertently revealing the significance of Wang Mingdao to the Chinese church even into the 1980s, Wang Weifan concludes his article by writing, "For the past ten years, whenever there has been a National Assembly of the Chinese Church, everyone has specifically prayed for Wang Mingdao, longing for a change of heart on his part."[122] If Stephen Wang is correct that Wang Weifan wrote his article due to political pressure after the Tiananmen event, the purpose of Wang Weifan's article was fulfilled. This article's main purpose was not to bring Wang Mingdao into the TSPM but to show that the TSPM continued to stand in solidarity with the CCP under the pressure of conformity in the aftermath of what happened in Tiananmen Square in May and June 1989. News of Wang Weifan's article reached the eighty-nine-year-old Wang Mingdao while he was living on Wukang Road. Wang responded that not only did he resist the Japanese at the risk of his life, but he never said anything about preferring the KMT over the CCP as the government of China and that he was told many times that "it is a crime to oppose the Three-Self Church."[123] Clearly, there are two divergent perspectives on why Wang Mingdao was arrested.

FINAL YEARS AND DEATH OF WANG MINGDAO

In October 1989, the director of a Western missionary organization visited Wang Mingdao at his home on Wukang Road with the express purpose of recording the second half of his life where his autobiography *The Last Fifty Years* had left off in the early 1950s.[124] When this unidentified man asked Wang who could write the second half of his life story, Wang suggested Stephen Wang, a close friend of his, who had been arrested as a member of the Wang Mingdao counterrevolutionary clique on August 8, 1955. Like Wang Mingdao, Stephen Wang was imprisoned until 1979 but subsequently immigrated to Canada.[125] In April 1990, Stephen Wang and his wife, Lu Minru 陸敏如, stayed with the Wangs on Wukang Road for three weeks and conducted the interviews that composed the account of Wang Mingdao and Liu Jingwen from 1949 to 1991 that makes up the 1997 book *Another Forty Years*, later translated in 2002 into English as *The Long Road to Freedom*.[126]

After the interviews with Stephen Wang, Wang Mingdao and Liu Jingwen continued to conduct Sunday morning worship services in their home until July 1991. On July 2, Wang began having difficulty speaking and was brought to the hospital to have CT scans, which revealed blood clots in and damage to his brain. On July 25, his ninety-first birthday, he could no longer talk. As worshippers began to gather at 69 Wukang Road on the morning of Sunday, July 28, 1991, Wang Mingdao died.[127] Liu Jingwen would follow less than a year later, succumbing to breast cancer complications on April 18, 1992.[128]

Wang Mingdao's death resulted in a profound outpouring of grief as well as a deep display of respect from Christians around the world. In fact, the deep display of respect had already begun in November 1990, to commemorate Wang Mingdao's ninetieth birthday.[129] Respected Chinese Christian leaders such as Thomas Wang, Stephen Wang, Jonathan Chao, and Wing Hung Lam, as well as former missionaries to China such as Arthur Reynolds, David Adeney, and Leslie Lyall paid tribute to the man whose "name would remain in the annals of Chinese church history." His death also brought a great sense of loss. Ying Fuk Tsang's reaction to the news of Wang's death likely expresses the feelings of many Chinese Christians when they heard the news: "My heart sank and his face came to my mind: 'The last of the giants of China's church has left the stage of history!'"[130] After Wang died, Jonathan Chao dedicated the following issue of his journal, *China and the Church* 中國與教會, to eulogize and remember Wang. Chao wrote that Wang's contribution to the Chinese church was as a pioneer in the development of indigenous Chinese churches, a traveling evangelist and revivalist, a fighter for theological truth against theological liberals, a virtuous example for Christians to follow, a soldier of Christ's cross under pressure, a person of genuine repentance, and one for whom God has redressed the injustices of his life.[131] Samuel Lamb (Lin Xiangao) 林献羔 (1924–2013), an influential unregistered house church leader in Guangzhou who was imprisoned for a similar period as Wang Mingdao for being "Wang Mingdao's henchman," described Wang as a father figure who would be given "a crown of faithfulness."[132] Allen Yuan (Yuan Xiangchen) 袁

相忱 (1914–2005), one of the church leaders in Beijing who along with Wang tried to resist joining the TSPM in 1955[133] but was later arrested on April 19, 1958, and who had spent twenty-one years in prison, said that Wang Mingdao was a servant greatly used by God in China. Yuan also mentioned that after knowing Wang for more than sixty years, having met with him before, during, and after his prison days, he could find no flaw in his lifestyle.[134] Finally, a full description of Wang's death process was described by an observant, Ming Yan 銘言, including the detail that it was during the opening prayer at 9:05 a.m., as the house church meeting began, that Wang Mingdao passed away. Interestingly, the author, who knew Wang personally, also includes an important fact that Wang impressed upon her in 1984. Ming Yan writes that Wang told her that many overseas people misunderstand that his opposition to the TSPM was opposition to the CCP or socialism. Ming Yan was careful to communicate that what Wang opposed was what was done in the name of Jesus that would rebel against Jesus's teaching and not any government system or party.[135] The inclusion of this detail says much about the Chinese house church movement in 1991. Unregistered house church Christians in China were careful to communicate that their resistance to the religious oversight of their churches by the TSPM did not mean that they rejected the CCP as the government of China. With Wang Mingdao gone, these Chinese Christians would now have to figure out the way forward without the presence of their "spiritual father" on 69 Wukang Road to consult.

CHAPTER SEVEN

The Theology of Wang Mingdao

After the preceding analysis of Wang's life and theology as it developed within its nearly century-long historical context, the following conclusions can be made based on this biographical reevaluation of his theology.

WANG MINGDAO AS THEOLOGIAN

What were the main themes of Wang's theology? Wang's life from the late-1920s to the mid-1950s was dominated by his articulation and defense of Fundamentalist Christian theology as opposed to Modernist Christian theology. Kevin Xiyi Yao has observed that a crucial distinction of a Fundamentalist in China during this time was willingness to publicly attack Modernism.[1] This articulation and defense of Fundamentalist theology and critique of Modernist theology set the fault lines for Wang's articles during these independent decades. The significant differences between what Wang understood as Modernist theology and his own Fundamentalist theology was summarized by Wang in a 1949 article titled "A Fortified City, an Iron Pillar, a Bronze Wall" in which Wang described Modernist theology:

> They [Modernists] say that God is only the great wisdom and knowledge of the universe, the great power, the world's truth, goodness, and beauty; Jesus is merely the world's most perfect, most noble, most ideal person; the miracles Jesus performed were just some of

> the records that the disciples had to assume after his death in order to spread his doctrine; Jesus's death was the highest form of "a sacrifice of life to preserve virtue complete,"[2] and "a letting go of life to choose righteousness";[3] Jesus's Resurrection was his [achievement of] "spiritual immortality and perpetual influence"; Jesus's Second Coming to rule is a symbol of the universal faith of humanity in him; and the Kingdom of Heaven coming is our using the teachings of Jesus to establish the ideal society.[4]

Wang believed that Jesus was the Son of God, that his miracles were literally true, that Jesus's death was not the Confucian ideal of virtuous martyrdom but was the price paid to free humanity from the penalty of sin, that Christ's resurrection was bodily, and that human beings could not affect the coming of the kingdom of heaven.

In his seminal 1955 article "We Are for the Faith!" Wang more fully articulated his theology on what he saw as the five main areas of divergence between Modernists and Fundamentalists:

> The first issue is related to the Bible itself. Fundamentalists consider that every word and phrase has been revealed by God and therefore contains no errors whatsoever. Modernists, using the methods of higher criticism, declare that the Bible, while a revelation from God, cannot be literally interpreted. . . . The Genesis account of the origin of man is a crucial point in this theological debate. The Fundamentalists say that man is the result of supernatural creation, while Modernists accept the theory of evolution and see man emerging by a process of natural development, possibly through spontaneous descent from the primates.
>
> The second issue between Modernists and Fundamentalists is with regard to the coming of Christ. Fundamentalists believe that His birth was supernatural, from the womb of a virgin. Modernists regard this story as allegorical; they do not deny the Incarnation, neither do they tie the Incarnation inseparably to the Virgin Birth.
>
> The third issue is the Atonement of Christ. Fundamentalists believe that Jesus' death on the Cross was a sacrifice to ransom man from sin; by this He turned the wrath of God into forgiveness. . . . But twentieth century Modernists see the Cross as a demonstration of

> God's love; because of this we may become one with God. It is not necessary for us to believe in a God of wrath who demands a price for our redemption.
>
> The fourth issue is the Resurrection. . . . Fundamentalists believe that Jesus' physical resurrection is an essential truth; otherwise Jesus could not have overcome death and decay. Modernists do not deny the Resurrection; neither do they insist that there must have been a physical resurrection. . . .
>
> The final issue between these two schools of theology is the Second Coming of Jesus. Fundamentalists, along with Paul and the primitive Christians, believe that Jesus will come in person very soon, upon the clouds back to the earth. Modernists consider the teaching about the Second Coming a form of poetic symbolism depicting the triumph of good over evil; they see the progress of the world taking place by gradual evolution and not by catastrophic change such as the Hebrew people expected in their historical hope for a Messiah.[5]

These theological emphases show no evidence of change from before Wang went into prison to after he was released. A curious part of his legacy among subsequent Chinese house church Christians is not necessarily found in his theology but in his practice of not joining the TSPM. The irony is that "We Are for the Faith!" is focused on distinguishing *theologically* between Fundamentalists and Modernists, which leads to practice.[6] Yet if these were Wang's theological emphases, which are not very different from Fundamentalist Christians in other parts of the world, why should Wang Mingdao be considered a Confucian Christian theologian?

It is now imperative to return to the original focus of this book on how the Chinese classics, sages, and histories shaped Wang Mingdao's Christian theology within his twentieth-century social context, which thus qualifies him to be considered a significant *Chinese* theologian, to more fully understand Wang Mingdao's thought. The previous chapters have detailed how, throughout the five stages of Wang's life, he continually mined the intellectual and moral resources of the two traditions of Christianity and Confucianism to develop his theology. As Archie Lee has observed to be true with other Asian Christians, Wang Mingdao did not sever his connection to Confucianism when he converted to Christianity.[7] In fact, he increasingly saw Christianity as the fulfillment of Confucianism and used the resources of both traditions to create his theology.

Wang never desired to create a comprehensive or systematic theology. He received a thorough bicultural education in the Christian and Confucian traditions while he was dependent on missionary Christianity. After his break with missionary Christianity in 1921, as an independent church leader, his theological works were constructed to meet contextual needs he felt required attention at the time. After his arrest, his prison works focused on writing to the government to clarify his situation and to defend those he felt had been wrongly accused. It is interesting to note that several of the people he defended while in Yinying were later rehabilitated by the CCP after Deng Xiaoping became paramount leader. One of Deng's reforms was the release of "counterrevolutionaries" like Wang. Wang's writings in this period were focused on seeking political rehabilitation for himself and those implicated with him. When he was released, Wang was shocked to discover that unregistered house church Christians in China honored him as a spiritual father.

During this mature stage of his spiritual father years, after the long period of contemplation at Yinying, Wang's theology took on different emphases. He was much more interested in writing about and discussing politics than he had been before. The decision he had made in 1924 to turn his back on the world, including its politics,[8] became impossible after his arrest in 1955. His personal moral failure, sufferings, and the time he had to review a broad scope of Chinese history in Yinying provided him with significant resources to minister to Chinese Christians who were coming out of the Cultural Revolution and were hoping to make a positive impact on the nation. Wang saw recovery from the previous years of "catastrophe" in China as possible through people pursuing a "spirit of righteousness," the primary virtue of which was truth telling. Both the Christian and Confucian traditions nourished his thought and allowed him to formulate a Chinese theology that was relevant to twentieth-century Chinese who were coming to visit him in Shanghai.

Wang's articles in *The Spiritual Food Quarterly* cover the major theological emphases he wanted to articulate at the time. He was always more interested in describing the practical working out of Christian theology through a life of upright moral character than he was in creating a systematic exposition of Bible doctrine. Therefore, Wang Mingdao's theology can be correctly categorized as a folk theology. Never convinced by what he saw as the Modernist emphasis on transforming culture while neglecting personal religious and moral transformation,[9] Wang always prioritized the individual in his theology.

THE SOCIAL SIGNIFICANCE OF WANG'S THEOLOGY

It would be an error to assume that because Wang prioritized the individual that his thought has no social significance, as Ng Lee-Ming has done.[10] Li Boxiong has noted that it was precisely because Wang's thought focused on the microlevel individual and not the macrolevel society that it provided help to Christians living in a socialist society.[11] As noted by Liang Shouhua, Wang's negative attitude toward people establishing the ideal society created a false impression that Wang had no concern for society.[12] Liang wrote an important article in 1998 titled "Independent Religious Beliefs' Effect on Society: A Reinterpretation of Wang Mingdao's Thoughts on Society"[13] in which he reinterprets Wang's thoughts on the social implications of Christianity. Liang notes that Wang is one of the most respected people in the modern Chinese church and that he is viewed as a model of faithfulness unto death by many Christians. He argues that even though some people claim Wang held an estranged, negative view toward society, Liang maintains that it is not difficult to see that Wang's writings have a social nature and modern significance because his thought does not escape reality but often responds to social situations. Therefore, in contrast to Ng Lee-Ming and Lam Wing-hung, Liang sees Wang's writings as being very meaningful to society.[14] Furthermore, Liang argues that Wang's attitude toward society was based on the Bible and on Wang's observations and concerns and that his dissatisfaction and distrust of society was in continuity with contemporary liberal academics and Marxists in China. Liang thinks that Wang's thought is conservative but modern and critically conservative and that he is even more critical than cultural and social activists of his time. He sees Wang as having maintained an independent, detached position that was not manipulated by secular power. Because his detached religious beliefs did not have a fixed political position, this allowed him a free and independent critique of all authority that did not meet his standard.[15] Liang's article attempts to show how the social situation Wang encountered affected his attitude toward society and that this attitude was appropriate and widespread in Chinese society at the time. Liang argues that critics have missed that Wang's teaching and thought have social implications. Due to historical factors and a limited period of development because of his arrest in 1955, Wang was not able to fully develop his ideas of how the gospel was to affect society. However, it is clear from his works that he was interested in the practical nature of how Christians should interact with society.[16] Liang interprets Wang's separation from the naivety of the Modernist theologians of his time as having allowed him to be a more independent critic of the powerful than they were. His high morality and suspicious spirit combined with this separation from society allowed him to be a more thorough and broader critic of society. This sort of transcendent critique was not loyal to any group or person, so he was able to become a properly objective critic, not controlled by the power of the political right or left.[17]

Lam Wing-hung's critique of Wang that his individual focus was inadequate to resist societal evil is more substantial because as Lam notes, macrolevel evil often requires macrolevel power to correct.[18] Lam states that social ideas received very little attention in Wang's writings mainly due to the fact that he promulgated the theological sequence of "first transform a person, then reform society." However, according to Lam, after people receive salvation, they will not necessarily naturally reform society.[19] Also, Lam claims that Wang's attacks on church and societal sin only led to ways of dealing with these macrolevel sins at the personal level. Lam argues that believers should resist societal evil and attempt to remove it or at least reduce it. Many organizational-level sins require organizational-level power and actions to destroy.[20] However, as Lam concedes, there has been no way to plan social movements in order to reform society in China in any way that is not approved by the CCP.[21]

This may be why after seeing the societal-level "catastrophe" of the Cultural Revolution, while not abandoning his focus on the individual, Wang in his mature stage continually pointed to the Confucian tradition's emphasis on the moral *leader*. Following the logic of *The Great Learning*, if the leader's actions are morally upright, individuals in society will be more accountable to have moral behavior, which has a far-reaching societal impact from individual to family to province to nation. Like Wei Zheng had done with Tang Taizong, it was the responsibility of officials to correct leaders when they deviated from correct moral action, even at the risk of their lives. Since Wang did this while in prison from 1963 until 1980, his words held great weight with Chinese Christians. In the final analysis, which Lam Wing-hung concedes, there has not been, nor is there currently, any way for religious Chinese to plan social movements to reform society in China in any way that is not approved by the CCP.[22] Therefore, Wang's emphasis is on the moral individual, particularly moral leaders and officials creating an impact on society in a positive direction, which *is* possible in China. This emphasis on the moral individual having a society-level impact has a solid historical basis throughout Confucian history and should be considered the social significance of Wang's mature theology. Several scholars have noted the importance in Confucian thought of the doctrine of the inner saint and outer king 內聖外王. The wisdom and virtue of an individual's inner life, the "inner saint," has a corresponding effect on their ability as a leader in society, the "outer king," to contribute to a healthy and productive sociopolitical environment.[23] Personal morality and public leadership are therefore inextricably connected in the Confucian tradition. Chinese Christians like Wang Mingdao who were deeply shaped by Confucianism therefore maintain this crucial connection between the individual and the social.[24]

WANG'S *SELECTIVE* USE OF CONFUCIAN THOUGHT

As to the question of *why* Wang used these Chinese sources in his writings, the reason seems to have evolved over time. As Archie C. C. Lee has noted, among other Asian Christians developing inseparable connections to the religious texts that shaped them before, or in Wang's case, at the same time, they encountered the Bible, Wang developed a deep connection to the texts of Confucianism in his youth. However, he did not mention Chinese sources very frequently in his writings before his years of conflict with the Japanese. Prior to this, Wang preferred to focus on explaining the Fundamentalist teachings of Christianity during the 1920s and early 1930s in his writings. This may have been influenced by the societal-level rejection of Confucianism during the May Fourth Movement as Chinese sought a new way forward, and Wang sought to provide the religious answers for Chinese with Fundamentalist Christian ideas unimpeded by Confucian concepts. However, during the war years beginning in 1938, Wang used familiar Chinese stories more frequently as common rallying points to promulgate his Confucian Christian vision of how to overcome the Japanese. After his years of contemplation in Yinying, he used Confucian in addition to Christian stories to instruct Chinese Christians coming to see him in Shanghai to guide those who hoped to make a positive impact in China with a "spirit of righteousness" after the devastation of the Cultural Revolution. In his "Rehabilitation Request Manuscript," when writing to Jiang Hua, Wang mentions very few Christian sources but refers to an enormous number of Confucian sources in his arguments requesting rehabilitation. Jiang Hua, as president of the Supreme People's Court, was a member of the CCP, which requires an official commitment to atheism. Bible verses would carry little intellectual weight for Wang's argument that he deserved political rehabilitation and might even have been interpreted as superstitious. However, since Jiang Hua was reform minded and the political climate had significantly changed due to Deng Xiaoping's reforms, Wang seems to have thought that referring to Confucian stories that extolled a moral vision for leaders and society would carry more convincing weight. Some may argue that since it was only during the 1980s that Wang declared himself to be a follower of Christ *and* Confucius that this may have been an apologetic attempt on Wang's part to convince Jiang Hua to grant Wang political rehabilitation and that I have read Confucianism retrospectively into his earlier periods or that he only came to this realization late in life. However, we have seen Wang going to the resources of *both* traditions again and again throughout his life to construct his uniquely Confucian Christian theology. Also, as evidenced by his refusal to admit to something that he felt was untrue in his prison release, it does not hold up with his character to think that he was simply trying to convince Jiang Hua by declaring himself Confucian as well as Christian in his "Rehabilitation Request Manuscript." Wang tells Jiang Hua that he has held a Confucian Christian worldview since his studies at Tsui Wen Academy.[25]

Yet, although it is true that Wang creatively used stories and teachings from both the Bible and the *Four Books* to construct his Confucian

Christian theology and although he stated that he accepted all of what the Bible taught,[26] he was *selective* in his use of the *Four Books*, saying that he accepted 99 percent of Confucius's teachings.[27] As detailed previously, Wang thought that Confucius's teaching to "return kindness with kindness, and injury with injury" was morally inferior to Jesus's command to "love your enemies." He saw Jesus's command to repay injury with kindness as being a superior teaching.[28] Wang rejected the Confucian tradition of sacrifice to the dead, mentioned in *Analects* 3.12, stating that as Christians, "we do not sacrifice to our ancestors, nor do we want our descendants to sacrifice to us."[29] In the spring 1948 volume of *The Spiritual Food Quarterly*, the issue before Wang described Confucius as "China's Sage,"[30] Wang wrote that "Confucius cannot compare to Jesus."[31] For Wang Mingdao, the sage of the nation did not have anywhere near the theological authority that the Son of God did. Similarly, although Wang had great respect for Mencius, he also disagreed with some of his teachings and said that we should not accept Mencius's lesson that to have no posterity is unfilial.[32] Wang also preferred Xunzi's interpretation of human nature being evil to Mencius's interpretation, enshrined in the *Four Books*, that human nature is good.[33] Wang also approved of the higher position of women in Christianity as opposed to the traditional Confucian moral injunctions for women to obey in turn their fathers, husbands, and sons.[34] In this book, as a corrective to the prevailing literature, particularly in English, I have attempted to show the lifelong influence of the Confucian tradition on Wang Mingdao. At the same time, it is clear that Wang's highest level of commitment in his theology was to the Bible.

WANG'S THEOLOGICAL METHOD

This naturally brings up the topic of Wang's theological method, or how he constructed his theology. Wang said during his independent stage that the basic principle he developed to guide his theology was that if a teaching was clearly written in the Bible, he accepted it; if it was not, he rejected it. Wang also said that he rejected any church tradition or regulation that he could not find a legitimate basis for in the Bible.[35] Wang would refer to reason 道理 as a guide in theological truth, as he did in articulating his preference for designating Jesus as the Son of God, as opposed to the "unclear reason" of the traditional Christian doctrines, which he viewed as being traditions passed on by people and not the "truth of the Bible."[36] Experience also played a role in whether Wang would give credence to a teaching. Although he prioritized the Bible in his interpretation of the issue of "spiritual tongues," his final comment on the issue in his autobiography was that he knew many people who did not speak in spiritual tongues but were morally sound Christians, and he knew of one man who spoke in these tongues but was morally reprehensible. His conclusion was based on his experience of the moral character of these people.[37] Experience of moral character also played a role in his warming toward John Sung and his cooling toward Watchman Nee.[38] Wang's statement that he studied "bitter toil theology"[39] can also be interpreted as the importance of experience in Wang's theology since what he formulated theologically, he had first experienced through hard work and suffering.

Despite their best efforts to turn their backs on "the world," in the 1950s, Fundamentalist Christians like Wang could no longer avoid political issues. When the CCP government arrested and imprisoned him, after about eight years of shock and grief, the scope of Wang's theological engagement during his prison years expanded to include political considerations as he wrote his suggestions to the government. Also during this time, his theological method expanded while in Yinying after he spent a long period thinking about God's engagement with China: Wang concluded that God had communicated the Way 道 (Dao) through Confucius in China until Jesus fully revealed the Way.[40] Although Wang never denied the highest priority given to the Bible in his theology, this broader perspective expanded his theological method to include other works that engaged with topics that the Bible did not necessarily touch on. Of particular interest due to his love of history, Wang was interested in the "spirit of righteousness" that can be observed in Confucian Chinese history, which illustrated how some Chinese worthies responded in righteousness to the challenges they faced. When articulating why he never used the word "patriotic," Wang said that the reason he did not use the word was because the Bible, the *Four Books*, and the ancient Chinese sages never used the term, revealing some of the components of the mature spiritual father's theological method.[41]

A comparison between John Wesley, another folk theologian, and Wang Mingdao could be made. When analyzing what sources Wesley utilized in the construction of his theology, some theologians have noted that he used *scripture*, *reason*, *tradition*, and *experience*, describing the four components of his theological method as the "Wesleyan Quadrilateral."[42] Using a similar idea to analyze Wang's mature theological method, a "Wangian Quadrilateral" emerges in which Wang constructs theology using *Christian scripture*, *reason*, *Confucian tradition*, and *experience*. The Christian Bible, the sixty-six books of the Old and New Testaments, is the main source and final authority for all theological issues for Wang. Although his statement that he did not use Bible commentaries was inaccurate since he referred to annotated study Bibles,[43] read Charles Spurgeon's *The New Testament Treasury*,[44] and translated a large number of English theological articles for *The Spiritual Food Quarterly*,[45] what does appear to be true is that what Wang interpreted the Bible to mean was not superseded by any other source in his theology. When, in 1933, Wang evaluated the significant spiritual activity that took place in Shandong Province, his first criteria for this spiritual activity being genuinely Christian was that it was consistent with the teaching of the Bible.[46] His interpretation of the Bible was closely rooted to a literal interpretation of the Christian scripture.[47] This method, described as "biblicism,"[48] on the one hand provided the theological justification to disagree with Christian Modernists who denied the virgin birth, resurrection, and Second Coming of Christ and on the other hand, gave him the biblical basis to disagree with other Fundamentalists over the doctrines of Christology and Trinity since the Bible does not record the philosophical statements required to articulate these teachings. It was what he described as his *reason* that brought him to claim that these two doctrines, enshrined in the Nicene and Constantinopolitan Creeds of Christianity, were simply traditions passed on by people and not the truths of God. *Experience*, particularly the experience of a person's moral character, also played a role in Wang giving credence to a teaching, but Christian scripture was always his final authority on theological matters.

Tradition was also important to Wang but not the traditions of Christianity. As early as 1935, Wang wrote about the value of the Confucian scriptures and histories in providing wisdom, noting that scholars in China paid attention to reading the Confucian classics 經, the *Four*

Books and Five Classics, as well as the histories 史, the twenty-four dynastic histories of China.[49] After his prison experience, Wang added a political dimension to his writings that he had avoided before his arrest. After he was released, he made his implicit conviction that Confucianism was part of God's revelation to humanity explicit in his writings and sermons. In his "Rehabilitation Request Manuscript," the main source of his mature theological thought, in addition to his sermons from Wukang Road in Shanghai, Wang reveals that the *Four Books* and the Chinese sages also provided resources for his theological reflection. Building on a lifetime of memorization and contemplation of these stories, Wang used the wisdom contained in the Confucian classics, sages, and histories to advance his points to Jiang Hua in requesting rehabilitation and to guide those unregistered house church leaders seeking his counsel who made the pilgrimage to Shanghai to visit the spiritual father. Nevertheless, for Wang, even the *Four Books* were subservient to the Bible as evidenced by the corrections Wang made to both Confucius on revenge and Mencius on posterity based on the later revelation of the Bible. The Chinese sages such as Qu Yuan, Xunzi, Wei Zheng, Zhang Xun, Wen Tianxiang, and others possessing a "spirit of righteousness" described in the dynastic history books also provided evidence of how God has guided the Chinese before Christ had been fully revealed in China to live morally upright lives. Sinologist Wang Gungwu 王賡武 has written on how these dynastic history books, beginning with Sima Qian's *Records of the Grand Historian*, to which Wang made many references in his works, constructed the framework for Chinese institutional memory with many Chinese finding the continuity of China's history key to their distinctiveness as a civilization.[50] Wang's inclusion of Confucian classics, sages, and histories in the construction of his mature theology distinguishes him as an important Chinese Christian theologian unsevered from his Confucian background and shows the continuity of God's action in the long history of the Confucian tradition in his thought.[51]

These four sources, *Christian scripture* as the highest authority, in addition to *reason*, *experience*, and the *Confucian tradition*, make up the "Wangian Quadrilateral," the sources of Wang Mingdao's theological method for his mature thought. The interaction of Christian scripture with the Confucian tradition was particularly influential in Wang's theology of God.

WANG'S GOD: THE "LORD ON HIGH" AND "GOD"

Wang's theology of God did seem to evolve, or at least he had time to more fully theologize on God due to his long contemplation of Chinese thought and history, while in prison. Not content with the vague descriptions of God as "the great wisdom and knowledge of the universe," Wang made what seems to have been an implicit understanding explicit when he connected the "Lord on High" or "Shang Di" of the Confucian classics with the God of Christianity during his spiritual father years.

In his mature thought revealed in his "Rehabilitation Request Manuscript," Wang argued that the materialism or atheism that the CCP promulgated in Chinese society after 1949 was detrimental to morality, since it removed the ideological constraints on immorality, and was also not in accord with the history of Chinese Confucian thought as revealed in the classics and other sage works. Wang argued that before Buddhism came to China, the most educated and intelligent Chinese of the ancient past, the Confucian literati, were theists. To prove his point, he quoted a vast array of Confucian authoritative texts.

> The scholars before the Emperor Ming 明帝 of the Eastern Han Dynasty welcomed Buddhism into China were all theists. They called God 神 "Heaven" 天 or "Lord on High"上帝. *The Book of Documents* says "Sacred counsels of vast importance, admirable words forcibly set forth! The ways of God are not invariable: on the good-doer he sends down all blessings, and on the evil-doer he sends down all miseries."[52] As well as "God is with you, said Shang-fu to the king. Have no doubts in your heart."[53] And also "Heaven, in giving birth to the multitudes of the people, To every faculty and relationship annexed its law. The people possess this normal nature, And they [consequently] love its normal virtue."[54] Confucius said, "Heaven produced the virtue that is in me. Huan Tui—what can he do to me?"[55] When Confucius was trapped by the Kuang people, he said, "Heaven produced the virtue that is in me, what can the people of Kuang do to me?"[56] He also said, "He who offends against Heaven, has none to whom he can pray."[57] As well as, "Wherein I have done improperly, may Heaven reject me! May Heaven reject me!"[58] Mencius said, "When Heaven is about to confer a great office

on any man, it first exercises his mind with suffering, and his sinews and bones with toil. It exposes his body to hunger."[59] He also said, "Though a man may be wicked, yet if he adjust his thoughts, fast, and bathe, he may sacrifice to God."[60] Xunzi said, "Heaven did not create the people for the sake of the lord; Heaven established the lord for the sake of the people."[61] It was only after the Eastern Han Dynasty brought in Buddhism to China that China worshiped idols. In the past, the Chinese only worshipped one God called "Heaven" or the "Lord on High."[62]

After positing that the ancient Confucians were theists, Wang goes on to contrast Mao Zedong's materialism with Confucius's theism and then makes the connection between the God of the Chinese and the God of the Bible: "Mao in *The Works of Mao Zedong* said: 'A thorough materialist is fearless.'[63] Confucius is not a materialist, so he said, 'There are three things of which the superior man stands in awe. He stands in awe of the ordinances of Heaven. He stands in awe of great men. He stands in awe of the words of sages.'[64] Joseph in the Old Testament was not a materialist, so when his master's wife (that lustful woman) tempted him to engage in adultery with her, he replied, 'How can I do such a great evil against God 神?'"[65]

Wang's prison years in which he had ample time to review the scope of Chinese history and what had happened in China after the CCP takeover confirmed to him that the God of the Confucian classics and sages was the same God of the Bible. This theological conviction led him to a practical conclusion that he tried to communicate in his spiritual father years to Jiang Hua, president of the Supreme People's Court of China, and most likely to those who visited him at his Shanghai house church who were trying to make sense of what had happened in China: to reject this God, as attested to in both the Confucian classics and the Bible, results in catastrophe. It seems that Wang Mingdao believed that both "Shang Di 上帝" and "Shen 神" were both appropriate terms for God, a view that many Chinese Christians share, but in his writings, he almost always preferred to use "Shen" when referring to God. He may have done this to distinguish between the Confucian revelation and the Christian revelation.[66]

WANG'S DOCTRINES OF CHRIST AND TRINITY

Whereas his mature thought on God seemed to have evolved over time, his early theology on the nature of Christ and the Holy Spirit seems to have been set for life in the early 1920s. Although Wang Mingdao is considered a spiritual father by Chinese unregistered house church Christians and is, or should be, considered a significant Chinese theologian due to his integration of Confucian and Christian thought, Wang's theology is somewhat controversial. He stated in 1922, at the beginning of his independent period, that "Jesus is the Son of God, not God, not Almighty, and not of one essence with God."[67] By stating that Jesus was "not of one essence with God 非與神一體," Wang was effectively breaking with the Christology of the Nicene Creed, a creedal statement of orthodox Christian theology formulated at the First Ecumenical Council of Nicea in 325. At this council, the theologians gathered finally settled on the teaching that Jesus was of the "same essence" (Greek *homoousion*) with God the Father.[68] In Wang's 1953 final revision of his most comprehensive theological treatise on Jesus titled *Who Is Jesus* 耶穌是誰?, despite the title, Wang does not provide any further articulation on his thoughts regarding the essence of Jesus, preferring to describe what Jesus *does* as the Son of God rather than who Jesus *is* in essence.[69]

During his early independent period in 1922, Wang also stated that the doctrine of the Trinity was erroneous.[70] Wang held this opinion and would discuss the "error of the Trinity" as late as 1952.[71] On August 14 and again on September 1, 1952, Wang was teaching on "correcting passed-on theological errors" including the doctrine of the Trinity.[72] By describing the doctrine of the Trinity, the teaching on the Godhead as three persons (Greek *hypostases*) of one essence (Greek *ousia*) 三位一體, as an error, Wang was also breaking with the teaching of the Constantinopolitan Creed, formulated at the Second Ecumenical Council of Constantinople in 381 resulting in a Nicene-Constantinopolitan Creed. At this second ecumenical council, the theologians assembled agreed on the divinity of the Holy Spirit, thus consolidating the Trinitarian formula of three persons of one essence.[73] Wang did not as clearly articulate the nature of the Holy Spirit as he did Christ. Wang again preferred to write about what the Holy Spirit *does* rather than who the Holy Spirit *is*.

In the few instances where Wang discussed the nature of the Holy Spirit, he said that "the Holy Spirit is given from God through Jesus Christ,"[74] and when he explained how the Holy Spirit descended, Wang said that Jesus promised the Spirit would come after his resurrection.[75] Since he posited that the doctrine of the Trinity was incorrect, Wang would not agree with the Constantinopolitan decision that the Holy Spirit was of one essence with God but rather used the biblical term "Holy Spirit 聖靈" or, occasionally, the "Spirit of God 神的靈" to refer to the Spirit.

These doctrines would bring him into conflict with Dora Yu and Jia Yuming in 1925 with Wang sticking to his unorthodox theological positions resulting in a painful separation between him and these other Fundamentalist Christians.[76] In Wang's 1951 article "God's Son Jesus" after several years of contemplation, Wang's favored theological description for Jesus was as "the Son of God 神的兒子" or, occasionally, "God's one and only Son" 獨生子, and he found it unfortunate that "there are some Christians who truly believe the truths recorded in the Bible, but they have accepted some teachings passed down by people in addition to the truths described in the Bible, using some eternally unclear reasoning, confusing many saints."[77] This "eternally unclear reasoning" almost certainly refers back to the conversations Wang had with Jia Yuming and Dora Yu when they attempted to convince Wang of the orthodox theological positions on Christ, using the language of Jesus being one essence with the Father, and the Godhead as a Trinity of three persons of one essence. With Wang being a biblicist, since the Bible did not use this philosophical language, he could not accept these teachings, but this stance did leave him open to theological attack as being unorthodox in his theology. K. H. Ting, in a veiled reference to Wang, mentioned that "among the opponents of the TSPM are some who deny the Trinity," which Wang quoted but did not offer a response to in "We Are for the Faith!"[78] The question of Wang's theology of Christ and the Trinity is still of significant interest today.[79]

Although Wang did teach his perspective on Christology and Trinitarian theology at the Christian Tabernacle and wrote his thoughts on his theology in his private diary, it seems that he did not see value in responding to K. H. Ting's comment on Wang's Trinitarian theology or in clarifying Wang's Christology beyond what he read in the Bible in his main theological publication, *The Spiritual Food Quarterly*, or in his later writings or sermons. On the one hand, Wang did not engage in speculation on the divinity of Christ beyond saying that he was the Son of God, but on the other hand, he also maintained that the description of Christ as a moral exemplar was insufficient in describing who Jesus Christ is. In short, Wang did not work out the full implications of these Christological and Trinitarian issues; instead of going into theological speculation, he was committed to simply write what the Bible recorded as to who Jesus and the Holy Spirit are.

As Andrew Louth has shown, the theologians who formulated the Nicene and Constantinopolitan Creeds borrowed extrascriptural philosophical concepts from the philosophy of Plotinus (204–270) in describing the Godhead as a Trinity of three persons of one essence.[80] At the time that the Nicene Creed was written, some theologians, as Wang Mingdao would centuries later, desired a more scriptural pattern to be followed in describing God and "were unhappy with the intrusion of philosophical and non-scriptural words" as definitions of Christian belief.[81] The desire to construct Christian theology as close as possible to the words of Christian scripture was not simply a development of twentieth-century Chinese Fundamentalists like Wang, but since he was not aware of these factors, where did his positions on Christ and the Trinity come from?

Ni Huiliang has written that Wang rejected Nicene Christology in favor of what Ni describes as a "relation-centric" perspective on the divine Father-Son relationship.[82] Ni asserts that Wang determined the nature of Jesus not by his essence but rather by his relationship with the Father as the Son of God. Ni believes that Wang's Christology is connected to the influence of the relational nature of Confucianism in which "the nature or role of a person is determined by the relationship that this person is in."[83] Ni writes that as a result, since for Wang, Jesus was God's Son and therefore, according to Wang's reasoning, not God, Wang rejected the doctrine of the Trinity as well. As discussed throughout this study, the influence of Confucian thought was strong in Wang's theology, but there seems to have been a more fundamental factor in Wang's rejection of these two orthodox doctrines: Wang could not accept a teaching that he did not find in the Bible.

The first indication we find in Wang's diary of a rejection of these two doctrines appears in the early 1920s. This was when he was attending a fellowship known as the Church of God—Zhu Dingcheng's church in Beijing that met in the home of an older Norwegian who was working in China. Iap Sian-Chin's contention that this Norwegian was Bernt Bernsten 賁德新 (1863–1933) is credible since Bernsten was a Norwegian in his sixties at the time, based in Beijing, and whose church had changed its name to the Church of God.[84] Wang also mentions having visited with Bernsten, or "Elder Ben 賁長老," several times from January 1921[85] until eventually breaking with Bernsten in January 1923 due to Wang being convinced that the doctrine of justification by faith was biblical, which Bernsten did not agree with.[86] However, before their break, it may explain why Wang began to have doubts in 1922 about the orthodox formulations of Christology and Trinity since he had listened to this older Norwegian teach on various theological topics and Bernsten rejected the doctrine of the Trinity.[87] Gene Ng's research has also shown that while Wang attended this fellowship, he wrote in his diary that he came to "know that God is One and not a Trinity."[88] Bernsten may have influenced Wang to reconsider the biblical basis of this teaching, as Bernsten seems to have convinced Paul Wei, founder of the True Jesus Church in China.[89] Wang eventually rejected Bernsten's teachings on salvation, finding Eric Pilquist's teachings on justification by faith more biblical, but Bernsten's teachings on the Trinity seem to have made Wang question the biblical basis of the doctrine. When Wang went back to look at the Bible, with his biblicist emphasis on the clear teaching of Scripture, he could not accept the philosophical formulations in orthodox Christology and Trinitarian theology, rejecting the teachings as unbiblical. Since many Christian Fundamentalists, such as Dora Yu and Jia Yuming, considered the doctrine of the Trinity a fundamental Christian belief and others such as Paul Wei and Wang Mingdao did not, it reveals that a greater variety of religious beliefs in Fundamentalist Chinese Christianity existed at the time than is sometimes recognized.[90] Independent Chinese Christians like Paul Wei and Wang Mingdao, empowered to break with tradition after the fall of the Qing dynasty and later the May Fourth Movement, established a new source of legitimacy through a literal interpretation of the Bible as a higher, divine authority apart from denominations and missionary agencies.[91] It seems that their time with Bernt Bernsten was formative in both men's rejection of the doctrine of the Trinity.

WANG MINGDAO'S THEOLOGICAL LIMITATIONS

Although Wang has been extremely influential in Chinese Christianity and should be considered a significant theologian, his theology, particularly in the areas of Christology and Trinitarian theology, are limited by his biblicist method of interpretation and a rare reliance on reason over the Bible in the construction of his theology. Wang's regular use of idiomatic expressions in his writings, both before and after prison, reveal his desire to be perceived as an intelligent, educated man despite his unspectacular educational achievements. It was not education per se that Wang objected to but rather, formal theological education. As Gloria Tseng has mentioned, Wang's distaste for formal theological education was a reaction to what he perceived as the domination of theological education in China by theological Modernists. However, as Tseng also indicates, this suspicion of theological education was regrettable due to the fact that it did not allow Wang to reach his full potential as a theologian.[92] After he was painfully deterred from pursuing his university education by his mother's illness and Yenching University's admission requirements, he later became convinced that theology schools in China were hotbeds of theological Modernism and wanted no part in them. At the beginning of his independent period, Wang began to prefer to study the Bible and other theological articles by himself. This allowed him to develop a contextual Confucian Fundamentalist Christian theology, but his emphasis on studying alone reinforced some blind spots in his thought. Wang's biblicism obscured the historical reality that previous generations of Christians had discussed the theological topics of Christ and the Godhead and collectively concluded that the Nicene-Constantinopolitan Creed contained the best representations of what Scripture taught.[93] With the theological context in China already intellectually fragile from the Modernist-Fundamentalist divide, any talk of moving away from the words of the Bible was a nonstarter for Wang. He persisted in a biblicist interpretation of Christology with Christ as the Son of God but not God, which resulted in a rejection of the doctrine of the Trinity. Wang's theology included a Father God, Son of God, and Spirit of God forming Wang's relational understanding of the Godhead in which only the Father is God in the orthodox sense of God's essence (*ousia*).

Because of this, Wang's theology does not fully capture what the Bible says about Jesus. The first chapter of John's Gospel reveals that "in the beginning was the Word, and the Word was with God, and the Word was God" (John 1:1). Wang's comments in 1927 on John 1:1 are that "the Word was with God in the beginning," but Wang stops short of identifying Jesus as God. Wang instead continued by writing that Jesus is "the head of all things God created" according to Colossians 1:15.[94] Later in 1952, when Wang interpreted the meaning of John 1:1 that Jesus is the Word, Wang states that "before Jesus came to earth, people could only hear the truth through God's words, [but] after Jesus came to earth, in addition to God's words, people could see God's truth from the Lord Jesus's life."[95] For Wang, Jesus revealed God as his one and only Son but was not God in his essence. Ni Huiliang is correct in attributing to Wang a relation-centric Christology with a preference for seeing Jesus as the Son of God,[96] but the Bible goes beyond Jesus's identity as merely the Son of God to affirming in John 1:1 that Jesus *is* God in the flesh. It is curious as to why Wang did not agree with the literal interpretation of John 1:1 that Jesus as the Word is God as the Nicene-Constantinopolitan Creed affirms. This is where the critics of Wang being a nonsystematic theologian have a valid point: Wang's Christology and resultant Trinitarian theology, while affirming *some* of what the Bible says about Jesus and God, does not affirm *all* that the Bible says about Jesus and God.

It is unfortunate that Wang did not have access to a premier theological institution of higher learning that would have allowed him to further develop his significant theological abilities.[97] Perhaps if he had been able to more fully understand that the early generations of Christians' contemplation of the Bible contained in the Nicene-Constantinopolitan Creed more adequately represented the teachings of Scripture than his did, Wang's theology could have been more fully orthodox. As it was, since the orthodox doctrines of Christology and Trinity utilized philosophical language, Wang viewed them as simply passed-on human traditions. Perhaps if he had been able to engage in a rigorous theology program that investigated the background of the Nicene-Constantinopolitan Creed from teachers he respected, he may have been able to see the biblical integrity of the creed.[98] Nevertheless, Wang's interpretation of John 1:1 is inadequately biblical and is a rare case in which his *reason*, trapped by his biblicist method of interpretation and possibly influenced by Confucian thought as Ni indicates, takes the upper hand in the construction of Wang Mingdao's theology over the Bible.

WHAT IS UNIQUE ABOUT WANG'S THOUGHT?

The blending of Confucian and Christian thought was not unique to Wang Mingdao. Christianity as the fulfillment of Confucianism was believed by other Chinese Christians like T. C. Chao, but what is unique about Wang's Confucian Christianity is that he did not embrace Modernist theology as Chao and many other Confucian Christians did but rather held to a Fundamentalist Christian theology that he blended with a Confucian worldview. Wang also differed from Jia Yuming who attempted to reconcile Confucian thought with Fundamentalist Christianity in that Wang rejected the orthodox doctrines of Christology and the Trinity. Wang saw the philosophical arguments for the doctrines as unbiblical traditions that had been passed on; he preferred the clear biblical description of Jesus as the Son of God, which caused the break between Wang and Jia in 1925. Also, Wang and other unregistered Chinese Christians found it problematic that Jia joined the TSPM[99] and eventually became vice chairman of the TSPM Standing Committee.[100] This has limited Jia's influence among unregistered house church Christians in China. Wang saw Christianity as the fulfillment of Confucianism's pursuit of the Way and used theological resources from both traditions to reinforce his arguments for *not* joining the TSPM. At both the beginning in Beijing and the end of his ministry in Shanghai, Wang provided leadership to churches meeting in his home as well as met with a significant number of Chinese Christians who came to seek his advice. These factors combined to create a unique position for Wang as a spiritual father to the unregistered house church movement. Although Watchman Nee has been very influential in the Local Church in China and around the world, his complicated legacy,[101] death while in prison in 1972, and lack of significant engagement with Confucian thought combine to make his contributions to the Chinese house church movement different and in some ways less influential than those of Wang Mingdao. Due to Wang's high level of personal integrity, his postprison years where he was able to retell his life story, and his deeply contextualized Confucian Christianity, Wang

Mingdao has become uniquely influential in the Chinese house church movement. One of these areas of influence has been in his ecclesiology.

WANG MINGDAO'S ECCLESIOLOGY

In terms of practice, Wang Mingdao based the Christian Tabernacle on what he considered a strict biblical model. Therefore, he rejected the practice of celebrating Christmas since the date of Jesus's birth was not clear in the Bible and he felt that many traditions had accrued around the holiday that brought unholy elements into the church.[102] He did not wear ceremonial attire or allow singers to wear robes, and he rejected adorning the church building with any cross, candles, or portraits of Jesus. Wang believed that these stemmed from Roman Catholic traditions and were secular means to draw people into the church. He advocated that the most important thing to draw people was the preaching of God's Word, particularly Christ's death and resurrection. Where this took place, a group would inevitably gather.[103] Wang wore a simple Chinese-style long gown while preaching. For decades, the Christian Tabernacle was furnished with wooden pews and a wide wooden pulpit where Wang preached. The bare white walls had the occasional sign with written characters on it, and Wang had a baptismal tank installed. Curiously, plants adorned the top and sides of the pulpit.[104] Apparently, this was seen as being in conformity to the biblical pattern. Wang seemed to be unaware of the fact that the purchase of a building for Christians to gather for worship was not in conformity with the biblical pattern. He simply preferred a streamlined Fundamentalist approach to church design. His house churches fit the biblical model better of locations where Christians gathered to both live and worship simultaneously.

In his thoughts on church identity, as detailed previously, Wang rejected both connecting with foreign missionary organizations as well as Chinese church networks such as Watchman Nee's Little Flock. He desired to lead a church independent of any influence outside of his own and a select group of leaders he handpicked such as Shi Tianmin to ensure that these people were living up to his standards of Christian holiness. Wang was extremely selective in whom he would allow to preach in his pulpit and whom he would baptize. He would only baptize those he was convinced had both faith in Christ and led a holy life. These select few were thus subsequently allowed to participate in the service aspects of the church. This type of quality control was the basis for his rejecting participation in both the North China Christian Union Group in the 1940s and the TSPM in the 1950s. It was imperative to Wang to remain separate from those he felt were not genuine Christians in any church organization. To maintain this level of control, he did not join the Christian Tabernacle with any network of Christians. Even among those he felt were genuine Christians, he did not unite because he did not find any biblical imperative to do so: "And even with true believers and faithful servants of God we can enjoy only a spiritual union. There should not be any kind of formal, organizational union, because we cannot find any teaching in the Bible to support it."[105] After his release from prison, although he had many significant friendships and was connected on a personal basis with scores of independent Chinese Christians, he never brought his Shanghai house church into any Christian network. Later Chinese Christians after becoming familiar with Wang's story have both followed Wang in his model of independent church life[106] and learned a lesson from his isolation after his arrest to form networks of mutual support.[107]

WANG MINGDAO AND SUFFERING

The physical and psychological suffering Wang endured during his prison years was not unique to the Christian experience in China, but as can be seen from the suffering of Lao She, Hu Feng, and countless others, it was common to all who offered intellectual resistance to the CCP during this period.[108] However, due to his resistance to the TSPM and subsequent arrest and imprisonment, many Christians have looked to Wang Mingdao as a model of faithfulness to God while enduring religious persecution, becoming known as a living "martyr for the faith."[109] To avoid a hagiographic light that is not accurate to Wang's history, it is important to admit his failures but still acknowledge that Wang was a man of unusual personal fortitude who almost certainly could have left prison had he simply joined the TSPM. By refusing, he endured two terms of imprisonment in which he suffered physical and psychological torture. What is evident when Wang's story is analyzed is that his response to suffering developed over time. There were different stages to Wang's response to personal suffering. During his first imprisonment beginning in 1955, Wang's Confucian Christian convictions collapsed under the combination of shock and disappointment of imprisonment, psychological terror, and beatings he received while in various prisons in Beijing. During this period, Wang lied to survive, was eventually released, passively refused to attend TSPM meetings, was reimprisoned in 1958, and continued his morally defeated life while in prison. This changed in 1963 when he received a life sentence. Surprisingly, this sentence changed his outlook and he began to write suggestions to the government. During this period, he began a more fearless written and spoken defense of what he thought was morally right. His behavior changed when he was transferred to the Datong Mining Camp and his defense of ousted political leaders resulted in a more aggressive form of physical torture. Wang was effectively silenced by this, but he was no longer willing to lie, at this point preferring being killed to lying.[110] He said that after 1965, he did not fear being shot or being in prison, but he could not stand to be tortured.[111] He did not write or speak out again until later while at Yinying Labor Camp when prison officials forbade such corporal punishment. Wang eventually returned to his written and spoken defense of what he thought was right, after the threat of torture was over, and he continued to do so after his release in Shanghai. His story shows that Wang responded to religious persecution in different ways depending on the severity of the persecution.

WANG'S THEOLOGICAL LEGACY: A DIVIDED CHINESE CHURCH

As a spiritual father to the unregistered house church movement, Wang's arrest for counterrevolutionary crime and ongoing lack of rehabilitation seems to be a major obstacle to reconciliation between the registered TSPM and the unregistered house churches. Some have argued that Wang's lack of participation in the TSPM was due to his individualism and the fact that he was hard to get along with.[112] In fact, Wang had several close relationships including meaningful friendships with Chen

Zigao, Shi Tianmin, John Sung, and Zeng Pingdao; Wang also grieved the loss of relationships such as what happened with Jia Yuming and Watchman Nee. However, it is true that Wang's perspective on the TSPM was binary. He believed that with regard to joining the TSPM, Chinese Christians were either on the side of God or the side of the devil. As mentioned previously, many sincere Christians in China were eager to see the Chinese church become independent from foreign control and freely joined with the TSPM with a sense that God was guiding the movement.[113] Any nuance of perspective on the TSPM was judged by Wang as compromise. His position by the summer of 1955, when the CCP and the TSPM were striving to create a united front, was no longer tolerated. The theological issues Wang laid out in "We Are for the Faith!" and his conclusion that he would not be willing to unite with "unbelievers" in the theology he thought fundamental made his arrest certain, but why he was arrested is still debated.

Philip Wickeri provides good insight that Wang in "We Are for the Faith!" was critiquing K. H. Ting's theology, but Ting, who emphasized mutual theological respect for such views as Wang's unorthodox perspective on the Trinity, critiqued Wang's politics. For Ting, mutual respect for diverse positions did not extend into politics.[114] The statements made by theologians connected with the TSPM that Wang was *not* arrested for opposition to the TSPM[115] do not match up with the historical data. As Thomas Harvey has observed, since in the 1950s Chinese context political essence and religious essence were connected, Wang's refusal to unite with the TSPM was seen as a betrayal of the nation.[116] Harvey's significant contribution is in explaining how it was political ideology that provided the foundation for the TSPM case against Wang. Harvey asserts that for the TSPM of the 1950s, political essence was the ground of human existence. Therefore, to the TSPM, Wang's religious beliefs were a "mere cloak" that hid his true essence. His religious views could only be understood according to his political ideology with his political essence defining his religious essence. This explains why, for those connected to the TSPM, Wang's refusal to unite with the TSPM was a betrayal not only of country but also of Christ and the church.[117] In other words, before 1955, Wang Mingdao thought that the argument was theological, but for the TSPM and CCP, it was entirely political. Days after Wang was arrested in 1955, H. H. Tsui (Cui Xianxiang) 崔

憲祥, the general secretary of the Church of Christ in China, undoubtedly upset with Wang for his critique of Tsui's theology in "We Are for the Faith!"[118] wrote, "Now, why then does Wang Mingdao oppose the Three-Self Movement? Very simply, it is because he opposes and hates the New China. . . . Wang Mingdao's madness is due to his hatred of Communism and the People's Government, it is not a matter of faith; this statement of his will fool no one."[119] This quote reveals that by July 1955, opposition to the TSPM was equated with opposition to the CCP. This correlation between the TSPM and the government makes clear that the reason Wang was arrested was almost certainly due to Wang's opposition to the TSPM.[120] His insistence that he was imprisoned not for any counterrevolutionary crime but only for opposing the TSPM continued until the end of his life.

Despite Wang's arrest, the issues he brought up in "We Are for the Faith!" have not been resolved even today, and so the Chinese church continues to be divided between registered and unregistered factions, a reality that again reiterates Wang's significance as a spiritual father to the house church movement. In fact, as Kao Chen-yang has reported, Wang's anti-TSPM ideology has legitimated the ministry of house church leaders outside of the TSPM. As a result, many modern unregistered house church leaders believe, in part due to Wang's writings and example, that the unregistered church is not an alternative to the official one but is the *only* divinely sanctioned church in China.[121] Wang's significance as a theologian is further evidenced by the fact that contemporary unregistered Chinese Christian leaders continue to bring up the issues he addressed in the 1950s as justification for not joining the TSPM. In 2010, Sun Yi 孫毅 of Shouwang Church 守望教會 in Beijing referred to Wang Mingdao's arguments in "We Are for the Faith!" as one of Shouwang Church's reasons for not joining the TSPM.[122] Furthermore, in August 2015, Wang Yi 王怡 of Early Rain Covenant Church 秋雨聖約教會 in Sichuan wrote his "95 Theses: The Reaffirmation of Our Stance on the House Church" as a memorial to the sixtieth anniversary of Wang Mingdao's arrest in 1955. In the article, Wang Yi describes Wang Mingdao as "a patriarch of the Chinese house church" and articulates his reasons based on Wang Mingdao's theology for Early Rain Covenant Church not joining the TSPM.[123] These examples show that Wang Mingdao's theology and personal example continue to be an obstruction to the reconciliation of the two factions. It seems that until the issues Wang brought up in "We Are for the Faith!" are dealt with in a manner acceptable to both sides, it is unlikely that there will be unity between unregistered house church and registered TSPM Christians in the Chinese church.[124]

THE STORY OF WANG MINGDAO AND CHINESE CHRISTIANITY

Just as the Christian faith itself is by nature a global story, so Wang Mingdao's story is an international one. His father, Wang Zihou, found employment at Peking Methodist Hospital as a Chinese doctor's apprentice and learned Western medicine from foreign missionaries. His death was an indirect result of being connected to the foreign missionary presence, which resulted in Wang Mingdao growing up without a father. His mother, Li Wenyi, was able to purchase a housing unit in Beijing due to Boxer indemnity funds given to her by the London Missionary Society (LMS). The LMS also provided funds for Wang to pursue his education at their Tsui Wen Academy and during his first year of a university prep program at a Methodist university. He taught at Martyr's Field School, which was run by the American Presbyterian mission. This experience convinced Wang to completely sever dependent connections with international missionary organizations, but he still interacted with a number of foreign missionaries he respected including Bernt Bernsten, Eric Pilquist, Arie Kok, Arthur Reynolds, David Adeney, and Leslie Lyall, among others.[125] Wang was mentioned several times in missionary journals such as the *Chinese Recorder*, which established an international reputation among Christians interested in China. After Wang's arrest in 1955 and grieving what they saw as the "loss of China" to the CCP, several former missionaries turned "China watchers" kept Wang's imprisonment after 1955 in the international news for years to come. They may have had a special affection for Wang in part because he did not write denouncements of missionaries or Western nations as other Chinese Christians had done.[126] They also admired his fortitude in going to prison to suffer for what they saw as religious reasons.[127] His autobiography *The Last Fifty Years* was loosely translated into English and subsequently into German and French. Overseas Chinese such as Stephen

Wang, Thomas Wang, Calvin Chao, Jonathan Chao, Theodore Choy, and Timothy Tow also kept Wang Mingdao's story alive around the world in international Chinese Christian communities, and his books continued to be published in Hong Kong, Singapore, and Taiwan. Wang received letters even while in prison from people overseas who were familiar with his story. The widespread nature of Wang's story is revealed by his inclusion in the 1978 Amnesty International report *Political Imprisonment in the People's Republic of China.* After his release from prison in 1980, a large number of Chinese as well as international visitors came to visit Wang and Liu Jingwen in Shanghai. He refused to meet with anyone connected, no matter how slightly, with the TSPM during his Shanghai years. As a result, the mood of Wang's surprise meeting with Billy Graham in 1988 seems to have in fact been much more tense than many of the reports reveal. However, the fact that Graham knew about Wang and persisted in the visit, despite being told three times by the Wangs not to come, reveals how important Wang's story had become in not only Chinese Christianity but in *world* Christianity. The ongoing inclusion of Wang Mingdao in international publications on Christianity, including this biography by a Canadian scholar, is proof of this fact as well.

However, Wang Mingdao's story is fundamentally a Chinese story. Wang never traveled outside of China any farther than Hong Kong and Macau, never wrote any articles in a language other than Chinese, and contextualized the Christian faith in a uniquely Chinese way by adopting elements of the Confucian tradition to create his theology. Spurning what he thought were the surface issues of Chinese contextualization such as architecture and song tunes, he sought what he felt was a deeper level of contextualization of the Christian message in Chinese history and morality by seeing Confucius's moral vision of following the Way (Dao) fulfilled by following Jesus Christ, the Word of God of John's Gospel, which itself is translated as the Way in the Chinese Bible.[128] He received a thorough Confucian education at Tsui Wen Academy where he developed a lifelong love for Chinese history and poetry. His life spanned nearly the entire twentieth century in five distinct stages that corresponded to larger sociopolitical movements taking place in China. He was deeply affected by the Boxer Rebellion, the May Fourth and May Thirtieth Movements, the Second Sino-Japanese War, and the Chinese Civil War and resultant CCP liberation and purge of "counterrevolutionaries," as well as Deng Xiaoping's Reform and Opening policies. He was personally acquainted with Cheng Ching-yi, Jia Yuming, Dora Yu, Watchman Nee, Zhang Yijing, Marcus Cheng, John Sung, David Yang, Z. T. Kuang, Allen Yuan, Samuel Lamb, T. C. Chao, Calvin Chao, Stephen Wang, Thomas Wang, Jonathan Chao, and Philip Teng, who were many of the most influential Chinese Christian leaders of the twentieth century. Even today, Wang Mingdao continues to be revered as a spiritual father to the unregistered house church movement.

In these ways, Wang's life story is a thoroughly Chinese story. His life tells the tale of twentieth-century Chinese Christianity as it fractured between Fundamentalists and Modernists in the 1920s and later again in the 1950s between registered TSPM and unregistered house church Christians. These fault lines continue to shape Chinese Christianity today. The story of Chinese Christianity in the twentieth century is impossible to tell without including the life of Wang Mingdao.

WORKS OF WANG MINGDAO

This bibliography provides full bibliographic references with annotation for Wang Mingdao's writings (primary sources) in both the original Chinese and in the English translation. For entries published in Chinese, the original title will be included in Chinese characters. The following entries are arranged chronologically according to publication date.

Wang Mingdao published *The Spiritual Food Quarterly* (*TSFQ*) from 1927 to 1955, usually in March, June, September, and December, for a total of 114 volumes. He was the primary writer but also included material he edited and translated from other sources, which he indicates at the beginning of each article. This is the main source of his writings.

Wang Mingdao, ed. *The Spiritual Food Quarterly* 靈食季刊. Peiping (Beijing): Spiritual Food Quarterly Press, 1927–55.

Wang also published several books and booklets on selected topics under the Spiritual Food Quarterly Press banner. Some of these were collections of articles he published in *TSFQ* but were revised and expanded. The following is a comprehensive chronological list of his book and booklet publications.

Wang Mingdao. *The Bride of Christ* 基督的新娘. Beijing: Spiritual Food Quarterly Press, 1926.

Wang Mingdao. *The Benefit of Suffering* 受苦有益. Beijing: Spiritual Food Quarterly Press, 1926.

Wang Mingdao. *Who Is Jesus Christ* 基督是誰? Beijing: Spiritual Food Quarterly Press, 1928.

Wang Mingdao. *The Resurrected Christ* 復活的基督. Beijing: Spiritual Food Quarterly Press, 1928.

Wang Mingdao. *The Second Coming of Christ* 基督再來. Beijing: Spiritual Food Quarterly Press, 1929.

Wang Mingdao. *How Long Will You Have a Divided Heart* 你們心持兩意要到幾時呢? Beijing: Spiritual Food Quarterly Press, 1929.

Wang Mingdao. *The Trumpet Call* 角聲. Beijing: Spiritual Food Quarterly Press, 1930.

Knight, George Halley. *In the Secret of His Presence* 隱密處的靈交. Translated by Wang Mingdao. Beijing: Spiritual Food Quarterly Press, 1930. Reprinted three times (4th edition in 1955).

Wang Mingdao. *Why I Believe the Bible Is God's Revelation* 我為甚麼信聖經是神所默示的.Beijing: Spiritual Food Quarterly Press, 1933. Reprinted two times (3rd edition in 1955).

Wang Mingdao. *The Peril of the Modern Church* 現代教會的危險. Beijing: Spiritual Food Quarterly Press, 1933.

Wang Mingdao. *Can People Establish God's Kingdom* 人能建設天國麼? Beijing: Spiritual Food Quarterly Press, 1933. Reprinted in 1951.

Wang Mingdao. *The Language of Christians* 王明道基督徒的言語. Beijing: Spiritual Food Quarterly Press, 1933. Reprinted two times (3rd edition in 1950).

Wang Mingdao. *The Spiritual Gifts Movement in the Light of Scripture* 聖經光亮中的靈恩運動. Beijing: Spiritual Food Quarterly Press, 1934.

Wang Mingdao. *An Admonition to Believers* 信徒針砭. Beijing: Spiritual Food Quarterly Press, 1935. Reprinted in 1951.

Wang Mingdao. *The True Meaning of the New Birth* 重生真意. Beijing: Spiritual Food Quarterly Press, 1935. Reprinted three times (4th edition in 1954).

Wang Mingdao. *To the Suffering Saints* 寫給受苦的聖徒. Beijing: Spiritual Food Quarterly Press, 1935.

Wang Mingdao. *Beware of the Devil's Tricks* 謹防魔鬼的詭計. Beijing: Spiritual Food Quarterly Press, 1935. Reprinted two times (3rd edition in 1954).

Wang Mingdao. *Distinguishing between the True and the False Gospel* 真偽福音辨. Beijing: Spiritual Food Quarterly Press, 1936.

Wang Mingdao. *Are All Men Sons of God* 普世人類都是神的兒子嗎? Beijing: Spiritual Food Quarterly Press, 1936.

Wang Mingdao. *The Gospel in Genesis 5* 創世紀第五章中的福音. Beijing: Spiritual Food Quarterly Press, 1936.

Wang Mingdao. *The Tallest Ladder on Earth* 世上最高的梯子. Beijing: Spiritual Food Quarterly Press, 1936. Reprinted in 1955.

Wang Mingdao. *Spiritual Gifts, Rewards, and Awards* 恩賜賞賜與獎賞. Beijing: Spiritual Food Quarterly Press, 1936. Reprinted in 1951.

Wang Mingdao. *Was Jesus Christ Really Raised from the Dead* 基督果真復活了麼? Beijing: Spiritual Food Quarterly Press, 1936.

Wang Mingdao. *Conduct in Society Common Sense for Christians* 信徒處世常識. Beijing: Spiritual Food Quarterly Press, 1936. Reprinted three times (4th edition in 1950).

Wang Mingdao. *Spiritual Food Fables Collection* 靈食寓言集. Beijing: Spiritual Food Quarterly Press, 1940. Reprinted in 1950.

Knight, George Halley. *The Days in Dense Cloud Darkness* 在密雲黑暗的日子. Translated by Wang Mingdao. Beijing: Spiritual Food Quarterly Press, 1941.

Wang Mingdao. *Christians and Marriage* 基督徒與婚姻. Beijing: Spiritual Food Quarterly Press, 1943.
Wang Mingdao. *Thankful People* 感恩的人. Beijing: Spiritual Food Quarterly Press, 1944. Reprinted in 1950.
Wang Mingdao. *What Money Can't Buy* 金錢不能買的幾樣東西. Beijing: Spiritual Food Quarterly Press, 1946.
Wang Mingdao. *In the Fiery Furnace and the Lion's Den* 在火窯與獅穴中. Beijing: Spiritual Food Quarterly Press, 1947. Reprinted in 1953.
Wang Mingdao. *The Christian Hymnal*. Beijing: Spiritual Food Quarterly Press, 1947.
Wang Mingdao. *Must Christians Keep the Sabbath* 基督徒必須守安息日麼? Beijing: Spiritual Food Quarterly Press, 1948.
Wang Mingdao. *To Young Christians* 寫給青年的基督徒. Beijing: Spiritual Food Quarterly Press, 1948.
Wang Mingdao. *The Last Fifty Years* 五十年來. Beijing: Spiritual Food Quarterly Press, 1950.
Wang Mingdao. *To the Suffering Saints* 寫給受苦的聖徒. Beijing: Spiritual Food Quarterly Press, 1950. Revised and expanded version.
Wang Mingdao. *To Young Christians* 寫給青年的基督徒. Beijing: Spiritual Food Quarterly Press, 1950. Revised and expanded version.
Wang Mingdao. *Our Lord* 我們的主. Beijing: Spiritual Food Quarterly Press, 1953.
Wang Mingdao. *On Being the Lord's Elite Troops* 作主精兵. Beijing: Spiritual Food Quarterly Press, 1953. Reprinted in 1955.
Wang Mingdao. *Look at These Men* 看這些人 (Vols. 1–2). Beijing: Spiritual Food Quarterly Press, 1953.
Wang Mingdao. *Remedies for Believers* 聖徒的藥石 (Vols. 1–2). Beijing: Spiritual Food Quarterly Press, 1954.
Wang Mingdao. *God's Seven Testimonies* 神的七個見證. Beijing: Spiritual Food Quarterly Press, 1954.
Wang Mingdao. *The Gracious Call* 施恩的宣召. Beijing: Spiritual Food Quarterly Press, 1954.
Wang Mingdao. *What Do We Gain Believing in Jesus Christ* 我們因信基督耶穌得了甚麼? Beijing: Spiritual Food Quarterly Press, 1954.
Wang Mingdao. *Discerning the True Gospel* 真偽福音辨. Beijing: Spiritual Food Quarterly Press, 1954. Revised and expanded version.
Wang Mingdao. *A Few Important Questions* 幾個重要的問題. Beijing: Spiritual Food Quarterly Press, 1955.
Wang Mingdao. *Messages for Our Time* 時代的信息. Beijing: Spiritual Food Quarterly Press, 1955.
Wang Mingdao. *We Are for the Faith* 我們是為了信! Beijing: Spiritual Food Quarterly Press, 1955.

In 1956, Wang Mingdao's confession, which he would later recant while in prison, was collected and published by the Three Self Patriotic Movement in the journal *Tianfeng.*

Wang Mingdao. "My Confession 我的檢討." *Tianfeng* 515 (October 1956): 7–9.

In 1963, Francis Jones translated and published a significant number of documents centered on the Three-Self Movement including Wang Mingdao's article "We Are for the Faith!" from 1955, a response to this article by H. H. Tsui (Cui Xianxiang) 崔憲祥, "A False Faith Cannot Fool People," in *Tianfeng* from 1955, and Wang Mingdao's "Self-Examination" or "Confession," from 1956.

Jones, Francis P., ed., *Documents of the Three Self-Movement: Source Materials for the Study of the Protestant Church.* New York: National Council of the Churches of Christ in the USA, 1963.

From 1976 to 1978, C. C. Wang (Wang Zhengzhong) edited in Taiwan a seven-volume collection of Wang Mingdao's writings titled, *Treasuries of Wang Ming Tao.* This collection was published during Wang Mingdao's imprisonment and did not receive his authorization. The names of the volumes are as follows: Volume 1: *The Narrow Gate* 窄門, Volume 2: *The Hard Road* 小徑, Volume 3: *Feeding the Spirit* 靈食, Volume 4: *The Overflow* 餘糧, Volume 5: *Call from Above* 天召, Volume 6: *On Reflecting* 借鏡, and Volume 7: *On Guard* 衛道.

Wang Mingdao. *Treasuries of Wang Ming Tao*王明道文庫 (Vols. 1–7). Edited by C. C. Wang. Touliu, Taiwan: Conservative Baptist Press, 1976–78.

In 1981, the Christian Literature Centre published a selection of Wang Mingdao's sermons.

Wang Mingdao. *A Collection of Mr. Wang Mingdao's Sermons* 王明道先生講道集. Hong Kong: Christian Literature Centre, 1981.

Some of the letters Wang Mingdao sent out after he was released from prison were recorded and shared in journals and magazines.

Wang Mingdao. "New Year's Letter from Wang Mingdao 王明道新年來信." *Evangelical Communications* 31 (1981): 1–2.

Several of Wang Mingdao's works were translated into English during the 1980s and 1990s. Arthur T. F. Reynolds, a China Inland Mission (CIM) missionary to China from 1933 to 1951, was personally acquainted with Wang Mingdao during his time in China. During Reynolds's retirement in England from 1981 to 1990, he translated and published into English several of Wang's works. Wang's works that have been translated into English are listed below chronologically according to translation date.

Wong Ming-Dao. *A Stone Made Smooth.* Translated by Arthur Reynolds. Southampton: Mayflower Christian Books, 1981. (Translation of *The Last Fifty Years*)

Wong Ming-Dao. *Spiritual Food.* Translated by Arthur Reynolds. Southampton:

Mayflower Christian Books, 1983. (Translation of twenty messages from *The Spiritual Food Quarterly*)

Wang, Ming-Dao. *A Call to the Church*. Translated by Theodore Choy. Fort Washington, PA: Christian Literature Crusade, 1983. (Translation of twenty messages from various books and booklets written by Wang Mingdao)

Wang Mingdao. *Building Virtue*. Translated by Wang Changxin. Hong Kong: Morning Star Publishing House, 1987.

Reynolds, Arthur, trans. *Strength for the Storm*. Singapore: Overseas Missionary Fellowship, 1988. (Sermons by Wang Mingdao and others)

Wang Ming-Dao. *Chinese Church Iron Man Wang Ming-Dao Looks at These People*. Translated by anon. Wheaton, IL: Conservative Baptist Press, 1988. (Translation of *Look at These Men*)

Wong Ming-Dao. *Day by Day*. Translated by Arthur Reynolds. Crowborough, UK: Highland Books, 1989. (Translation of devotional material from nineteen different books and booklets written by Wang Mingdao)

Wang Ming Tao. *Wang Ming Tao and Charismatism*. Translated by Timothy Tow. Singapore: Christian Life Publishers, 1989.

Wong Ming-Dao. *The Spiritual Gifts Movement*. Translated by Arthur Reynolds. Southampton: Mayflower Christian Books, 1990. (Translation of Wang's *The Spiritual Gifts Movement in the Light of Scripture*)

Wang Ming Tao. *God's Grace in Suffering*. Translated by Ding. Hong Kong: Living Books for All, 1993.

Wang Ming Tao. *On Temptation*. Translated by Timothy Tow. Singapore: Far Eastern Bible College Press, 1997. (Translation of six essays from *The Spiritual Food Quarterly* and *Proverbs for Christian Living*)

In the 1980s, several of Wang's Shanghai sermons were recorded and later shared on YouTube.

Wang Mingdao. "A Strong Wall, an Iron Pillar—Wang Mingdao's Testimony 堅城鐵柱-王明道見證." Sermon. No Date. https://www.youtube.com/watch?v=NbYbk3vrmr4&list=PLeyV8uWMaMm0TfMS-koWZ3JEaveoadkqC&index=3.

Wang Mingdao. "Wang Mingdao's Critique of Watchman Nee to Warn Preachers and Christians 王明道講道指責倪柝聲給傳道人與基督徒的警戒." Sermon. No Date. https://www.youtube.com/watch?v=HiXhBUy4ZZ0&list=PLeyV8uWMaMm0TfMS-koWZ3JEaveoadkqC&index=4.

Wang Mingdao. "Wang Mingdao Sermon 02—Come Out from Babylon 王明道講道02 - 從巴比倫出來." Sermon. No Date. https://www.youtube.com/watch?v=lWenH5ndAAE.

Wang Mingdao. "Wang Mingdao's Sermon 02—Guard against Two Kinds of Leaven; To Serve the Lord One Must Be Holy 王明道讲道02 - 防備兩種酵; 侍奉主要聖潔." Sermon. No Date. https://www.youtube.com/watch?v=Dz_wQ7_by1g&list=PLeyV8uWMaMm0TfMS-koWZ3JEaveoadkqC&index=5.

Wang Mingdao kept a diary from 1915 to 1955, each year one volume, for a total of forty-one volumes. His diary was confiscated when he was taken into custody in 1955 and was returned to him when he was released with the exception of the 1954 volume. Hong Kong's Spiritual Rock Publishers published a selected volume of the diaries in 1997 more focused on the later period until 1955. The full collection of diaries (with the exception of the 1954 volume) was entrusted by Wang Mingdao's son Wang Tianduo to the Hong Kong Alliance Bible Theological Seminary's Christianity and Chinese Culture Research Center in order to copy and eventually publish at some point in the future.

Wang Mingdao. *Selections from Wang Mingdao's Diary* 王明道日記選輯. Hong Kong: Spiritual Rock Publishers, 1997.

In 2013, Ying Fuk Tsang collected and edited *Wang Mingdao's Last Confession*. This book is a set of fifteen editions of an appeal and twenty unfinished pages written by Wang Mingdao in 1982–83 to the director of China's Supreme People's Court. This is Wang's "Rehabilitation Request Manuscript": his attempt to have his conviction of being a counterrevolutionary reassessed. It represents a significant resource in Wang Mingdao's later thought.

Wang Mingdao. *Wang Mingdao's Last Confession* 王明道的最後自白. Edited by Fuk Tsang Ying (Xing Fuzeng). Hong Kong: Logos Publishers, 2013.

CCLM Publishing Group 華宣出版社 in Taiwan has republished the full collection of *The Spiritual Food Quarterly* from 2012 to 2014. In addition to *The Spiritual Food Quarterly*, CCLM has also reprinted several other works by Wang Mingdao between 2012 and 2013. This edition by CCLM is a reprint of the original version of Wang's writings and represents the new standard in the study of Wang Mingdao's theology. These works are also available in searchable digital format through Google Play. They are arranged chronologically according to the original publishing date.

Wang Mingdao. *The Spiritual Food Quarterly* 靈食季刊 (1927–55). Reprint. New Taipei City: CCLM Publishing Group, 2012–14.

Wang Mingdao. *Look at These Men (Part One)* 看這些人(上) (1935). Reprint/ New Taipei City: CCLM Publishing Group, 2013. (A compilation work)

Wang Mingdao. *The Last Fifty Years* 五十年來 (1950). Reprint. New Taipei City: CCLM Publishing Group, 2012.

Wang Mingdao. *But Do God's Will and Don't Ask about the Future* 但遵神旨，莫問前程 (1952). Reprint. New Taipei City: CCLM Publishing Group, 2012. (A compilation work)

Wang Mingdao. *Look at These Men (Part Two)* 看這些人 (下) (1953). Reprint. New Taipei City: CCLM Publishing Group, 2013. (A compilation work)

Wang Mingdao. *Our Lord* 我們的主 (1953). Reprint. New Taipei City: CCLM Publishing Group, 2012. (A compilation work)

NOTES

NOTES TO CHAPTER ONE

1. Lin and Chang, *An Injured Brave*, 108.

2. Covell, *Confucius, the Buddha, and Christ*, 226.

3. My translation of Ying Fuk Tsang's phrase 平反遺稿. Where it seems helpful for clarity, the Chinese characters are included in this study.

4. See Wang Mingdao and Ying Fuk Tsang, *Wang Mingdao's Last Confession*, 384–86. Ying, in his appendix 3, provides Wang Mingdao's publication directory in Chinese. See the Wang Mingdao bibliography in this book for an updated English version. Since *Wang Mingdao's Last Confession* has a prominent role in the research for this study, there is distinction made in this book between the sections written by Wang Mingdao, which are the fifteen documents and twenty loose pages that were intended to be sent to Jiang Hua, the president of the Supreme People's Court of China, and the sections written by Ying Fuk Tsang, which are the introduction, footnotes, conclusion, and four appendixes. This is done by naming the person at the beginning of the footnote. For example, Wang Mingdao, *Last Confession*, with page number, or Ying, *Last Confession*, with page number. This work is abbreviated as *Last Confession* in this book.

5. For the sake of clarity, Wang preferred to self-publish his sermons in *The Spiritual Food Quarterly* rather than rely on others to record them. See Wang Mingdao, *The Last Fifty Years*, 203. In 1951, Wang published an expanded version of his autobiography *The Last Fifty Years*, which included previously unknown details about his father. This work is abbreviated as *Fifty Years* in this book.

6. That Wang was the main source of the articles written in *The Spiritual Food Quarterly*, see Wang Mingdao, *Fifty Years*, 209.

7. CCLM Publishing Group 華宣出版社 in Taiwan recently republished a large number of Wang Mingdao's works including the full collection of *The Spiritual Food Quarterly*. Many of these works are also available in searchable digital

format through Google Play. All references to *The Spiritual Food Quarterly* in this book are from the CCLM edition.

8. See Ying, *Last Confession*, 5.

9. Ying, *Last Confession,* 5. See Wang Mingdao, *Selections from Wang Mingdao's Diaries.*

10. This document is available in English in Jones, *Documents of the Three Self-Movement*, 117–21.

11. S. Wang, *The Long Road to Freedom*, 170. This work is abbreviated as *The Long Road to Freedom.*

12. This is the date given by Ying, *Last Confession*, 6.

13. Some of the introductory material that was later included in the *Last Confession* was originally published in 2010 as Ying, "A Counterrevolutionaries' Final Words," 319–54.

14. See Ying, *Last Confession*, 5.

15. A simple search on YouTube using the Chinese characters 王明道講道 (Wang Mingdao preaching) produces several results.

16. Wong Ming-Dao, *A Stone Made Smooth*, trans. Arthur T. F. Reynolds. This autobiography by Reynolds was translated from English into German—see *Wang Ming-tao: Ein Stein wird geschliffen* (A stone made smooth), unnamed translator—as well as French—see *Wang Ming-tao: Façonné par la main du Maître* (Shaped by the hand of the Master), trans. Thomas Roder.

17. See the Wang Mingdao bibliography in this book for Arthur Reynolds's significant contribution in translating Wang's works into English from 1981 to 1990.

18. See Bays, *A New History of Christianity in China*, 155n41. Since the English translation of Wang's autobiography is not an accurate translation, I refer to the original Chinese version republished by CCLM in this book.

19. Jones, *The Church in Communist China*, 103–10.

20. Jones, *Documents of the Three Self-Movement*, 99–114, 117–21.

21. Reynolds, *Pathway to Glory*, 17–21.

22. The interesting story of how *Another Forty Years was* written is documented in S. Wang, "How *Another Forty Years* Was Written."

23. Wang Changxin, *Another Forty Years.*

24. S. Wang, *The Long Road to Freedom*. This English translation was supervised and approved by Stephen Wang. See S. Wang, *The Long Road to Freedom*, 8. Since the English version is an accurate translation, I refer to the English version in this book with supplemental details added from the Chinese version, *Another Forty Years.*

25. Shi, *Sixty-Three Years.*

26. Lin and Chang, *An Injured Brave.*

27. See Ying, "Counter-Revolution in the Revolutionary Era," 97–147.

28. For a thorough discussion of the secondary sources on Wang Mingdao, see Payk, "Revisiting the Life and Theology of the Confucian-Christian Wang Mingdao," 15–24.

29. Starr, *Chinese Theology*, 4.

30. See Kao, "The Cultural Revolution and the Post-Missionary Transformation of Protestantism in China."

31. Kao, "The House Church Identity and Preservation of Pentecostal-Style Protestantism in China," 207–19.

32. Kao, "The House Church Identity and Preservation of Pentecostal-Style Protestantism in China," 211.

33. Kao, "The House Church Identity and Preservation of Pentecostal-Style Protestantism in China," 212–14.

34. Lyall, *Three of China's Mighty Men*, 155. Ying, *Last Confession*, vii.

35. Chao, "A Brief Outline of Mr. Wang Mingdao's Contribution to Chinese Churches," 2–3.

36. Harvey, *Acquainted with Grief*, 9.

37. Cook, "Wang Mingdao and the Evolution of Contextualized Chinese Churches," 219.

38. Lui, *Development of Chinese Church Leaders*, 136.

39. Kao, "The House Church Identity and Preservation of Pentecostal-Style Protestantism in China," 211.

40. Cook, "Fundamentalism and Modern Culture in Republican China," 3.

41. Cook, "Fundamentalism and Modern Culture in Republican China," 9.

42. Cook, "Fundamentalism and Modern Culture in Republican China," 185.

43. Cook, "Wang Mingdao and the Evolution of Contextualized Chinese Churches," 209–23.

44. Cook, "Wang Mingdao and the Evolution of Contextualized Chinese Churches," 209.

45. Cook, "Wang Mingdao and the Evolution of Contextualized Chinese Churches," 219.

46. Ng, *Christianity and Social Changes in China*, 163–64.

47. Lam, *Wang Ming-Tao and the Chinese Church*, 232.

48. Cook, "Fundamentalism and Modern Culture in Republican China," 3.

49. Cook, "Wang Mingdao and the Evolution of Contextualized Chinese Churches," 209. However, Richard Cook, as one of the reviewers of this book for Notre Dame Press, has recently indicated that he is "largely persuaded" by the new information presented in this book that Wang should be considered a Confucian Christian theologian.

50. Zhang Zhiyi 張執一 (1911–83), deputy minister of the United Front Work Department of the CCP Central Committee, described Wang in this way. At the third National Conference of Christianity held in 1981, he criticized Wang Mingdao by

name and said, "There are also a few people like Wang Mingdao who are pawns of foreign reactionary forces." See Wang Mingdao, *Last Confession*, 67n34.

51. See John Wesley, *John Wesley*, iii.

52. See Maddox, *Responsible Grace*, 16.

53. Lee, "Cross-textual Hermeneutics and Identity in Multi-Scriptural Asia," 182.

54. Wang Mingdao, *Last Confession*, 266.

55. Wang Mingdao, *Fifty Years*, 43.

56. See Maddox, "The Recovery of Theology as a Practical Discipline," 650–72. For the nonsystematic nature of much of Chinese theology, see Starr, *Chinese Theology*, 280.

57. Li Kaihuan, "Wang Mingdao's Theology," 110.

58. For example, Wang believed that T. C. Chao (Zhao Zichen) 趙紫宸 at Yenching University 燕京大學 and later K. H. Ting (Ding Guangxun) 丁光訓 at Nanjing (Jinling) Union Theological Seminary 金陵協神學院 were theological Modernists who promulgated a "social gospel" that in Wang's opinion ignored personal salvation. See Wang Mingdao, "How Many Gospels Are There," 137–38. Kevin Xiyi Yao writes, "A common view among the Fundamentalists was that the Modernists' strongholds were schools." See Yao, *The Fundamentalist Movement among Protestant Missionaries in China*, 101. See also Wang Mingdao, *Fifty Years*, 87 and 157 to see Wang's negative evaluation of studying theology. These evaluations must be read in light of Wang's perception that "studying theology" inevitably would mean enrollment in a Modernist institution, thus his preference for personal Bible study.

NOTES TO CHAPTER TWO

1. Yamane, "Narrative and Religious Experience," 177–78.

2. Wang Mingdao, *Fifty Years*, 9.

3. Wang Mingdao, *Fifty Years,* 20.

4. Wang Mingdao, *Fifty Years*, 19.

5. For a detailed analysis of the background factors that led to the Boxer Rebellion, see Bickers, "Introduction," xi–xvii.

6. Bickers, "Introduction," xiii. Lian Xi estimates the number of Chinese Christians seeking shelter in the Beijing legation was more than three thousand people. Lian Xi, *Redeemed by Fire*, 111.

7. Wang Mingdao, *Fifty Years*, 19.

8. Wehrle, *Britain, China, and the Antimissionary Riots, 179–80.* Wang Mingdao, *Fifty Years*, 32.

9. Cohen, "Humanizing the Boxers," 183.

10. One such account is given in Cohen, "Humanizing the Boxers," 186.

11. Wang Mingdao, *Fifty Years*, 20.

12. In 1951, shortly after publishing his autobiography, Wang Mingdao read an article by Lu Wantian 鹿完天 titled "Record of the 1900, Beijing Incident" in which Lu describes Wang Zihou's suicide. Lu dates Wang's suicide to June 22, 1900, at 5:00 a.m. in the garden of the Huashen Temple. See Wang Mingdao, *Fifty Years*, 21. See also Lu Wantian, "Record of the 1900 Beijing Incident," 27.

13. Wilcox, "Psychiatric Morbidity, Violent Crime, and Suicide," 514–23. The article reports a threefold greater risk of suicide for suicide descendents.

14. The West Lake undoubtedly appealed to Wang Mingdao's poetic side during his melancholic period of release from prison. Bai Juyi 白居易 (772–846 CE), a poet Wang Mingdao read, wrote several poems about West Lake including a poem titled "Walking in Spring by West Lake" 錢塘湖春行. See Graham, *Poems of the West Lake*, 15.

15. Wang Mingdao, *Fifty Years*, 227.

16. Wang Mingdao, *Last Confession*, 61.

17. Porter, "The Boxers and the Hospitals," 294. The hospital is named "Methodist Episcopal" Hospital, Peking in the list. See also, "The Situation in the North," 276.

18. See The History of Western Medicine in China, Indiana University Library, "Hopkins Memorial Hospital."

19. Lim et al., *National Medical Association of China Medical Guide, 1928*, 32–33. See also the key and map for the physical location of the hospital, which was located at the corner of Hatamen and Legation Streets very close to the Forbidden City. However, when Wang Zihou worked at the hospital, it seems that it was located at the MEC mission compound, which was located on Filial Piety Alley, very close to the Hatamen entrance. See Ewing and Ewing, *Death Throes of a Dynasty*, 74n8. A good map of the Legation Quarter in 1900 is available in Moser and Yeone, *Foreigners within the Gates*, 88–89.

20. Wang Mingdao, *Fifty Years*, 19. This author has translated 中國醫士 as Chinese doctor's apprentice since they were not full doctors 醫師. In 1896, there were nine men studying to become doctors in all the missionary hospitals in Beijing (Peking). See Neal, "Medical Teaching in China," 91. However, there were two levels to this training. One level of missionary training was given to "native doctors," and the other was for "native assistants," who were not as fully trained as the "native doctors." It is not always clear in the missionary literature when missionaries are writing about training Chinese in medicine if they are talking about "native doctors" or "native assistants." It is also possible that the two groups were separated in the course of training, which lasted several years. See Cohen, "Christian Missions and Their Impact," 10:575.

21. Lim et al., *National Medical Association of China Medical Guide, 1928*, 33.

22. Lim et al., *National Medical Association of China Medical Guide, 1928*, 32.

23. Bashford, *China and Methodism*, 111. Also "Hopkins, N. S., North China."

24. Lim et al., *National Medical Association of China Medical Guide, 1928*, 32.

25. Bashford, *China and Methodism,* 113. See also "Lowry, George D., North China."

26. Porter, "The Boxers and the Hospitals," 296. Also, Thompson, *William Scott Ament and the Boxer Rebellion*, 221. However, during the Boxer Uprising, Dr. Hopkins was listed as being in Tsunhua (遵化 Zunhua), Hebei, most likely at the Tsunhua Methodist Hospital. See "Personal Notes," 309.

27. Hopkins and Lowry, "Hospital Reports," 149. Dr. Hopkins's MEC biography states that he was involved in training many Chinese doctors in eye surgery in connection with Hopkins Memorial Hospital. "Nehemiah S. Hopkins, M.D., Passes."

See also the mention of these two doctors in the work at Peking Methodist Hospital in Mullowney, "Report of the Peking Hospital," 206–9.

28. For medical missionaries' preference to choose Christian Chinese men to be their assistants, see Renshaw, "Accommodating the Chinese," 181. Also, "Christian character" was an expectation of Chinese assistants. See Main, "Hospital Reports," 186. See section on "Students."

29. Beebe, "Our Medical Students," 2.

30. Wang Mingdao, *Fifty Years*, 21.

31. Jeremiah was described as being "an iron pillar," as noted by Wang, in Jeremiah 1:18. Wang Mingdao, *Fifty Years*, 22.

32. Wang Mingdao, *Fifty Years*, 22. Dried Fish Lane is 幹魚胡同 and Sweet Rain Lane is 甘雨胡同. They have a very similar pronunciation in Chinese. Many lane (hutong) names were changed in Beijing during the Republican period from "vulgar" to more "cultured" names. See Dong, *Republican Beijing*, 74.

33. Cohen, *History in Three Keys*, 56. The value was calculated by Cohen in 1997 to be US$333 million to be paid in thirty-nine annual installments with 4 percent interest on unpaid principal.

34. Wang Mingdao, *Fifty Years*, 22. She was renting one housing unit, but the sale was for the whole housing complex of seven units and four sheds. She eventually modified the complex to include fourteen rooms, which housed herself with her two children, her mother, two sisters with their own families, and eight unrelated families for a total of ten family members and over thirty people. Despite Wang's comment that his mother, Li Wenyi, was not very intelligent, she did seem to possess some entrepreneurial skills. See Wang Mingdao, *Fifty Years*, 23.

35. Wang Mingdao, *Fifty Years*, 22.

36. Wang Mingdao, *Fifty Years*, 256. His father was almost certainly highly intelligent to be selected to become a doctor's assistant, as only those deemed highly intelligent were selected by foreign doctors to become Chinese doctor's assistants. See "Medical Education in China," 127.

37. Wang Mingdao, *Fifty Years*, 256.

38. Wang Mingdao, *Fifty Years*, 24.

39. Rawski, "Elementary Education in the Mission Enterprise," 138.

40. Xie and Su, "Chinese Translations of John Bunyan's *The Pilgrim's Progress*," 114–41.

41. See Li Zipeng, "Late Qing Chinese Christian Literature," 280.

42. S. Wang, *The Long Road to Freedom*, 220. Unfortunately, there is very little mention of Wang's maternal grandmother in the biographies.

43. Wang Mingdao, *Last Confessio*n, 52–53.

44. Wang seems to have completely lost contact with his father's side of the family after Wang Zihou's suicide.

45. Wang Mingdao, *Fifty Years*, 26.

46. See Wu, *The Monkey and the Mon*k, 48. The passage is also found in Chinese in Yu, *The Journey to the West* 西遊記, 3.24. The lingzhi mushroom 靈芝草 that his uncle indicates Wang will need to eat to become immortal has a long history in Chinese medicine and is also referred to in *The Journey to the West.* Anthony C. Yu translates the mushroom as "the nine-leaf divine agaric," which to those who are nourished by it, according to the classic novel, "would remain indestructible for a thousand years and luminous in all ages." See Yu, *The Journey to the West*, 3:218.

47. The English name in YMCA documents is Tsui Wen Academy 萃文學校, but to provide more precise information on Wang's education, the elementary primary, elementary senior, and middle school at Tsui Wen Academy will be named in order to distinguish them in Wang's chronology.

48. See Wang Xiaojing, "The Church Unity Movement," 48, 55.

49. See Bickers, "New Light on Lao She, London, and the London Missionary Society," 24.

50. Wang Gungwu, *China Reconnects*, 95.

51. Wang Mingdao, *Fifty Years*, 26.

52. See Tsai, "Scriptures and Their Popularization," 145.

53. Wang Mingdao, *Last Confession*, 179–210. The fact that he wrote these quotations, even though he could no longer read due to his deteriorating eyesight in 1982, indicates his memorization of the quotes.

54. Wang Mingdao, *Fifty Year*s, 26 and *Last Confessio*n, 52. There were two assistant teachers: Mr. Xu's son, who was a medical student, and his son's friend, both of whom are not named. Wang Mingdao, *Fifty Years*, 26.

55. See Dunch, "Science, Religion, and the Classics," 64.

56. Rawski, "Elementary Education in the Mission Enterprise," 142.

57. Wang Mingdao, *Fifty Years*, 27.

58. *Book of Rites*, Record on the Subject of Education, 12. Wang Mingdao has several references to the *Five Classics* 五經 (*Classic of Poetry*, *Book of Documents*, *Book of Rites*, *Book of Changes*, and the *Spring and Autumn Annals*) in *Fifty Years* and *Last Confession.* The traditional view is that Confucius was the editor of the *Five Classics*, which Wang Mingdao subscribed to.

59. Sima Qian, *The Grand Scribe's Records*, 1:153–54. These records, the first and most influential of the twenty-four dynastic histories of China, are foundational to historical knowledge in China.

60. Chinese Ancient Poetry. Chen Ziang 陳子昂, "On a Gate Tower at Yuzhou 登幽州臺歌"; Wang Mingdao, *Fifty Years*, 27.

61. S. Wang, *The Long Road to Freedom*, 212. Zhen Pindao would be the Hanyu Pinyin transliteration, but I retain Ma Min's transliteration for clarity.

62. *Mencius*, Gaozi I, 6.2. For a more nuanced perspective on Mencius's statement that human nature is good, see Van Norden, "Mencius," section 3, The Goodness of Human Nature.

63. See *Biographies of Outstanding Women* 列女傳, Maternal and Polite, Zou Meng Ke Mu, 1–9.

64. Wang Mingdao, *Fifty Years*, 29.

65. Wang Mingdao, *Fifty Years*, 30.

66. Wang Mingdao, *Fifty Years*, 258.

67. Wang Mingdao, *Fifty Year*s, 31. We can see with Wang's analysis of himself as both a radical and a conservative he is interpreting himself in ways that he would not have been aware of as a preteen. We must always remember that his autobiography *Fifty Year*s is an account that has been interpreted with specific goals in mind. However, this does not mean that his account is fictional.

68. See Furth, "Intellectual Change," 12:350–54.

69. Cohen, "Christian Missions and Their Impact," 544.

70. The complex interplay of ideas at the time in China is laid out in Cao, "Adoption of Christian Anthropology," 317.

71. The political situation during these years is described in detail in Young, "Politics in the Aftermath of Revolution," 12:237–46.

72. Wang Mingdao, *Fifty Years*, 32.

73. The *Educational Review* was a journal produced in the early twentieth century in Shanghai that was focused on providing information on education in China and was heavily influenced by Christian missionaries. The November 1910 issue indicates that at the time, there were two schools in Peking that were operated through the auspices of the LMS under the leadership of the "Chinese Church Council." See "Day Schools in Chihli," 14. These two schools appear to be Tsui Wen Elementary and Middle School for boys that Wang Mingdao attended and the affiliated girls' school that Wang mentions in Wang Mingdao, *Fifty Years*, 32.

74. Wang Mingdao, *Fifty Years*, 32–33.

75. See Cook, "Wang Mingdao and the Evolution of Contextualized Chinese Churches," 211, 217.

76. Wang Mingdao, *Fifty Years*, 33.

77. Gene Ng 吳劍麗, a professor who has access to Wang's complete diary at Alliance Bible Seminary in Hong Kong, notes that even in Wang's unpublished diary, he does not mention this classmate's name. Gene Ng, Facebook message to the author, April 19, 2021.

78. 認識神 can be translated as "to know God" or "to gain an understanding of God." Since this is Wang's religious conversion narrative, I prefer the former translation.

79. See Wang Mingdao, *Fifty Years*, 80.

80. Wang Mingdao, *Fifty Years,* 95.

81. Wang Mingdao, *Last Confession*, 56–57.

82. Wang Mingdao, *Last Confession*, 52.

83. Lam Wing-hung sees these two issues, what happens after death and moral cultivation, as being the two main concerns of Wang Mingdao's early life. See Lam, *Wang Ming-Tao and the Chinese Church*, 21. However, Wang continued to fear death even after his conversion to Christianity. See Wang Mingdao, *Fifty Years*, 45.

84. *The Book of Rites: The Great Learning*, 2.

85. Wang Mingdao, *Last Confession*, 52. See also *The Book of Rites: The Great Learning*, 2.

86. See T. C. Chao, "A Chinese Delegate Looks at Tambaram," 463–64. Also T. C. Chao, "The Articulate Word," 485–86.

87. Wang Mingdao, *Fifty Years*, 34.

88. See Zia, *The Protestant Missions in China*, xv–xvii.

89. Chu, "Early 20th Century Chinese Christian Writers," 197–98.

90. Chu, "Early 20th Century Chinese Christian Writers," 200. Some believe that it was because of H. L. Zia's writings that the publications of the YMCA made a significant impact on the thinking men of China during the early twentieth century. See Lacy, *A Hundred Years of Chinese Methodism*, 192.

91. Zia, *Friendly Talks with Students*, unnumbered publisher's page. Wang likely read the previous 1912 edition since the 1914 edition was published in August 1914, and he indicates reading the book around May 1914.

92. Zia, *Friendly Talks with Students*, table of contents 2–4. The original contributions by H. L. Zia were part 1, section 1. Entering School: Hints to New Students, 12. How to Use a Dictionary, part 2, section 2. The Value of Evening Schools, 3. How to Spend a Vacation Profitably, and 5. How I Learned to Read English. Since Zia was the editor of the book, the various authors' ideas can be considered to represent Zia's perspectives on the topics.

93. Zia, *Friendly Talks with Students*, part 1, 11.

94. Zia, *Friendly Talks with Students*, part 1, 20.

95. Zia, *Friendly Talks with Students*, part 1, 29. Although in this section Zia recommends reading modern authors instead of ancient, his strong emphasis on the practical discipline of Christianity shapes his thought with a Confucian Christian character.

96. Wang Mingdao, *Last Confession*, 153–54.

97. Zia, *Friendly Talks with Students*, part 2, 7–8.

98. Zia, *Friendly Talks with Students*, part 2, 46.

99. See Zia, *Selected Works of Xie Honglai*, xxvii, 293–306. However, as the translator of influential American Modernists Harry Emerson Fosdick 富司迪 and

Sherwood Eddy 艾迪, H. L. Zia's theology may have been more Modernist than Wang Mingdao realized. See Zia, *Selected Works of Xie Honglai*, xxxiv. Wang Mingdao described Fosdick as a leading Modernist thinker and notes that the YMCA translated his works but did not make mention of Zia's translation of Fosdick. See Wang Mingdao, "We Are for the Faith!" 136–37. Wang described Sherwood Eddy as a preacher of the Modernist gospel. See Wang Mingdao, "Does Dr. Sherwood Eddy Preach the Gospel?" 245–47.

100. See G. Ng, "The Shaping Influence of the Chinese YMCA on the Young Wang Mingdao," 159–94. Ng's article shows from Wang's unpublished diary that H. L. Zia and the YMCA had a deep influence on Wang between 1915 and 1920 before the split between Fundamentalists and Modernists in China.

101. Wang Mingdao, *Fifty Years*, 34.

102. Zhu Xi, *Interlinear Analysis of and Collected Commentaries on the Four Books, Commentary on Analects* 7.6.

103. *Book of the Later Han*, Biography of Geng Yan, 12.

104. Wang Mingdao, *Fifty Years*, 44.

105. Wang Mingdao, *Fifty Years*, 37. Wang recalled that when he went to visit H. L. Zia's grave in 1925, Wang's commitment to the practical aspects of Christian life was in part due to Zia's influence.

106. See Guo, "Protestant Christian Elementary Education in China," 630–32. Research into YMCA records reveals that there were more Christians at Tsui Wen than Wang Mingdao thought, although the number of baptized students remained quite low and the number of baptisms decreased over time. See *China's Young Men* 10: 77, 327. Also, *China's Young Men* 11: 460. It is almost certain that Wang would only have considered the baptized students as being true Christians. There are only three years of *China's Young Men* available that include statistics on Tsui Wen Academy. Coincidentally, the years that are available range from 1913 to 1915, bookmarking the years of Wang's conversion.

107. Wang himself was able to master English to the level that he was later able to translate English theological works into Chinese such as four books by George Halley Knight (1835–1917), including *In the Secret of His Presence* (1906) and *In the Cloudy and Dark Day* (1910). See Wang Mingdao, *Fifty Years*, 209. He was also able to "skillfully" converse with English-speaking foreign visitors even into his later years. See Lin and Chang, *An Injured Brave*, 133. However, he did not publish any works in English.

108. See Lutz, "Middle Schools," 12–13.

109. No explanation is offered in *China's Young Men* for the dramatic drop-off in Christians at Tsui Wen Academy. See *China's Young Men* 10: 77, 327. Also, *China's Young Men* 11: 460.

110. A Chinese teacher acted as the directing teacher in the frequent absence of the principal, Thomas Biggin.

111. Wang Mingdao, *Fifty Years*, 35–37.

112. Wang Mingdao, *Fifty Years*, 37. Even though he had many enemies at Tsui Wen Middle School, Wang also developed a close friendship in 1916 or 1917 with a student named Chen Zigao 陳子誥, but he makes mention of it only later in life. Wang respected Chen's morality and knowledge and was deeply concerned when Chen later wavered in his Christian faith. See Wang Mingdao, *Fifty Years*, 132.

113. Wang Mingdao, *Fifty Years*, 44–45.

114. Originally from the *Later History of the Five Dynasties* 新五代史, book 32, 10.

115. Wang Mingdao, *Fifty Years*, 45. He mentions in Wang Mingdao, *Last Confession*, 265, the biography on Abraham Lincoln that he read while in middle school, but the first character could not be discerned by the editor due to Wang's illegible handwriting. The reference is to __英雄, which is translated __Heroes. Since he was an avid reader of H. L. Zia's works, he may also have read, Zia, *World Leaders*, which contained a biography of Abraham Lincoln in Chinese translated by H. L. Zia.

116. Lian Xi thinks that the deteriorating political situation in Beijing also motivated his desire to become a politician. See Lian, *Redeemed by Fire*, 113. However, Wang makes no mention of a political source of motivation to enter politics.

117. *Mencius*, Teng Wen Gong 1, 4.16.

118. Wang Mingdao, *Fifty Years*, 45–46.

119. Wang Mingdao, *Fifty Years*, 47.

120. Wang uses the idiom 人強勝天 "man can conquer nature," a concept that is universal as well as Chinese. The idea appears in China at least as early as the unofficial dynastic history *The Lost Book of Zhou* 逸周書, Wenzhuanjie, 1. I use "heaven" in the translation because Wang's use of the idiom is clearly referring to resisting God.

121. Here, Wang uses another idiom, 以卵擊石 "to strike a stone with an egg," from the *Romance of the Three Kingdoms* 三國演義, 43.11. He frequently used idioms in *Fifty Years*. It is not known whether he read these classics, as idioms are commonly used in Chinese writing, but his use of idioms reveals that he is attempting to convey that he is an educated, or at least, a well-read man despite his unspectacular formal educational achievements.

122. Wang Mingdao, *Fifty Years*, 48.

123. See Wang Mingdao, *Last Confession*, 55n6.

124. Wang does not mention that the Yenching Women's College, also known as the North China Union Women's College (founded 1905), and the School of Theology (founded 1906), itself a union of three schools, were also part of the merger that resulted in Yenching University. See Hin Wong, "The Formal Opening of Yenching University," 348, as well as West, *Yenching University and Sino-Western Relations*, 34–35.

125. Wang Mingdao, *Fifty Years*, 49. The university preparatory program Wang entered existed in a similar format in the American school system known as an associate degree awarded after a course of postsecondary study lasting two years.

126. Not to be confused with National Peking University 北京大學 (founded 1898).

127. This would be thought of today as the first year of university studies, and in fact, Wang describes it as such in Wang Mingdao, *Fifty Years*, 54.

128. The preparatory program was likely composed of general subjects to prepare students for the rigors of university education. He mentions a course in May 1919 that he took on English history in which the teacher inspired him to work for moral reform in China like John Wesley did in England. See Wang Mingdao, *Fifty Years*, 61. Even the first two years of the undergraduate program at Yenching University were composed of general subjects with students specializing in certain fields of study only in their third year. See Hin Wong, "The Formal Opening of Yenching University," 349–50.

129. See Schwartz, "Themes in Intellectual History," 12:407.

130. Wang Mingdao, *Fifty Years*, 51. Wang uses the idiom 相依為命. His education until the completion of his first year of university was supplemented by a lifelong love of reading that provided him with a rich vocabulary full of idiomatic expressions. He said that of all his possessions, he treasured his books the most. See Wang Mingdao, *Fifty Years*, 247.

131. Wang Mingdao, *Fifty Years*, 51.

132. Shaw, *An American Missionary in China*, 47. Wang said that the person he wrote to was a Western missionary but did not name him.

133. Wang Mingdao, *Fifty Years*, 52. The disappointment from the complete lack of response from Stuart may be why he always wrote back to those who requested his ministry even when he rejected the request, an onerous task considering he would become one of the most famous Christians in China in the 1930s, and encouraged John Sung to do so as well. See Wang Mingdao, "Mr. Song Shangjie [John Sung] Has Died," 152.

134. For budget information on Yenching University, see West, *Yenching University and Sino-Western Relations*, 36–37.

135. Wang Mingdao, *Fifty Years*, 51–52.

136. "Encountering Sorrow 離騷" is an extremely influential poem from the *Songs of Chu* 楚辭, a collection of poetry from the ancient Chinese state of Chu. Until the twentieth century, the traditional view has been that Qu Yuan wrote "Encountering Sorrow." See Knechtges and Chang, *Ancient and Early Medieval Chinese Literature*, 127. Wang normally accepts traditional authorship of Classical Chinese and Christian writings.

137. Qu Yuan's biography is recorded in Sima Qian, *The Grand Scribe's Records*, 7:295–302.

138. Wang Mingdao, *Fifty Years*, 52–53.

139. Hawkes, *Chu Tzu*, 34.

140. Wang Mingdao, *Last Confession*, 54.

141. See Schwartz, "Themes in Intellectual History," 407.

142. Hu Suh, "Intellectual China in 1919," 354.

143. Ling, "The Other May Fourth Movement," 4.

144. Bays, *A New History of Christianity in China*, 107.

145. Wang Mingdao, *Fifty Years*, 55.

146. Cohen, *History in Three Keys*, 52. See also Ketler, *The Tragedy of Paotingfu*. Baoding was translated in missionary literature as Pao-ting or Paotingfu.

147. See "Missionary News," 264.

148. Not to be confused with his grandfather Walter Lowrie or his uncle Walter Macon Lowrie 婁理華 (1819–47) as some have done. See "In Remembrance," 181–82.

149. Originally born in Shanghai in 1856, James Walter Lowrie was the son of Reverend Reuben Lowrie. He left Baoding to work in Shanghai from 1910 to 1925, later returning to Baoding until his death in 1930. See Shavit, *The United States in Asia*, 310, as well as "Rev. James W. Lowrie," *New York Times*, January 29, 1930.

150. Zhang Jing, "The Spread and Development of Early Christianity," 200.

151. Wang Mingdao, *Fifty Years*, 59. Wang does not provide this man's name.

152. Wang Mingdao, *Fifty Years*, 56.

153. Wang Mingdao, *Fifty Years*, 57.

154. Wang Mingdao, *Fifty Years*, 60. However, Wang always resisted the term "pastor" for his role as a church leader. See Wang Mingdao, *Fifty Years*, 171.

155. The following list is from Wang Mingdao, *Fifty Years*, 60.

156. Wang uses the idiom 利己損人. *The Old Book of Tang* uses the nearly identical idiom 損人益己. See *The Old Book of Tang* 舊唐書, book 92, 31.

157. Wang uses the idiom 恃強凌弱. Used in the famous Ming dynasty story collection *Stories to Caution the World* 警世通言, book 3, 3.

158. Wang uses the expression 諂富輕貧. A poor man who does not flatter and a rich man who is not proud meets minimal ethical standards for Confucius. See *Analects* 1.15.

159. Wang uses the idiom 爾虞我詐. This is an idiom that developed out of *Mr. Zuo's Commentary on Chun Qiu* 左傳, Duke Xuan, Year 15.2. See James Legge's translation, "We will not deceive you; do not you doubt us." *The Chinese Classics, Vol. V: The Chun Tsew with the Tso Chuen*, 5:328.

160. Wang uses the idiom 鬥角勾心. One of Wang's favorite Tang poets, Du Mu 杜牧, uses the same idiom but in reverse order, 鉤心鬥角, in his Efang Palace Poem to describe how the halls of the palace rivaled one another in splendor, which evolved into the idiom of people rivaling with one another. See Chinese Ancient Poetry. Du Mu 杜牧, "Efang Palace 阿房宮賦."

161. Wang Mingdao, *Fifty Years*, 60–61.

162. The Western theology degree he had in mind was likely the bachelor of divinity degree (BD, presently known in North America as the master of divinity, or MDiv, degree). T. C. Chao had completed the BD degree at Vanderbilt University in

1917 and went on to become a famous theologian at Yenching University beginning in 1926, the school where Wang had originally hoped to complete his university studies. See *Biographical Dictionary of Chinese Christianity*, "Zhao Zichen."

163. Wang Mingdao, *Fifty Years*, 62.

164. See "Members of the Educational Association of China," n.p. There are few biographical details available for Thomas Biggin. He was an Englishman ordained with the LMS who held various leadership roles in the society, and Wang does not mention him when he retells his story of studying at Tsui Wen or this conversation until he recalls his experience at Martyr's Field Presbyterian school, but Wang respected Biggin for his honesty and integrity. See Wang Mingdao, "Saints Who Fall Ill Should Remember This," 168.

165. Wang Mingdao, *Fifty Year*s, 65. Wang does not describe Han Xin's story, confident his readers will understand the reference as soon as Han Xin's name is mentioned.

166. Han Xin's biography is recorded in Sima Qian, *Records of the Grand Historian*, 163–84. His death by beheading is recorded on p. 182.

167. Wang Mingdao, *Fifty Years*, 67.

168. According to Gene Ng, this colleague's name was Zhang Zian 張子安 based on Wang's unpublished diary entries. See Ng, "The Shaping Influence of the Chinese YMCA on the Young Wang Mingdao," 188–90. Wang does not mention his name in *Fifty Years* for some unknown reason.

169. Wang used the expression 天之驕子. See *Book of Han* 漢書, Biography of Xiongnu, part 1, 70.

170. Wang Mingdao, *Fifty Years*, 70.

171. See Isaiah 6. This mystical prayer experience lasted from around 10:00 p.m. to 1:00 a.m.

172. Wang Mingdao, *Fifty Years*, 71.

173. See Wang Mingdao, *Last Confession*, 100. In 1966, Wang wrote over a hundred pages in Datong Labor Camp to refute two articles given to him by a prison official because he felt the articles slandered the missionary schools and hospitals.

174. For example, the Swedish missionary Eric Pilquist, see Wang Mingdao, *Fifty Years*, 95; the Dutch diplomat Arie Kok, see Wang Mingdao, *Fifty Years*, 128; as well as James Hudson Taylor III, see Lin and Chang, *An Injured Brave*, 138.

175. Lian Xi notes that a recent battle between two warlord factions had resulted in the central government becoming weakened and unable to pay these soldiers for several months resulting in their plan to attack the Presbyterian mission compound. See Lian, *Redeemed by Fire*, 114. Lian indicates a nationalist impulse in Wang due to the impact of the May Fourth Movement.

176. From Matthew 26:52.

177. Wang Mingdao, *Fifty Years*, 72.

178. See Harvey, *Acquainted with Grief*, 18, 176n12.

179. Wang Mingdao, *Fifty Years*, 74–75.

180. Wang Mingdao, *Fifty Years*, 80.
181. Wang Mingdao, *Fifty Years*, 77.
182. Wang Mingdao, *Fifty Years*, 77.
183. From 1 Samuel 15:22.
184. Wang Mingdao, *Fifty Years*, 78.
185. From Matthew 16:25.
186. Lian Xi notes that the Apostolic Faith Mission 使徒信心會 emerged in 1909 as a group of twenty-six foreign missionaries who were Pentecostal in theology. See Lian, *Redeemed by Fire*, 46. Zhu Dingchen must have been one of their Chinese converts who went on to become a preacher with the mission.
187. Wang Mingdao, *Fifty Years*, 79.
188. Later, Wang had a baptismal tank 浸池 in the church he led, the Christian Tabernacle. See Wang Mingdao, *Fifty Years*, 168. He was not convinced that others had to follow him in being baptized in natural waters.
189. Wang Mingdao, *Fifty Years*, 79–80.
190. Wang names Shi as his "old friend" 老友 who would take over responsibility for ministry including preaching at the Christian Tabernacle when Wang was away on preaching trips. See Wang Mingdao, *Fifty Years*, 163. Shi Tianmin translated several English articles into Chinese and contributed several original articles of his own for *The Spiritual Food Quarterly*.
191. S. Wang, *The Long Road to Freedom*, 93.
192. "Pentecostal group" would be the direct translation but "Pentecostal movement" is the older preferred English nomenclature. It refers to a broad movement of Christians who emphasize the gifts of the Holy Spirit and should not be confused with the Pentecostal Church, which is one of the churches within the movement.
193. Wang Mingdao, *Fifty Years*, 80.
194. Wang Mingdao, *Fifty Years*, 81. In 1934, in the midst of a significant Pentecostal activity in Shandong Province, Wang would write a booklet on the Spiritual Gifts movement in which he would discuss several of these issues in detail. See Wang Mingdao, *The Spiritual Gifts Movement*.
195. Inouye, *China and the True Jesus*, 82. Also Lian, *Redeemed by Fire*, 43.
196. Lian, *Redeemed by Fire*, 68.
197. Lian, *Redeemed by Fire*, 115.
198. Wang Mingdao, *Fifty Years*, 71.
199. Nedostup, *Superstitious Regimes*, 6–11. "Superstitious" groups were contrasted at the official level with "religious" groups. Those organizations considered superstitious were despised by the educated and even at times considered illegal while those considered official religious groups retained a degree of respect and legality. An explanation for this contrast is offered by Goossaert and Palmer: "As religion was considered a strong, moralizing, and unifying force behind the Western nation-states, it was, in this early period, generally received by Chinese intellectuals as something positive. 'Science' often came to be the touchstone in dividing between

'religion' [compatible with science] and 'superstition' [unscientific]." See Goossaert and Palmer, *The Religious Question in Modern China*, 50.

200. Wang Mingdao, *Fifty Years*, 71.

201. See *The North China Famine*, vii–viii.

202. Wang Mingdao, *Fifty Years*, 82.

203. The "filial son" 孝子 that Wang strove to be is an ideal that is encouraged in the Confucian classics. See *The Book of Rites*, Qu Li 1, 19: "A filial son will not do things in the dark, nor attempt hazardous undertakings, fearing lest he disgrace his parents. While his parents are alive, he will not promise a friend to die (with or for him), nor will he have wealth that he calls his own."

204. Wang Mingdao, *Fifty Years*, 83.

205. Wang Mingdao, *Fifty Years*, 84.

206. Knight, *In the Secret of His Presence*, 203–4. George Halley Knight was a Scottish Free Church minister and one of Wang's favorite authors.

207. G. H. Knight particularly emphasized the importance of *individual* prayer and Bible study: "He [the well-nourished Christian] draws strength out of deep heart-intercourse with God, out of the secret study of the Word, out of private prayer; but these things he has to *seek*: he must go in search of the water, for the water will not come to him." Knight, *In the Secret of His Presence*, 156.

208. See Sandeen, *The Roots of Fundamentalism*, xv–xvii.

209. It is interesting that Wang's friend John Sung was also thought to have had a mental breakdown in 1927 while studying at Union Theological Seminary in New York. It should be noted that Sung's mental state did appear to show signs of a genuine mental-emotional breakdown. However, the period of rest and study that each man had, Wang at Dayou Village in 1921 and Sung at Bloomingdale Hospital in 1927, was characterized in their own narratives by both future Chinese Fundamentalist Christian leaders to be their theological training period. See Lim, *The Life and Ministry of John Sung*, 65–68. Also, Li and Smalley, "A Chinese Christian Leader Revisited," 96–98. More recent scholarship has shown how Sung's breakdown is more complicated than he himself described. See Ireland, *John Song*, 21–23.

210. Wang's description of the beauty of Dayou Village makes one wonder what poems or events came to his mind in the shadow of the Summer Palace, which had been an imperial garden of the Qing dynasty. For a landscape being a repository of texts for Chinese Christians, see Starr, *Chinese Theology*, 92.

211. Wang Mingdao, *Fifty Years*, 88–89. Wang returned home six times during his time in Dayou Village with a total of sixty-two days being actually spent in his cousin's home.

212. However, it appears that Wang participated in YMCA evangelism teams earlier as a street preacher in 1917. See Ng, "The Shaping Influence of the Chinese YMCA on the Young Wang Mingdao," 175.

213. Wang Mingdao, *Fifty Years*, 88–89.

214. Bays, *A New History of Christianity in China*, 108. Bays describes this allegation as an ongoing process of realization between 1921 and 1925.

215. The Chinese Christian spirit in response to the May Fourth Movement is reflected in part by T. C. Chao's statement in 1924 that "the indigenous church . . . will be one entirely supported by Chinese money, wholly governed by Chinese Christians, completely reorganized to suit the Chinese genius, and freely enriched by Chinese thought on theological definitions and modifications. See T. C. Chao, "The Indigenous Church (1924)," 177.

216. Wang Mingdao, *Last Confession*, 104–5. This anti-theist idea in Wang's thought will be discussed later in this book.

NOTES TO CHAPTER THREE

1. Bays, *A New History of Christianity in China*, 109–10.

2. In Wang's diary, he records the characters for Cheng Ching-yi's name as 誠靜宜, but the 誠靜怡 characters are the more common way to write Cheng's name in Chinese.

3. See Wang Xiaojing, "The Church Unity Movement in Early Twentieth-Century China," 109–15.

4. According to Lian Xi, this LMS church on Rice Market Street was connected to the Tsui Wen Academy that Wang attended, but Lian provides no evidence to verify this statement. See Lian, *Redeemed by Fire*, 111. Alternative evidence seems to indicate that the LMS church connected to the Tsui Wen Academy was Gangwashi Church 缸瓦市教會, or as it was known in English, the Peking West City New Church. See Bickers, "New Light on Lao She," 24–26.

5. Wang Xiaojing, "The Church Unity Movement in Early Twentieth-Century China," 89–91. Also, *Biographical Dictionary of Chinese Christianity*, "Cheng Jingyi."

6. As recorded in the *World Missionary Conference* 1910, 352–53.

7. Shi, *Sixty-Three Years*, 20.

8. *Wang Mingdao's Diary*, 8.

9. *Wang Mingdao's Diary*, 15. The missionaries were possibly troubled by Wang, a layperson, baptizing people but more likely by the fact that some of these people had already been baptized by sprinkling and Wang was encouraging them to seek rebaptism by immersion. Both reasons may have prompted the missionaries to want Wang to leave Hebei.

10. See Exodus 3:1.

11. Wang used the idiom 盡美盡善 "perfect," whose Chinese literary source is found in Confucius's statement in the *Analects* that "the Master said of the Shao that it was perfectly beautiful and also perfectly good." See *Analects* 3.25.

12. Wang Mingdao, *Fifty Years*, 91.

13. Wang Mingdao, *Fifty Years*, 98. The dates in the narrative of Wang's autobiography *Fifty Years* begin to become mixed up at this point as Wang focused on emphasizing certain themes in each chapter. This prompted Arthur Reynolds in his English translation, *A Stone Made Smooth*, in order to make Wang's story clearer, to rewrite Wang's story linearly according to date. However, he also edited out several important Chinese elements of Wang's story.

14. Iap Sian-Chin has offered compelling evidence that this older Norwegian man was Bernt Bernsten 貢德新. See Iap, "Bernt Bernsten," 98–99.

15. Wang Mingdao, *Fifty Years*, 94.

16. Eric Pilquist's early history until 1904 can be found in Onsager, "On Fire for China." Pilquist's later history is available at Adventism in China, "Pilquist E."

17. Wang uses justification by faith 因信稱義 and salvation by faith 因信得救 interchangeably.

18. The connection between Bernsten and Pilquist is indicated in Tiedemann, "The Advance of Pentecostalism in China," 200.

19. Wang Mingdao, *Fifty Years*, 95. One wonders if the discovery of the doctrine of salvation by faith was the reason he penned the article and translated the song "The East Will Sing" on April 1, 1923, in an otherwise difficult year. See Wang Mingdao, "The East Will Sing," 75–76.

20. Wang Mingdao, *Fifty Years*, 96–97. This translation work is likely one of the sources for the many English articles Wang translated and included in *The Spiritual Food Quarterly*.

21. On Wang's critical attitude toward and independence from foreign Christian missions but love for individual missionaries whom he felt integrated their beliefs with their lives, see Lyall, *Come Wind Come Weather*, 38. Also, Adeney, *China*, 53. Both Lyall and Adeney knew Wang personally.

22. *Wang Mingdao's Diary*, 17. See also Ng, "The Shaping Influence of the Chinese YMCA on the Young Wang Mingdao," 190n177.

23. *Wang Mingdao's Diary*, 18. There is no capitalization in Chinese characters.

24. *Wang Mingdao's Diary*, 28, August 11, 1923.

25. Wang Mingdao, *Fifty Years*, 98.

26. Wang Mingdao, *Fifty Years*, 98.

27. *Wang Mingdao's Diary*, 28. He discussed with a Mr. Hua 華 the "mistaken idea of the Trinity 三一的謬誤."

28. *Wang Mingdao's Diary*, 28. He preached on six evidences that Jesus is God's Son and clarified the "absurdity that Jesus is God 耶穌為神說之謬妄."

29. Wang Mingdao, *Fifty Years*, 91–92.

30. Wang Mingdao, *Fifty Years*, 115.

31. In 1921, Jia Yuming began publishing *Spiritual Light Magazine*. See *Biographical Dictionary of Chinese Christianity*, "Jia Yuming 賈玉銘."

32. See Kwok, "The Christ-Human and Jia Yuming's Doctrine of Sanctification," 145–65.

33. Nee began publishing this journal in 1923 and in 1925 began publishing another journal, the *Christian* 基督徒報. See Lian, *Redeemed by Fire*, 164–65. For Wang's reading of these journals, see *Wang Mingdao's Diary*, 50, October 9, 1924, and 119, April 22, 1926.

34. Ying, "Watchman Nee in the Eyes of Wang Mingdao," 137. This article is the main source for the relationship between Wang Mingdao and Watchman Nee. Between 1924 and 1925, Wang and Nee exchanged fifteen letters before the relationship soured. Ying's article is important as it is the first to address the rift that developed between Wang and Nee, two "giants" of the Chinese church.

35. In Wang's diary entry for March (no day), he writes that he preached at 南苑馮軍 including the name Feng, which he omits in *Fifty Years*. See *Wang Mingdao's Diary*, 31.

36. The sincerity of Feng Yuxiang's conversion to Christianity is debated. See Sheridan, *Chinese Warlord*, 52–54.

37. See Sheridan, "The Warlord Era," 12:314–15.

38. See Sheridan, *Chinese Warlord*, 122.

39. Wang describes his response to what he saw at the camp by using the idiom 疾首痛心, "to grieve and lament," originally found in Mr. Zuo's Commentary on Chun Qiu 左傳, Duke Cheng, Year 13.2.

40. Sheridan indicates that there were 4,500 baptisms at the Nanyuan camp with Feng desiring genuine conversions based on the requirement that the soldiers provide evidence of some knowledge of basic Christian tenets and a report from superiors that they were living moral lives. See Sheridan, *Chinese Warlord*, 122. Wang obviously had a different opinion of the soldiers' Christian knowledge and moral integrity.

41. Wang Mingdao, *Fifty Years*, 92. Despite Feng Yuxiang's Christian profession of faith and admiration for the sages of ancient China, Wang was much more impressed with Feng's superior in the Zhili clique of warlords, who would become Feng's adversary after the Beijing coup in 1924, the Confucian general Wu Peifu 吳佩孚 (1874–1939). See Wang Mingdao, *Last Confession*, 89–92.

42. *Wang Mingdao's Diary*, 42.

43. Wang Mingdao, *Fifty Years*, 92.

44. *Wang Mingdao's Diary*, 15. It was Wang's friend Chen Zigao who refuted the preacher on this occasion.

45. See Yao, *The Fundamentalist Movement*, 282, 287.

46. Wang Mingdao, *Fifty Years*, 93.

47. *Wang Mingdao's Diary*, 50.

48. Wang Mingdao, *Fifty Years*, 93. These booklets would later become content in Wang's quarterly journal *The Spiritual Food Quarterly*, which he began publishing in 1927.

49. Wang Mingdao, *Fifty Years*, 114–15.

50. Bays, *A New History of Christianity in China*, 111–13.

51. *Wang Mingdao's Diary*, 61.

52. Wang Mingdao, *Fifty Years*, 226–27; Shi, *Sixty-Three Years*, 21.

53. The actual name is "Spiritual" Christians or "Spiritualists" 屬靈派.

54. *Wang Mingdao's Diary*, 78, June 2, 1925.

55. Ying, "Watchman Nee in the Eyes of Wang Mingdao," 135–36n14.

56. See *Wang Mingdao's Diary*, 57. The most vocal speaker against Wang appears to have been Dora Yu. See Ying, "Watchman Nee in the Eyes of Wang Mingdao," 136.

57. *Wang Mingdao's Diary*, 78, June 2, 1925.

58. Ying, "Watchman Nee in the Eyes of Wang Mingdao," 136.

59. *Wang Mingdao's Diary*, 28, August 10–11, 1923.

60. *Wang Mingdao's Diary*, 79, June 4, 1925.

61. Despite the fact that Dora Yu and Jia Yuming now considered Wang a Modernist. Many years later, Wang was in Shanghai and he saw Dora Yu walking on the street. Out of respect for his elder, Wang bowed to Yu, but she responded with, "Wang Mingdao, you preacher of heresy, are you still preaching?" See Lin and Chang, *An Injured Brave*, 123.

62. Wang Mingdao, *Fifty Years*, 116.

63. Ying, "Watchman Nee in the Eyes of Wang Mingdao," 138–39.

64. *Wang Mingdao's Diary*, 80.

65. Shi, *Sixty-Three Years*, 6.

66. Wang Mingdao, *Fifty Years*, 117.

67. Wang Mingdao, *Fifty Years*, 118.

68. *Wang Mingdao's Diary*, 92.

69. *Wang Mingdao's Diary*, 93, August 19, 1925.

70. *Wang Mingdao's Diary*, 94.

71. *Wang Mingdao's Diary*, 95.

72. Ying, "Watchman Nee in the Eyes of Wang Mingdao," 141. This detail is from the unpublished diaries of Wang Mingdao, since August 26 is not included in the published diary.

73. Ying, "Watchman Nee in the Eyes of Wang Mingdao," 141.

74. Unfortunately, there is no further articulation of their conversation on the Trinity in Wang Mingdao's diaries and Watchman Nee makes no mention of Wang in his written works. It is likely that Nee's closer use of biblical language for describing the "three one God" was more acceptable to Wang than Jia Yuming's Trinitarian language. However, according to Lian Xi, Nee later thought of Wang Mingdao's Christian Tabernacle as a "halfway house." Nee was clearly not impressed by Wang, as will be revealed, and thus makes no recorded comments on the man himself. See Lian, *Redeemed by Fire*, 171, 275n64.

75. Before their relationship soured, Wang says that during this time, he loved Nee very much. See Ying, "Wang Mingdao Discusses Chinese Church Leaders and Affairs," 82.

76. Wang Mingdao, *Fifty Years*, 118.

77. He started to open to the idea of getting married at least as early as September 28, 1924, but Jia Yuming confirmed his thoughts. See *Wang Mingdao's Diary*, 48.

78. Wang Mingdao, *Fifty Years*, 228–29.

79. Shi, *Sixty-Three Years*, 1.

80. Shi, *Sixty-Three Years*, 6–7. Wang Mingdao said that he had great love and respect for his father-in-law (Wang Mingdao, *Fifty Years*, 136–37) and that when his mother-in-law died in 1974, he wept and lost any desire he previously had to leave prison, as his main desire in leaving would have been to see her. See Wang Mingdao, *Last Confession*, 149.

81. Shi, *Sixty-Three Years*, 1. Mary Vaughan High School, named after a CMS missionary who donated two thousand dollars to build a school for girls in Hangzhou, was established in 1909 as one of the first schools to provide females with a high school education in East China. See Bond, "The One for the Many," 447.

82. Shi, *Sixty-Three Years*, 4.

83. Shi, *Sixty-Three Years*, 5–6.

84. Shi, *Sixty-Three Years*, 18. By November 1925, it seems that Liu Jingwen had finished her studies at Mary Vaughn High School and was a teacher. See Wang Mingdao, *Fifty Years*, 229.

85. Wang Mingdao, *Fifty Years*, 233.

86. Shi, *Sixty-Three Years*, 19; italics added.

87. *Wang Mingdao's Diary*, 103, November 29, 1925. She was not a familial aunt, but Wang uses the phrase as a term of affection common in Chinese society for an older woman. She was the person who introduced Wang to the family on June 26. Aunt Li's full name is Li Jingqian 李靜謙.

88. Wang Mingdao, *Fifty Years*, 231.

89. Wang Mingdao, *Fifty Years*, 233. One of the places he preached was in the Methodist churches of Nanjing where, leading up to Easter Sunday in 1926, Wang preached to congregations of over one thousand people. A missionary observer commented that "though his sermons ran over the ordinary length in time yet he held his audiences and was able to pass over to them his contagious earnestness." This is the first mention of Wang Mingdao (Wang Ming-tao) that I have been able to find in English. See "On the Field," 373.

90. Wang Mingdao, *Fifty Years*, 231–32.

91. Wang Mingdao, *Fifty Years*, 236.

92. Wang Mingdao, *Fifty Years*, 232.

93. Wang Mingdao, *Fifty Years*, 119.

94. Wang Mingdao, *Fifty Years*, 120, 232.

95. Wang Mingdao, *Fifty Years*, 203.

96. For a detailed list of the contents of the 114 issues of *The Spiritual Food Quarterly* in English, see Payk, "Revisiting the Life and Theology of the Confucian-Christian Wang Mingdao," 207–66.

97. Wang Mingdao, "Publication Announcement," 9.

98. Wang Mingdao, "Martin Luther's Prayer," 17. The main events of the Diet of Worms in relation to Luther took place on April 16–18, 1521. Wang does not reveal the document source he used for Luther's prayer.

99. See Bays, *A New History of Christianity in China*, 112.

100. Wang felt the impact of the anti-Christian movement in China during the late 1920s and made mention of it in *The Spiritual Food Quarterly*. See Wang Mingdao, "The Story of Zhang En and Wang Yi," 239.

101. Wang Mingdao, *Fifty Years*, 124.

102. Wang Mingdao, *Fifty Years*, 125.

103. Wang Mingdao, "Editor's News" (Summer 1928), 116.

104. *Wang Mingdao's Diary*, 46–47, September 20, 1924.

105. See Sheridan, "The Warlord Era," 317.

106. See Eastman, "Nationalist China during the Nanjing Decade," 13:124.

107. Wang Mingdao, *Fifty Years*, 125, 232.

108. Shi, *Sixty-Three Years*, 17.

109. Wang Mingdao, *Fifty Years*, 234.

110. Wang Mingdao, *Fifty Years*, 235.

111. Wang Mingdao, *Fifty Years*, 236–37.

112. Wang Mingdao, *Fifty Years*, 239.

113. Wang Mingdao, *Fifty Years*, 264.

114. Wang Mingdao, *Fifty Years*, 238.

115. See Exodus 20:12.

116. Wang Mingdao, *Fifty Years*, 239.

117. See Genesis 2:24 and Ephesians 5:31.

118. Wang Mingdao, *Fifty Years*, 239.

119. Tseng, "Bathsheba as an Object Lesson," 61.

120. Wang Mingdao, *Fifty Years*, 126.

121. Shi, *Sixty-Three Years*, 137. Wang Mingdao undoubtedly went back to pay the bill when he arrived home on July 17, but Liu Jingwen was upset about this event even into her senior years.

122. Nor in *The Spiritual Food Quarterly*. True to his word that the journal would not include news on current affairs in the initial 1927 issue, Wang Mingdao did not share in the editor's news section for July 1929 that his son was born. See Wang Mingdao, "Editor's News" (Fall 1929), 186.

123. Wang Mingdao, *Fifty Years*, 263.

124. Wang Mingdao, *Fifty Years*, 243.

125. Wang Mingdao, *Fifty Years*, 247.

126. Shi, *Sixty-Three Years*, 151.

127. Shi, *Sixty-Three Years*, 44.

128. *Wang Mingdao's Diary*, 364, July 6, 1951.

129. S. Wang, *The Long Road to Freedom*, 39. Also, *Wang Mingdao's Diary*,

383, January 1, 1952.

130. Currently known as China Agricultural University 中國農業大學 after a merger in 1995 with Beijing Agricultural Engineering University.

131. Wang Mingdao, *Last Confession*, 73n37. The Chinese Academy of Sciences consistently ranked as one of the top research organizations in the world. See "Ten Institutions That Dominated Science in 2015." As of April 2020, the Shanghai Institutes for Biological Sciences was reformed and renamed.

132. Shi, *Sixty-Three Years*, 131.

133. Wang Mingdao, *Fifty Years*, 126.

134. See *Biographical Dictionary of Chinese Christianity*, "張亦鏡 (Zhang Yijing)." He is also known as Zhang Wenkai 張文開.

135. See Kwok, "Theology of Religions and Intertextuality," 70.

136. Wang Mingdao, *Fifty Years*, 127. Wang was also dismayed that year after having read Cheng Ching-yi's 誠靜怡 "Pentecost Era Church," 2–7. In Wang's opinion, Cheng's description in the article of Jesus's resurrection as not a physical resurrection but that Jesus's "spirit did not die" and his "personality lives on" revealed Cheng to be a Modernist. See Wang Mingdao, "After Reading Pentecost Era Church," 208–9.

137. Ying, "Watchman Nee in the Eyes of Wang Mingdao," 143.

138. *Wang Mingdao's Diary*, 151.

139. As noted by Ying, "Watchman Nee in the Eyes of Wang Mingdao," 144.

140. Wang Mingdao, *Fifty Years*, 128. Wang Mingdao, "Editor's News" (Fall 1930), 234.

141. Shi, *Sixty-Three Years*, 150.

142. Chang, *Forgotten Diplomacy*, 172n117, 321.

143. Wang trusted Kok's religious beliefs and personal integrity enough to allow him to occasionally preach at the church in his absence. See Arthur Reynolds's comment in Wong Ming-Dao, *A Stone Made Smooth*, introduction.

144. See Krabbendam, "Three-Way Chess," 230–33. In 1931, John Sung met Wang at one of these meetings in Arie Kok's home.

145. See Tiedemann, "The Advance of Pentecostalism in China," 209.

146. Wang Mingdao, *Fifty Years*, 128. Kok's residence was at 4 Xiaobaofang Lane 小報房胡同. One of the places Wang preached at when he left Beijing was the Effie Sears Memorial School in Pingdu 平度, Shandong Province. Wang's preaching at the meeting, which provided "rich spiritual food" to the attendees, was recorded in the Southern Baptist Convention's Annual for 1930 and is the first mention of Wang Mingdao (Wong Ming Tao) that I have been able to find that would have been for a Western audience outside of China. See *Annual of the Southern Baptist Convention 1930*, 208.

147. Wang Mingdao, *Fifty Years*, 163. Wang mentions that Shi Tianmin was filling in for him at the church in Beijing as early as the spring of 1927. See Wang Mingdao, "Editor's News" (Spring 1927), 69.

148. Wang Mingdao, *Fifty Years*, 244–45.

149. Wang Mingdao, *Fifty Years*, 129–30. An interesting note to make considering that the stone pillars are covered with dragons. It would be hard to imagine a Western Fundamentalist Christian at the time saying the same thing.

150. Cui Hui wrote the poem "Yellow Crane Tower 黃鶴樓" and Li Bai wrote the poem "Seeing Off Meng Haoran for Guangling at Yellow Crane Tower 黃鶴樓送孟浩然之廣陵."

151. Wang Mingdao, *Fifty Years*, 131.

152. See Sima Qian, *The Grand Scribe's Records*, 7:299–301.

153. See Wang Mingdao, *Fifty Years*, 131. *Wang Mingdao's Diary*, 169, May 14 and 18, 1932.

154. See Bays, *A New History of Christianity in China*, 97, 138.

155. Wang Mingdao, *Last Confession*, 139–40.

156. Wang said the article was published shortly after his trip to Changsha and the content of this article fits Wang's description. See Chiang, "The Principles of Jesus concerning National Salvation," 5–8.

157. Chiang, "The Principles of Jesus concerning National Salvation," 7.

158. Wang Mingdao, *Last Confession*, 140.

159. Wang Mingdao, *Last Confession*, 143. A more sympathetic view of the genuineness of Chiang Kai-shek's Christian faith is presented in Taylor, *The Generalissimo*, 108–9. However, Taylor does note the contradictory nature of some of Chiang's actions to the Christian faith he professed on p. 590.

160. It should be noted that Wang did not make this critique publicly in 1932 but rather in 1982 to Jiang Hua, the president of the People's Supreme Court, who would have had no affection for Chiang Kai-shek. However, Wang was willing to critique the famous Christian evangelist Sherwood Eddy during this period for what he saw as Eddy's Modernist gospel. See Wang Mingdao, "Does Dr. Sherwood Eddy Preach the Gospel?" 245–47. Wang did not critique political leaders publicly but focused his literary efforts on religious affairs before his arrest.

161. Yue Fei's story is told in History of the Song Dynasty 宋史, biography 124, Yue Fei and Zi Yun. See the Chinese Text Project, www.ctext.org.

162. Wang Mingdao, *Last Confession*, 85.

163. Wang Mingdao, *Fifty Years*, 131.

164. Lian, *Redeemed by Fire*, 129. Lian uses Wang's 1929 article from *The Spiritual Food Quarterly*, "Watch Out for Thieves," as representing Wang's opinion on these issues. Although Lian exaggerates Wang's disregard for the physical world, Lian's book *Redeemed by Fire* provides outstanding research on Chinese Christianity in the twentieth century.

165. Thus, he later urged Western missionaries to learn about Chinese social customs and sense of propriety to effectively preach the gospel in China. See Wang Mingdao, "More Important than Work," 34.

166. See Wang Mingdao, "Watch Out for Thieves," 176–77.

167. Wang also appreciated beautiful natural landscapes. In the midst of preaching appointments, during breaks he would enjoy seeing the scenic spots of the area such as the mountains and stalactite-filled caves in Guilin 桂林, Guangxi Province, which he described as beautiful beyond imagination. See Wang Mingdao, *Fifty Years*, 138.

168. Wang Mingdao, *Fifty Years*, 132–33.

169. Wang Mingdao, *Fifty Years*, 131–32. Wang visited Robert Morrison's grave while in Macau.

170. See Wang Mingdao, *Last Confession*, 97.

171. Tseng, "Revival Preaching," 179.

172. Wang Mingdao, "The Gospel in Genesis 5," 185–97. Wang, knowing he had a gift in preaching, also made efforts to develop his preaching ability and read Robert Thomas Bryan's *Practical Preaching Skills* 實用講道術 in 1932. See *Wang Mingdao's Diary*, 170, July 3, 1932.

173. According to Lim Ka-Tong, during Sung's Beijing revival services, seven hundred people, many of whom were intellectuals, were converted. See Lim, *The Life and Ministry of John Sung*, 152–54.

174. The best treatment of this complicated period of Sung's life is described in Ireland, *John Song*, 21–23.

175. Bays, *A New History of Christianity in China*, 138.

176. Wang Mingdao, *Fifty Years*, 133.

177. Lim, *The Life and Ministry of John Sung*, 116–17.

178. Song Shangjie, *The Diary of John Sung*, 83. John Sung has the date of their meeting somewhere between January 5 and January 13, 1931. Since the meetings at Kok's house were on Sundays, January 11, 1931, is most likely the date of Wang and Sung's first meeting.

179. The time period (1931), and the fact that Wang says that he met Sung when the church was still meeting in a brother's home, indicates that the two met in Arie Kok's home while Wang was conducting services there. See Wang Mingdao, "Mr. Song Shangjie [John Sung] Has Died," 149–50. Also, Sung mentions that the meeting he attended was on Xiaobaofang Lane 小報房胡同, which was Kok's home address. See Song Tian-Zhen, *The Diary of His [John Sung's] Spiritual Life*, chap. 4, pt. 1. Kok endeavored to develop a network of Fundamentalist Christians, and so his home was a natural place to connect John Sung and Wang Mingdao.

180. Wang Mingdao, *Fifty Years*, 162.

181. He dates the beginning of the Christian Tabernacle to 1933 in Wang Mingdao, *Last Confession*, 97.

182. Wang Mingdao, *Fifty Years*, 133.

183. Wang Mingdao, *Fifty Years*, 133.

184. Wang Mingdao, *Fifty Years*, 196.

185. Wang Mingdao, *Fifty Years*, 134.

186. As observed in Cook, "Fundamentalism and Modern Culture in Republican China," 29.

187. Wang Mingdao, *Fifty Years*, 163–64.

188. Wang Mingdao, *Fifty Years*, 136, 245–46. Wang uses the term 慈愛 "love, affection, kindness" to describe Liu Delin's treatment of Wang. This adjective is particularly used to describe an affectionate love a parent has for a beloved child. In the absence of his birth father, Wang Zihou, Liu Delin seemed to be a very significant father figure in Wang's life. See also *Wang Mingdao's Diary*, 206, September 11, 1934.

189. *Wang Mingdao's Diary*, 207. Ying, "Watchman Nee in the Eyes of Wang Mingdao," 146. Ying explains that Nee at this time used the name Little Flock 小群 to refer to his church, but it later became known as Local Church 基督徒聚會處 when under the leadership of Li Changshou.

190. See Witness Lee, *Watchman Nee*, 41–43.

191. Ying, "Watchman Nee in the Eyes of Wang Mingdao," 147.

192. Wang uses the phrase 併吞六國, 統一天下, which refers to the Qin wars of unification in the third century BCE in which the Qin emerged as the victor of the Warring States Period. The other six states were the Han (Hann) 韓, Zhao 趙, Yan 燕, Wei 魏, Chu 楚, and Qi 齊.

193. Wang uses the idiom 貴為天子, 富有四海, which originally comes from the biography of Qin Shihuang in Sima Qian, *The Grand Scribe's Records*, 1:164.

194. Wang Mingdao, *Fifty Years*, 139.

195. Wang Mingdao, *Last Confession*, 264–65.

196. See Sima Qian, *The Grand Scribe's Records*, 1:147, 1:155. Wang also quotes the Tang poem by Zhang Jie 章碣, "Book Burning Pit 焚書坑."

197. *Mencius*, Gong Sun Chou I, 3.

198. Wang is referring to Confucius leaving public service in the State of Lu. See *Analects* 18.4. The full story is told in Szuma Chien, *Selections from Records of the Historian*, 9.

199. *Mencius*, Gong Sun Chou I, 3.

200. Lim, *The Life and Ministry of John Sung*, 191.

201. Wang describes his conditions for a preacher at his church in Wang Mingdao, *Fifty Years*, 196. On January 8, 1936, when he was back in Beijing, Wang went to the bus station to see John Sung off from Beijing, and the two did not see each other again for several years. See *Wang Mingdao's Diary*, 219.

202. *Wang Mingdao's Diary*, April 30, 1935.

203. Wang Mingdao, "The Evils of the Modern YMCA," 94–106. See also Ng, "The Shaping Influence of the Chinese YMCA on the Young Wang Mingdao," 192.

204. Wang Mingdao, *Last Confession*, 87. The idiom is 恨我入骨.

205. Wang Mingdao, "The Sin of the Modern YMCA," 95–96.

206. Wang Mingdao, "The Sin of the Modern YMCA," 100–101.

207. Wang Mingdao, "The Sin of the Modern YMCA," 102.

208. Wang Mingdao, *Last Confession*, 106. Wang's article and other critiques like it of the leaders of the YMCA would prompt Liang Xiaochu 梁小初, director of the National Association of the Chinese YMCA from 1935 to 1950, to indirectly respond in an article published in the YMCA's magazine on July 15, 1936, titled "The YMCA and the Spiritualists 青年會與屬靈派." Liang's article is reproduced in Ying, *Last Confession*, 377–82. Since Wang saw several leaders in the YMCA as "unbelievers," these same people who would later become leaders in the TSPM, this would set him against the movement from when he first heard about it in the early 1950s.

209. *Wang Mingdao's Diary*, 219, February 7, 1936.

210. Wang Mingdao later described Chao's *Life of Jesus* as being a model of Chinese Modernist literature. See Wang Mingdao, "We Are for the Faith!" 147.

211. *Wang Mingdao's Diary*, 221, March 12, 1936.

212. See Bays, *A New History of Christianity in China*, 124–28.

NOTES TO CHAPTER FOUR

1. Brook, "Christianity under the Japanese Occupation," 323–24.

2. Wang Mingdao, *Fifty Years*, 164.

3. Wang Mingdao, *Fifty Years*, 140–41, 164.

4. Wang Mingdao, *Fifty Years*, 143. In his 1933 reflection on miraculous healings, he stated that "I have with my own eyes observed such healing." His 1936 experience in the river further convinced him, but it should be noted that Wang thought that God does not miraculously heal in the same way as recorded in the Bible because "there is not the same need for these things today." Wang Mingdao, "The Spiritual Gifts Movement in the Light of Scripture," 223. In English, Wang Mingdao, *The Spiritual Gifts Movement*, 15–16.

5. The battle for Beijing is described in Eastman, "Nationalist China during the Sino-Japanese War 1937–1945," 13:550.

6. Wang Mingdao, *Fifty Years*, 166. The location at 42 Shijia Lane is about a thirty-minute walk east of the Forbidden City.

7. Wang Mingdao, *Fifty Years*, 166.

8. In 1939, Wang would more fully articulate this vision for the ideal church and what he felt were unhelpful traditions in Wang Mingdao, "Is This a Good Phenomenon or Not?" 82–87.

9. Wang Mingdao, *Fifty Years*, 167–68. Two pictures of the Christian Tabernacle during the first service on August 1, 1937, are in Shi, *Sixty-Three Years*, 6.

10. Ying, "Watchman Nee in the Eyes of Wang Mingdao," 147–48. Nee's *Rethinking the Work* was republished in English as *The Normal Christian Church Life*. Nee's ecclesiology, which includes the idea of one city, one church, is articulated in Watchman Nee, "Not Wider than a Locality."

11. *Wang Mingdao's Diary*, 237, March 2, 1938.

12. Also in the spring of 1939, Wang moved into the Christian Tabernacle to overcome an illness and found that it made life easier for his family to live apart from his mother and sister, and so he moved out of his mother's home. See Wang Mingdao, *Fifty Years*, 263.

13. Wang Mingdao gives the year 1939 for this meeting, but it is uncertain as recorded in Ying, "Watchman Nee in the Eyes of Wang Mingdao," 149–50, and Ying, "Wang Mingdao Discusses Chinese Church Leaders and Affairs," 82.

14. Jonathan Spence estimates that during the massacre in Nanjing, twenty thousand Chinese women were raped, thirty thousand Chinese soldiers were killed, and twelve thousand Chinese civilians were murdered. Spence, *The Search for Modern China*, 448.

15. *The Spiritual Food Quarterly* taken as a whole was overwhelmingly dominated by Wang's interpretation of the Bible with thousands of biblical references and quotes, yet nearly every issue also contains translated works from Western Christians. However, Wang crafted his interpretation of the Bible and selected articles to translate in a way that appealed to a Chinese Fundamentalist Christian audience and made many references to Classical Chinese sources as well.

16. See Knight, *In the Cloudy and Dark Day*.

17. Wang Mingdao, "A Small Elm Tree on the City Wall," 236. *The School Sayings of Confucius* 孔子家語, Guanzhou 3.

18. Wang Mingdao, "Their Sorrows Shall Be Multiplied That Hasten after Another God," 138. *The Analects* 14.43.

19. Wang Mingdao, "A Very Important Role," 23. *The Enlarged Writings of Worthies* 增廣賢文, 178.

20. Wang Mingdao, "Scared to Death," 53. *Nancun Chuogenglu* 南村輟耕錄, book 30, 10.

21. These Chinese sources continue to appear more frequently during the 1940s in *The Spiritual Food Quarterly* with Wang making regular references to the *Four Books and Five Classics* as well as Chinese poets and histories until 1953 when his conflict with the TSPM leaders took over his focus.

22. *Mencius*, Teng Wen Gong II, 7.2.

23. Wang Mingdao, "My Opinion of Spiritual [Ministry] Work," 226.

24. The article is Wang Mingdao, "The Meaning of [the Word] Church," 87–102. He does not mention Nee by name, but it is clear from the content of the article that Nee is the person Wang is referring to.

25. Nee published *The Orthodoxy of the Church* 教會的正統 in 1945, which was a collection of messages preached earlier. In the book, he stated, "How can we say that there is such a thing as a Christian synagogue [tabernacle] and yet not bring in Judaism? The Lord says that they are the synagogue of Satan." See Watchman Nee, "The Orthodoxy of the Church."

26. Wang Mingdao, "The Meaning of [the Word] Church," 89.

27. Wang Mingdao, *Fifty Years*, 179. A reference to the biblical story in the book of Exodus, in particular, Exodus 3:7. This story was originally written by Wang after the Japanese were defeated in World War II and left China in Wang Mingdao, "Their God Is Still Our God," 144–63.

28. For the historical context of Wang's resistance to the North China Christian Union, see Ying, "Wang Mingdao and the North China Christian Union," 103–16. The broader political context is described in Brook, *Collaboration*.

29. Timothy Brook's research confirms Wang's assessment with the ultimate goal of the union group being the formation of a single Protestant Christian group in China that would be "amenable to the hegemony of the occupation state." See Brook, "Christianity under the Japanese Occupation," 332.

30. All churches in Beijing at the time, both churches connected with foreign missions and independent Chinese churches like the Christian Tabernacle, were under the same pressure to join the union or face closure. See *Wang Mingdao's Diary*, 266. December 10, 1942.

31. Wang Mingdao, *Fifty Years*, 181.

32. Wang Mingdao, *Fifty Years*, 183–84.

33. *Life* magazine reported that Wu's funeral was so grand that it was "the most impressive funeral ever seen in Republican China." See "Peking Gives Wu Pei-Fu, China's Honest War Lord, a Fine Princely Funeral," 30–32.

34. Elison, "Japan Wars on Mr. Wu," 25, 45–49.

35. Wang Mingdao, *Last Confession*, 89–92.

36. Wang Mingdao, *Last Confession*, 144–45, 229. See also his articles around the time describing his disdain for this type of "compromise" in Wang Mingdao, "This Is the Lord Jesus's Disciple," 29, and Wang Mingdao, "The Uncompromising Christ," 68–72.

37. According to Thomas Wang (Wang Yongxin) 王永信, who attended the Christian Tabernacle at the time. See Thomas Wang 王永信, "'Faithful unto Death,'" 28:40.

38. Harvey, "Sermon, Story, and Song," 145. Harvey's emphasis on Wang's biblical interpretation is understandable since the focus of his article is on Wang's sermonizing and not the contextualization of the Christian message in China.

39. For the context of the rebellion, see Beckwith, *Empires of the Silk Road*, 145.

40. Wang Mingdao, *Fifty Years*, 189.

41. Wang Mingdao, *Fifty Years*, 190.

42. See Vala, "Failing to Contain Religion," 68–69.

43. Ying, "Wang Mingdao and the North China Christian Union," 135.

44. Wang Mingdao, *Fifty Years*, 191.

45. It should be noted that Wang received a visit from Yanaihara Tadao 矢内原忠雄, a Japanese Christian and first director of the Institute of Social Sciences at the University of Tokyo, who was critical of Japan's invasion of China. He visited

with Wang Mingdao in 1942 while he was in Beijing and encouraged Wang in his refusal to cooperate with the Japanese-controlled North China Christian Union Group. See Matsutani Yosuke, "Yanaihara Tadao and China," 97–123.

46. See Cook, "Wang Mingdao and the Evolution of Contextualized Chinese Churches," 210.

47. Wong Ming-Dao, *A Stone Made Smooth*, 210. Chapter 10 recounts Wang's conflict with the Japanese during the Japanese occupation of China focused on the period 1939–43.

48. Wang Mingdao, *Last Confession*, 77.

49. See *The Old Book of Tang* 舊唐書, chap. 194. The story may have come to Wang from a different source, but *The Old Book of Tang* appears to be the story's original source.

50. Lian, *Redeemed by Fire*, 193.

51. Lim, *The Life and Ministry of John Sung*, 236–37.

52. Song Tian-Zhen, *The Diary of His Spiritual Life* [of John Sung], chap. 6, pt. 1 (March 20, 1940). Wang Mingdao, "Mr. Song Shangjie [John Sung] Has Died," 150.

53. See Song Tian-Zhen, *The Diary of His Spiritual Life* [of John Sung], chap. 6, pt. 3 (August 1, 1941). Also, *Wang Mingdao's Diary*, 262, April 15, 1942.

54. Wang Mingdao, "Mr. Song Shangjie [John Sung] Has Died," 151.

55. Wang Mingdao, "Mr. Song Shangjie [John Sung] Has Died," 149–57. Wang Mingdao's son, Wang Tianduo, described the sermon as "one of the most touching sermons I ever heard." S. Wang, *The Long Road to Freedom*, 16.

56. *Conduct in Society Common Sense for Believers* 信徒處世常識 was originally published serially in *The Spiritual Food Quarterly* from issue 20 in the winter of 1931 to issue 37 in the spring of 1936 in sixteen parts and was later collected and edited into book form, which Wang published first in 1936. Wang further distilled it into nineteen "Maxims for Believer's Conduct in Society," 170–71.

57. Wang Mingdao, "Mr. Song Shangjie [John Sung] Has Died," 153. However, Daryl Ireland's research has revealed that John Sung was a much more complicated person than Wang realized. See Ireland, *John Song*, particularly chap. 1.

58. Ying, "Wang Mingdao Discusses Chinese Church Leaders and Affairs," 80. The quote of Confucius is from *The Analects* 5.10.

59. In a 1948 article on the importance of moral character, Wang may have made a veiled reference to Watchman Nee's famous book *The Spiritual Man* 屬靈人 when he said that reading the book was like being in a fog and that not only did the people who read it not become more spiritual, but the testimony of the author's life brought shame to God's name and harmed many people. See Wang Mingdao, "More Important than Work," 38.

60. Ying, "Watchman Nee in the Eyes of Wang Mingdao," 158.

61. Wang Mingdao, "Editor's News" (Spring 1948), 75.

62. The most detailed research on this period of Wang's life can be found in

Ng, "The Situation of the Christian Tabernacle and Wang Mingdao's Preaching," 233–54.

63. Wang Mingdao, "Editor's News" (Fall 1945), 115.

64. Wang Mingdao, *Fifty Years*, 152, 264.

65. Mrs. Pan, the woman who connected Wang to the Beijing church network in 1925, also died on August 26, 1948. Wang said that due to her support for his ministry, the two developed a deep relationship and he respected her devout piety. See Wang Mingdao, *Fifty Years*, 152–53.

66. Originally published in Wang Mingdao, "In Memory of Mother," 258–78, he revised and republished it in Wang Mingdao, *Fifty Years*, 256–70.

67. Wang Mingdao, *Fifty Years*, 263–64. See *Han Shi Waizhuan* 韓詩外傳, book 9, 3.

68. Revealing the influence of Chinese folk religion 民間信仰 on Christianity in China during the Republican period.

69. In Chinese folk religion, it is thought to be unlucky to die in the brick kang bed, and the change of clothes is thought to prepare the deceased for the next life. See Naquin, "Funerals in North China," 39.

70. Wang Mingdao, *Fifty Years*, 266–67.

71. Whyte, "Death in the People's Republic of China," 292.

72. Compare Wang Mingdao, *Fifty Years*, 266–67 with Reynolds's complete lack of description of these events in Wong Ming-Dao, *A Stone Made Smooth*, 209.

73. See Mark 6:3.

74. See Wang Mingdao, "To Glory in Your Shame," 107. The word "sage 聖人" can also be translated as "saint." Wang quoted *The Analects* 9.6.

75. Wang Mingdao, *Fifty Years*, 153. See also Ng, "The Situation of the Christian Tabernacle and Wang Mingdao's Preaching," 252–53. Ng indicates that throughout these years, Wang was deeply affected by the civil war and he felt that people needed to hear the gospel more than ever.

76. Harvey, *Acquainted with Grief*, 109.

77. Wang Mingdao, *Last Confession*, 54–55.

78. For example, Thomas Harvey's PhD dissertation was almost entirely focused on the conflict between Wang and the TSPM between 1954 and 1955. See Harvey, "Changing Heaven's Mandate," 10. Ying Fuk Tsang has also covered the conflict between Wang and the TSPM from 1950 to 1955, closely describing the war of words in Wang's *Spiritual Food Quarterly* and the TSPM's *Tianfeng*, in Ying, "Counterrevolution in the Revolutionary Era," 100–131.

79. See S. Wang, *The Long Road to Freedom*, 11–12, and Wang Mingdao, *Last Confession*, 55–56.

80. See Bays, *A New History of Christianity in China*, 161–62.

81. See S. Wang, *The Long Road to Freedom*, 11. For details on the delegation and the TSRM, see Ying, "Anti-imperial Patriotism and Religious Reform," 91–141.

82. An English translation of the Christian Manifesto is available in Jones,

Documents of the Three-Self Movement, 19–20, and Harvey, *Acquainted with Grief*, 163–65.

83. Y. T. Wu, "Where Is God 上帝在那裡?" 7–10; *Wang Mingdao's Diary*, 360, May 29, 1951; S. Wang, *The Long Road to Freedom*, 27.

84. Y. T. Wu, *Darkness and Light*; *Wang Mingdao's Diary*, 507, May 27, 1955. Wang was reading Wu's book to do research for his article "We Are for the Faith!" which indicates that he had read *Darkness and Light* earlier.

85. Wang Mingdao, *Last Confession*, 132.

86. *Wang Mingdao's Diary*, 377, November 20, 24, and 27, 1951.

87. S. Wang, *The Long Road to Freedom*, 20. For Nee's article, see Lian, *Redeemed by Fire*, 200, 281n90, 314. Lian indicates the original article, which is difficult to find, is available in Ren Zhongxiang 任鐘祥, *A Brief History of the Shanghai Christian Local Church* 上海基督徒聚會處簡史, 22.

88. The meetings with Yan Jailei are recorded in *Wang Mingdao's Diary*, 419 and 422. John Wu reports that the signature list had thirty-five thousand signatures of Nee's followers on it. See Wu, *Understanding Watchman Nee*, 47.

89. Chirot, *Modern Tyrants*, 187.

90. Ying, "Wang Mingdao Discusses Chinese Church Leaders and Affairs," 83. More context is provided in Ying, *Anti-imperialism, Patriotism, and the Spiritual Man*, 102–9.

91. See Witness Lee, *Watchman Nee*, 190.

92. Ying, "Wang Mingdao Discusses Chinese Church Leaders and Affairs," 84. Nee died in prison on May 30, 1972.

93. The Jesus Family 耶穌家庭 was forced to disband in 1952. Its leader, Jing Dianying 敬奠瀛 (1890–1957), originally joined the TSRM but was later denounced and imprisoned where he died from cancer in 1957. The True Jesus Church 真耶穌教會 joined and accepted the leadership of the TSRM with its leader Isaac Wei (Wei Yisa) 魏以撒 (1900–?) arrested in 1951, pledged support for the TSRM and subsequently disappeared. See Bays, *A New History of Christianity in China*, 161–63 and Lian, *Redeemed by Fire*, 200. The Bread of Life Church 靈糧堂, due to the political situation in China, moved its headquarters to Hong Kong in 1949 and eventually to Taipei, Taiwan, in 1954. See Tiedemann, *Reference Guide to Christian Mission Societies in China*, 245.

94. S. Wang, *The Long Road to Freedom*, 43–45.

95. Wang Mingdao, *Last Confession*, 135. The story of Wu Zetian's name change goes back to *The Old Book of Tang* 舊唐書, book 6, Empress Ze Tian, 12.

96. Wang Mingdao had read Wang Zizhong's works including "Avoiding Reality 躲避現實" and "The Resurrection of Christ 基督的復活" and determined that he was an "unbeliever." See *Wang Mingdao's Diary*, 482–83, December 24, 1953. The other members of the four-person delegation were Zhao Fusan 趙復三, Jiang Yizheng 蔣翼振, and Yin Jizeng 殷繼增. It is difficult to determine the precise date of the visit because Wang's 1954 diary was never returned after being confiscated in 1955.

97. Wang Mingdao, *Last Confession*, 118. Despite Wang's questioning his patriotism, it does seem that Z. T. Kuang provided cooperative resistance to the Japanese. For a more sympathetic treatment of Kuang during the Second Sino-Japanese War, see Ying, "Wang Mingdao and the North China Christian Union Group," 138–40. Ying sees Kuang as taking the role in the Japanese-controlled union group to keep the Chinese church open during the war. Had he refused the role, Kuang believed that the church in China would be forced to close.

98. Wang had read Marcus Cheng's article "聖誕認罪禱文 Christmas Confession Prayer." See *Wang Mingdao's Diary*, 483, December 24, 1953. On April 4, 1955, apparently upset by Cheng's participation in the TSPM, Wang dreamed that he was rebuking Cheng so vehemently in his sleep that he woke Liu Jingwen up. See *Wang Mingdao's Diary*, 498.

99. The other members of the five-person delegation were Chen Jianzheng 陳見真, Zhu Guishen 竺規身, and Xie Yongqing 謝永欽. Since they were of high social status in the church and were all of senior age, they were called the Five Old Men of Shanghai 上海五老.

100. S. Wang, *The Long Road to Freedom*, 48.

101. Wang Mingdao, "Be Faithful to God and Not Concerned about People's Feelings," 237. However, there were two men who came to visit Wang after the Five Old Men from Shanghai whom he thought "were believers" and he did meet them but did not shake their hands due to their participation in the TSPM. See Ying, "Wang Mingdao's Counter-revolutionary Clique," 113. My guess, due to his personal knowledge of their beliefs and later affiliation with the TSPM, is that one may have been Jia Yuming whom Wang knew from his previous cooperation with him in 1925. The other may have been David Yang (Yang Shaotang) 楊紹唐 whom Wang was personally familiar with and respected. See Ng, "The Situation of the Christian Tabernacle and Wang Mingdao's Preaching," 234n4 as well as Wang Mingdao, "A Conscientious Girl," 175. Yang wrote a letter to Wang in 1951 encouraging him to participate in the TSRM. See *Wang Mingdao's Diary*, 381, December 27, 1951. Wang lamented when he heard that Jia and Yang joined the TSRM, along with Marcus Cheng, as recorded in his diary on November 25, 1952. See *Wang Mingdao's Diary*, 426.

102. Wang Mingdao, "We Are for the Faith!" 134–74. This article was published in the last issue of the journal before Wang's arrest on August 7, 1955, and remains a classic of Chinese Fundamentalism during the period. An English translation is available in Jones, *Documents of the Three-Self Movement*, 99–114.

103. See Goldman, "The Party and the Intellectuals," 14:237.

104. Wang Mingdao, "We Are for the Faith!" 138–39. See Wang's article "Can We Trust That the Miracles in the Bible Are True?" 141–44.

105. Wang Mingdao, "We Are for the Faith!" 139–41. See Wang's translation of George P. Tasker's article "Jesus's Virgin Birth," 12–16.

106. Wang Mingdao, "We Are for the Faith!" 141–42. See Wang's article "The Cross of Christ," 19–26.

107. Wang Mingdao, "We Are for the Faith!" 142–45. See Wang's article "The Resurrected Christ," 27–39.

108. Wang Mingdao, "We Are for the Faith!" 145–46. See Wang's article "Christ's Second Coming," 13–20. Wang in this article and the following two parts reveals his premillennial theological orientation toward Christ's Second Coming.

109. See Marchal, "Lü Zuqian's Political Philosophy," 197–99. Donlai was an alternative name for Lü Zuqian. See also Wang Mingdao's article, "To Neglect a Warning Is to Court Disaster," 162, for another reference to Lü Zuqian.

110. *Wang Mingdao's Diary*, 260–62, January 16 and February 3, 1942.

111. *Wang Mingdao's Diary*, 512, July 7, 1955.

112. Wang was also translating a number of Western Christian writers, particularly in the early 1950s, the works of the American Presbyterian James R. Miller (1840–1912). Wang translated many of Miller's works in nearly every issue of *The Spiritual Food Quarterly* from issue 74, summer 1950 to issue 114, summer 1955, including a significant portion of Miller's books *In Green Pastures* and *A Life of Character.*

NOTES TO CHAPTER FIVE

1. A translated English version of the *Last Confession* would be a great contribution to Chinese Christian knowledge, but the book would be difficult to translate since the manuscript is not one document but fifteen versions of the request with twenty loose pages. Nearly every page contains Chinese idioms and historical references, some of which are obscure.

2. S. Wang, *The Long Road to Freedom*, 93.

3. S. Wang, *The Long Road to Freedom*, 95.

4. Ying, "Wang Mingdao's Counter-revolutionary Clique," 134n160. The third session of the National People's Congress in Beijing in Chinese is 北京市一屆人大三次會議.

5. S. Wang, *The Long Road to Freedom*, 104.

6. S. Wang, *The Long Road to Freedom*, 94. This detention center was in the west section of Beijing at 19 Weed Haze Lane with twenty-four prison cells in each of the north and south prisons. See Encyclopedia Knowledge, "Caolanzi Prison Former Site 草嵐子監獄舊址."

7. S. Wang, *The Long Road to Freedom*, 106–7.

8. S. Wang, *The Long Road to Freedom*, 108.

9. S. Wang, *The Long Road to Freedom*, 121–22.

10. Shi, *Sixty-Three Years*, 99. Liu Jingwen's story from her arrest on August 8, 1955, to her release on September 30, 1956, is told on pp. 95–100.

11. S. Wang, *The Long Road to Freedom*, 126–27.

12. S. Wang, *The Long Road to Freedom*, 129. An English translation of Wang

Mingdao's confession can be found in Jones, *Documents of the Three-Self Movement*, 117–21, and Harvey, *Acquainted with Grief*, 167–73.

13. S. Wang, *The Long Road to Freedom*, 130.

14. The reference was to Canadian newspapers, which I have been unable to find but several American newspapers had reported on Wang Mingdao's arrest. See Thorkelson, "More Saloons than Churches Reported"; Thrapp, "Faction Blamed in China Arrest"; Thrapp, "Southland Parish"; and Barrington, "Panel Cites Threat Posed by Marxism." Wang's "religious persecution" was also reported in 1956 by the Australian newsman Alfred Francis James who inquired about him during an interview with an official from the Religious Affairs Bureau in China. See James, *Reports on Deputation of Australian Churchmen to Mainland China*, 11.

15. S. Wang, *The Long Road to Freedom*, 130. See Wang Mingdao, "The Evils of the Modern YMCA," 94–106.

16. See Cheng, "A New Commandment," 15–16. In 1957, during the Hundred Flowers Campaign 百花齊放, some leaders within the party encouraged citizens to openly express their views on the CCP. Marcus Cheng criticized the government for their harsh treatment of religious believers. However, this was soon followed in mid-1957–1958 by the Anti-Rightest Campaign 反右運動 in which Mao Zedong himself denounced Cheng as a rightest. Y. T. Wu, the leader of the TSPM, led the attack against Cheng who was kicked out of the TSPM and later died in 1963. See Bays, *A New History of Christianity in China*, 168, and Bush, *Religion in Communist China*, 226.

17. See Wang Mingdao, "My Confession 我的檢討," 7–9.

18. S. Wang, *The Long Road to Freedom*, 134; Shi, *Sixty-Three Years*, 99. Wang describes her as a "hostage" being held to pressure him to read his confession in Wang Mingdao, *Last Confession*, 230.

19. See Lo, "Confucian Ethic of Death with Dignity," 315.

20. See Sima Qian, *The Grand Scribe's Records*, 7:299. Qu Yuan's suicide is still remembered annually by Chinese during the Dragon Boat Festival on the fifth day of the fifth month of the lunar calendar.

21. See Wang Mingdao, *Last Confession*, 147.

22. Hawkes, *Chu Tzu*, 89.

23. S. Wang, *The Long Road to Freedom*, 140.

24. Wang Mingdao, *Last Confession*, 61.

25. S. Wang, *The Long Road to Freedom*, 141.

26. S. Wang, *The Long Road to Freedom*, 143. T. C. Chao would come under attack in 1956, accused of being a collaborator with American imperialists, and lost his position at Yenching University. He suffered terribly during the Cultural Revolution and died in 1979. See Glüer, "The Legacy of T. C. Chao," 165.

27. S. Wang, *The Long Road to Freedom*, 141.

28. S. Wang, *The Long Road to Freedom*, 150; Wang Mingdao, *Last Confession*, 109.

29. S. Wang, *The Long Road to Freedom*, 152. The name of the Gongdelin Detention Center is only in the Chinese version. See Wang Changxin, *Another Forty Years*, 84. It was located at 1 Gongdelin Road.

30. S. Wang, *The Long Road to Freedom*, 152. Again, the name of the Zixin Road Detention Center, which was commonly referred to as the South Detention Center 南所, is provided only in the Chinese version. See Wang Changxin, *Another Forty Years*, 84. It was located in the Xuanwu District 宣武區 on 11 Zixin Road close to Taoranting Park 陶然亭公園.

31. The timeline for their stay in Zixin Road Detention Center is not precise, but it seems they remained there until 1964 or 1965.

32. S. Wang, *The Long Road to Freedom*, 162–63, 166.

33. S. Wang, *The Long Road to Freedom*, 169.

34. Stephen Wang indicates that Wang Mingdao recalled writing "dozens of books" refuting his previous confession with each book consisting of a hundred pages. These books, if they still exist, have not been made available to the public. S. Wang, *The Long Road to Freedom*, 170–71.

35. S. Wang, *The Long Road to Freedom*, 173. The period for writing the retraction of his confession and his suggestions for the government appears to be the fall of 1963 until the end of 1964. Wang's suggestions for the government, if they still exist, have not been made available to the public.

36. See Goldman, "The Party and the Intellectuals," 218.

37. S. Wang, *The Long Road to Freedom*, 174.

38. S. Wang, *The Long Road to Freedom*, 174. See also *The Analects* 15.15.

39. S. Wang, *The Long Road to Freedom*, 176.

40. Bickers, "New Light on Lao She," 24–26.

41. See Goldman, *An Intellectual History of Modern China*, 226. Some believe that Lao She was murdered as an intellectual target of the Cultural Revolution. See Becker, "The Mystery of Lao She."

42. Wang Mingdao, *Last Confession*, 100.

43. The date of Wang's transfer to Datong, Shanxi Province is not precise in any of the sources but seems to have taken place shortly after May 1966.

44. Liu Jingwen was transferred in the beginning of 1965 to the Tongxian County Labor Camp 通縣勞改所 east of Beijing and then back to Beijing Prison's sock factory 襪廠勞改 in 1966. In 1969, she was transferred to Handan's Farm Labor Reform Farm 邯鄲勞改農場 in Hebei Province. She was supposed to be released upon completion of her sentence in April 1973 but instead, in September of 1973, was transferred to Shijia Village's Labor Reform Farm 石家莊勞改場 since convicts who had completed their sentences were required to work in a place specified by the government. She stayed in Shijia Village until September 1976 when she was transferred to Xingtaitang Village Farm 邢台唐莊農場 in Hebei Province. She was finally released in 1977 when she moved to Shanghai to live with her son, Wang Tianduo, and his family. See Shi, *Sixty-Three Years*, 103–5, 112.

45. S. Wang, *The Long Road to Freedom*, 185.

46. See Kung Lee Wang, "China's Mineral Industries in 1967," 435. For the crucial contribution that "reform through labor" prisoners made to the national economy in Mao's China, see Dikötter, *Mao's Great Famine*, 289.

47. Wright, *Coal Mining in China's Economy and Society*, 87.

48. For the complex array of motivations for the Cultural Revolution, see Spence, *The Search for Modern China*, 603–4.

49. See, for example, Li Siqun 黎斯群, "Wu Han—The Zealot of the Jiang [Chiang Kai-shek] Dynasty, Deputy of American Imperialism 吳晗-蔣家王朝的策士, 美帝的幫辦"; Sun Yusheng 孫玉升, "Wu Han, What Qualifications Do You Have to Represent the People? 吳晗，你有什麼資格代表人民? "; "Peng Dehuai and His Backstage Crimes Cannot Escape 彭德懷及其後台罪責難逃"; Zhang Yifei 張益飛, "The Great Traitor Liu Shaoqi Will Be Expelled from the Party Forever 把大叛徒劉少奇永遠開除出黨大快人心! "

50. Wang Mingdao, *Last Confession*, 102.

51. S. Wang, *The Long Road to Freedom*, 182. See also *The Analects* 2.22.

52. See Wang Mingdao, *Last Confession*, 101. Wang's direct quotation 拔刀相助 actually comes from Wu, *The Scholars* 儒林外史, 12:9. *The Scholars*, which due to many quotations of the work by Wang in the *Last Confession* makes it likely that he read the book, is a classic novel completed in 1750 that praises exemplary Confucian morality while at the same time criticizes overly ambitious scholars. An English translation of Wang's quote reads "Whenever I see injustice done, I must draw my sword to avenge the injured." See Wu Jingzi, *The Scholars*, 162.

53. Wang recounts the date of his five months of torture in Datong to be 1968 in Wang Mingdao, *Last Confession*, 85, 102. Since they are recalled by Wang in 1982, they are best guesses, but the timeline does correspond to the denunciations of Wu Han and others beginning in 1966. See Spence, *The Search for Modern China*, 604.

54. Ying, *Last Confession*, 33. Wang came to believe that the catastrophic consequences of the Cultural Revolution were due to the China's embrace of atheism. He thought that the thoroughgoing materialistic ideology of the CCP resulted in a lack of fear of the consequences for breaking the law and violating what he thought was natural morality.

55. S. Wang, *The Long Road to Freedom*, 182–83. For the story of the Stams, see *Biographical Dictionary of Chinese Christianity*, "Elisabeth Alden 'Betty' Stam."

56. Wang Mingdao, *Last Confession*, 101–2. Although he had been beaten while in prison in Beijing, a more aggressive form of torture 肉刑 was inflicted on Wang while at Datong by a former KMT air force officer, a Mr. Wu 吳, who did it to have his prison sentence reduced. See S. Wang, *The Long Road to Freedom*, 183–85.

57. See Wang Mingdao, *Last Confession*, 85. 改造 can also be translated as "transform" or "remold."

58. Wang names Zhan in S. Wang, *The Long Road to Freedom*, 183 and identifies him as a Methodist 衛理公會 pastor in Wang Mingdao, *Last Confession*, 101.

Little is known about Zhan except that Wang Mingdao said that he studied theology in America after the Japanese surrender in China where he spoke out against the CCP, was arrested for having spoken against the CCP when arriving back in China in 1958, and was sentenced to life imprisonment. He took the opportunity to denounce Wang in both Datong and Yinying to successfully reduce his sentence. After leaving China, Zhan disingenuously aligned himself with Wang Mingdao on overseas speaking tours as having suffered in prison for his faith. See S. Wang, *The Long Road to Freedom*, 183–84, 194.

59. S. Wang, *The Long Road to Freedom*, 185; Wang Mingdao, *Last Confession*, 108–9. Most likely, the works of Francis Jones, Arthur Reynolds, and other "China watchers" had kept news of the Wangs alive in Europe and North America. See also the mention of "sketchy reports" in 1968 that Wang was still alive in prison in Bush, *Religion in Communist China*, 262.

60. See Mühlhahn, "Remembering a Bitter Past," 110.

61. Mühlhahn, "Remembering a Bitter Past," 111.

62. Wang Mingdao dates his transfer to Yinying Labor Camp to be the spring of 1970, but Stephen Wang, who investigated Wang Mingdao's story, dates the transfer to April 1968. This reveals the fluid nature of some of the dates while Wang was imprisoned since they were recalled by him in his senior years and it was during a tumultuous period of Chinese history where few records have been released, if they even exist, regarding prisoners in Datong or Yinying Labor Camps. See Wang Mingdao, *Last Confession*, 102, and S. Wang, *The Long Road to Freedom*, 194.

63. Wang Mingdao referred to this place as Yinying Prison 蔭營監獄 in Wang Mingdao, *Last Confession*, 56. Datong is located in the north of Shanxi Province, while Yinying 蔭營, 293 kilometers south of Datong, is a small town in the north of Yangquan County 陽泉縣 in the east of Shanxi Province. The labor camp was situated on a hill outside of the small town. See S. Wang, *The Long Road to Freedom*, 211.

64. Wang Mingdao, *Last Confession*, 102.

65. S. Wang, *The Long Road to Freedom*, 195.

66. Wang Tianduo visited his father alone in the spring of 1973, with his wife and daughter in 1974, and with Liu Jingwen, who was allowed two weeks of holidays from her work program to visit relatives, in 1975. See S. Wang, *The Long Road to Freedom*, 197.

67. Wang Mingdao, *Last Confession*, 102.

68. Wang Mingdao, *Last Confession*, 76. It seems that not only was Wang allowed to read because he was now seventy-three years old, but he also did not have to work because some people within the government continued to hold on to the hope that Wang would eventually work with the TSPM and varied between hard (Datong) and soft (Yinying) tactics in order to convince him to do so.

69. He wrote that "the majority of the books I read are historical." Wang Mingdao, *Last Confession*, 53.

70. Wang Mingdao, *Last Confession*, 166.

71. Wang Mingdao, *Last Confession*, 224.

72. Wang Mingdao, *Last Confession*, 166. Unfortunately, this is one of the pages that is incomplete and nowhere else in the manuscript does Wang continue his thought on the difference between Mencius and Xunzi on human nature. Another name for Xunzi is Xunkuang 荀況.

73. See, for example, Wang Mingdao, "The Human Heart," 104–5. In this article, Wang matches Bai Juyi's description of the indefensibility of the human heart with the Bible's description of the treacherousness of the human heart.

74. On Mencius's thought that human nature is good, see *Mencius*, Teng Wen Gong I, 1, as well as *Mencius*, Gaozo I, 6.

75. On Xunzi's belief that human nature is evil, see *Xunzi* 23:1–24, "Human Nature Is Evil." An English translation is available in *Xunzi: A Translation and Study of the Complete Works*, 3:139–62.

76. During the Song dynasty, the influential scholar Zhu Xi 朱熹 (1130–1200) approved of Mencius's statement that human nature was good and solidified the *Four Books* as the core curriculum for classical Chinese education with Mencius as Confucius's interpreter. Zhu Xi believed that Xunzi's philosophy was erroneous, which resulted in Xunzi's interpretation of Confucius, along with his thought that human nature was evil, being generally rejected by educated Confucians. See Goldin, "Xunzi," 9, particularly "Xunzi's Reception after His Death."

77. Wang Mingdao, *Fifty Years*, 28–29.

78. See, for example, his description of the sinfulness of modern people in Wang Mingdao, "Look at These Ninevites," 14.

79. See Wang Mingdao, *Last Confession*, 185, 187, 190. Wang mentions, after quoting part of Wen Tianxiang's "Song of the Spirit of Righteousness," that he admired people like Wen ever since he was at Tsui Wen Middle School. See Wang Mingdao, *Last Confession*, 77. It seems that Wang Tianduo brought his father a book while at Yinying that contained some of Wen Tianxiang's poetry.

80. See China Knowledge, "Wen Tianxiang."

81. See S. Wang, *The Long Road to Freedom*, 212. Although Wang had apparently memorized the entire poem, his quotations in Wang Mingdao, *Last Confession*, 77 and 190 are abbreviated versions.

82. This Zhang refers to Zhang Xun 張巡, to whom Wang referred to rally the leaders of the Christian Tabernacle to resist participation in the Japanese-led North China Christian Union in 1942. Zhang Xun had lost most of his teeth due to grinding them while in battle at Sui Yang. See *The Old Book of Tang* 舊唐書, chap. 194.

83. See Wen Tianxiang 文天祥, "The Song of the Spirit of Righteousness 正氣歌." This translation of the "Song" by Feng Xinming includes historical annotation for the poem with detailed information on the Chinese heroes referred to in the poem.

84. Wang Mingdao, *Last Confession*, 69, 262.

85. As noted by Ying, *Last Confession*, 28.

86. Wen Tianxiang's original Chinese poem is 孔曰成仁，孟曰取義，惟其義

盡，所以仁至。讀聖賢書，所學何事，而今而後，庶幾無愧。See Wang Mingdao, *Last Confession*, 69, 84.

87. Wang Mingdao's original Chinese poem is 先知成仁，使徒取義，受命傳道，首重剛毅。熟讀《聖經》，洞曉真理，堅貞不屈，頂天立地。See Wang Mingdao, *Last Confession*, 69, 262.

88. Wang Mingdao, *Last Confession*, 118.

89. To add to his grief, he found out through a letter from his son sent to the prison that his mother-in-law, Zhang Meiyun, died in early 1974. This news devastated Wang as he said that his main desire in leaving prison was to see her again. See Wang Mingdao, *Last Confession*, 149, and Shi, *Sixty-Three Years*, 14–15.

90. The complex story of how Lin went from CCP hero to villain is told in Spence, *The Search for Modern China*, 616–17.

91. The Gang of Four was made up of Mao's wife, Jiang Qing 江青, Zhang Chunqiao 張春橋, Yao Wenyuan 姚文元, and Wang Hongwen 王洪文, who would eventually serve as scapegoats for the excesses of the Cultural Revolution.

92. See Spence, *The Search for Modern China*, 635. For some of the many criticisms leveled against Lin Biao at the time that Wang Mingdao would have read while in Yinying, see Criticism Group of the Military and Political University 軍政大學大批判組, "The Gun Must Always Be in the Hands of the Party and the People 槍杆子要永遠掌握在黨和人民手裡"; Jia Heng 嘉衡 and Chun Shu 春樹, "The Reactionary Essence of Lin Biao and His Group Advocating for 'Determining Power' 林彪一夥 鼓" 決定動力 "的反動實質."

93. See, for example, "Criticize Confucius's Reactionary Thought and Take the Road of Uniting the Workers and Peasants 批判孔子反動思想走與工農相結合的道路"; Feng Chunxiang 馮春祥, "Criticizing Confucius's Fallacy of Studying and Being an Official 批判孔子的讀書做官的謬論."

94. Spence, *The Search for Modern China*, 636. Some of the articles that criticized Confucius but praised Qin Shihuang include Peking University and Tsinghua University's Criticism Group 北京大學; 清華大學大批判組, "On the Violence of Qin Shihuang 略論秦始皇的暴力"; Gu Shouhai 穀守海, "Lin Biao Cursed Qin Shihuang as an Attack on the Dictatorship of the Proletariat 林彪咒罵秦始皇就是攻擊無產階級專政"; Wei Jin 衛今, "Looking at the Book Burning of Qin Shihuang from the Yinqueshan Bamboo Slips 從銀雀山竹簡看秦始皇焚書."

95. Wang Mingdao, *Last Confession*, 258. If these documents still exist, they have not been made available to the public.

96. See, for example, "Confucius Kills Shao Zhengmao"; Tang Xiaowen 唐曉文, "What Does Confucius's Killing of Shao Zhengmao Tell Us 孔子殺少正卯說明了什麼?"

97. Wang Mingdao, *Last Confession*, 103. The story of Confucius's execution of Shao Zhengmao is told in Szuma Chien, *Selections from Records of the Historian*, 9. This is currently the only English translation available for the biography of Confucius. The execution of Shao is also told in *Xunzi* 28.2. An English

translation is available in *Xunzi* 3:245.

98. S. Wang, *The Long Road to Freedom*, 199; Wang Mingdao, "To Glory in Your Shame," 107.

99. Ching, *Confucianism and Christianity*, 52.

100. Feng Youlan 馮友蘭, *A History of Chinese Philosophy* 中國哲學史.

101. See Internet Encyclopedia of Philosophy, "Feng Youlan."

102. Feng Youlan 馮友蘭, *On Confucius* 論孔丘.

103. Wang Mingdao, *Last Confession*, 103. Wang was also familiar with the Neo-Confucian scholars Huang Yanpei 黃炎培 (1878–1965) and Chen Shutong 陳叔通 (1876–1966), commenting that they would have been heartbroken had they lived to see the Criticize Confucius Movement in Wang Mingdao, *Last Confession*, 104. These are the only references I have found that Wang makes to Neo-Confucian scholars. Wang makes no references to Liang Shuming 梁漱溟 (1893–1988), one of the most famous Neo-Confucian scholars of the twentieth century.

104. Tang Xiaowen 唐曉文, "What Does Confucius's Killing of Shao Zhengmao Tell Us 孔子殺少正卯說明了什麼?"

105. Wang said that after 1965, he did not fear being shot or being in prison, but he could not stand to be tortured. See Wang Mingdao, *Last Confession*, 102.

106. A reference to *The Analects* 9.5. This reference to "the people of Kuang" refers to when Confucius was imprisoned in the town of Kuang 匡 because he resembled a criminal but was released after five days without injury owing his release to "heaven's cause of truth." The story was explained by Sima Qian with an English translation available in Szuma Chien, *Selections from Records of the Historian*, 10.

107. He expressed these thoughts he had in 1975 to Jiang Hua in 1982 in his "Rehabilitation Request Manuscript." See Wang Mingdao, *Last Confession*, 258–59.

108. As seen from his comments on Daoism after reading a book on Han Xiangzi 韓湘子, one of the Eight Immortals of the Daoist pantheon. See *Wang Mingdao's Diary*, 154, July 5, 1930.

109. See Wang Mingdao, *Last Confession*, 81.

110. Some scholars have argued that Christian missionaries such as the Jesuits found in Confucianism a theism that they were looking for but was in fact not true to Confucianism. See Rainey, "Confucianism and Tradition," 227–44. Nevertheless, several Chinese Confucian Christians such as T. C. Chao and Wang Mingdao held the belief that Confucianism was theistic.

111. Chao saw divine revelation in the thought of Confucius and Mencius as being continuous with the later revelation of the incarnate Word in Jesus Christ. See T. C. Chao, "A Chinese Delegate Looks at Tambaram," 463–64.

112. T. C. Chao publicly rejected his earlier Confucian Christian religion, but it is difficult to know whether this was a declaration made under duress similar to Wang's experience in 1958. See Glüer, "T. C. Chao Revisited," 179, 196.

113. "Religion."

114. For example, Stephen Wang indicates that it was due to a London-based

human rights organization's campaign that political prisoners were released in 1979. See S. Wang, *The Long Road to Freedom*, 205. The organization he is likely referring to is Amnesty International. See *Amnesty International Report 1978*, 154–58.

115. See *Political Imprisonment in the People's Republic of China*, 153–54.

116. "Rehabilitation of Rightists Announced in China."

117. According to Chao, *A History of Christianity in Socialist China*, 284n56. The fact that Carter asked Deng about several matters of concern to Christians in early 1979, including the status of political prisoners in China provided to him by Amnesty International, makes it quite possible that the two men discussed Wang Mingdao. See Sterba, "Carter, Ending China Trip, Stresses Taiwan Issue." Also, Jimmy Carter, "The United States and China." However, I have been unable to find direct evidence that proves that Jimmy Carter discussed Wang Mingdao's imprisonment with Deng Xiaoping.

118. For the refocus on economic development, see Goldman, "The Post-Mao Reform Era," 407. For correcting and healing some of the excesses of the Mao era, including the distinction made between true "counterrevolutionaries" and those who made "wrong statements" and were involved in "sectarian activities" by the Supreme People's Court of China in 1980, see Ying, *Last Confession*, 329.

119. Wang Mingdao, *Last Confession*, 133. See "Member of the Standing Committee."

120. Wang Mingdao, *Last Confession*, 55–56. This document, if it still exists, has not been made available to the public.

121. Wang Mingdao, *Last Confession*, 133.

122. S. Wang, *The Long Road to Freedom*, 206–8.

123. Wang Mingdao, *Last Confession*, 76–77.

124. Mühlhahn, "Remembering a Bitter Past," 110–11.

125. Kao, "Reassembling Christianity," 12.

126. Mann, "Scene-Setting," 631; Starr, *Chinese Theology*, 78.

127. S. Wang, *The Long Road to Freedom*, 209.

128. Wang wrote that he had memorized the huge number of classical Chinese quotes he used as his preface to his "Rehabilitation Request Manuscript," with the exception of Xunzi, many years ago in Wang Mingdao, *Last Confession*, 166. Since he was writing in 1982, it is likely he was referring to his days at Tsui Wen Academy, but it is also possible that he put to memory, or at least refreshed his memory on, many of these classical quotations while at Yinying since he was there in the 1970s.

NOTES TO CHAPTER SIX

1. S. Wang, *The Long Road to Freedom*, 212.

2. The date provided by Wang in Wang Mingdao, *Last Confession*, 83.

3. A descriptive phrase used by Kao Chen-yang in his PhD dissertation

investigating Protestantism in post-Mao China. See Kao, "The Cultural Revolution and the Post-missionary Transformation of Protestantism in China," 179. As well as in Kao, "The House Church Identity and Preservation of Pentecostal-Style Protestantism in China," 211. Wang has also been called "the symbol of the house church movement" in Lui, *Development of Chinese Church Leaders*, 136. He is referred to as the first "patriarch" of the house church movement in Aikman, *Jesus in Beijing*, 47.

4. Hong Kong's Morning Star Publishing 晨星出版社 published Wang Mingdao's works in the 1970s. See Wang Mingdao, *Last Confession*, 66, 67n31.

5. Taiwan's Conservative Baptist Press 浸宣出版社 published a seven-volume *Treasury of Wang Mingdao* 王明道文庫 from 1976 to 1978 edited by Wang Zhengzhong 王正中. This was the standard collection of Wang's works until the republication of *The Spiritual Food Quarterly*, *The Last Fifty Years*, and some of Wang's other writings by Taiwan's CCLM Publishing Group 華宣出版社 in the 2010s. Wang Mingdao's works are still banned in China.

6. Wang Mingdao, *Last Confession*, 78.

7. This explains why many younger Chinese went to visit Wang after 1980. See Kao, "The Cultural Revolution and the Post-missionary Transformation of Protestantism in China," 192–93.

8. For Chao's prolific training sessions in China, see Rourke, "Jonathan Chao." Chao greatly admired Wang Mingdao and endorsed his theology. See J. Chao, "A Brief Description of Mr. Wang Mingdao's Contribution to Chinese Churches," 3.

9. Li Boxiong, "Wang Mingdao's Contribution to Popular Theology," 22.

10. Lui, "Development of Chinese Church Leaders," 143. Lam Wing-hun also stated that Wang's theology was representative of conservative mainstream theology in 1980s China. See Lam, *Wang Ming-Tao and the Chinese Church*, 4, 227.

11. Wang Mingdao, *Last Confession*, 83, 226.

12. For example, some described being with Wang in the 1980s as like being in the presence of an angel or a biblical character. See Brother David and Gilbert, *Walking the Hard Road*, 16 and 19.

13. S. Wang, *The Long Road to Freedom*, 214.

14. See Chinese University of Hong Kong, "Chung Chi Campus Newsletter," 11 ("Obituary").

15. Ng, *Christianity and Social Changes in China*, 133–69. The book is a revised version of Ng's PhD dissertation, "Christianity and Social Change."

16. Wang Mingdao, *Last Confession*, 66.

17. Ng, *Christianity and Social Changes in China*, 133.

18. Ng, *Christianity and Social Changes in China*, 163–64.

19. As noted in Ying, *Last Confession*, 66–67n34. See Zhang Zhiyi, "Speech of the Deputy Minister," 19.

20. Wang Mingdao, *Last Confession*, 66–67. Many Chinese Christian leaders were insulted when this term was ascribed to their names during the accusation

campaign in the 1950s including Z. T. Kuang. See Ying, *Christianity's Failure in China*, 88.

21. According to Chang Kuan-Ing 章冠英, the helper who lived with Wang from 1982 to 1991. See Lin and Chang, *An Injured Brave*, 98.

22. See Xu Bin, "Memory and Reconciliation in Post-Mao China," 51–54.

23. Ying Fuk Tsang calculates that from October 1978 to the end of 1981, courts at all levels in China reversed more than 301,000 unjust cases 冤假錯案 involving more than 326,000 parties. See Ying, *Last Confession*, 18–19.

24. Jiang Hua's report, given on June 7, 1983, is translated into English in Jiang Hua, "On the Work of the Supreme People's Court, June 7, 1983," 1:295–300.

25. The date Ying Fuk Tsang provides in Ying, *Last Confession*, 6. Wang dates one of the documents that makes up the manuscript at 1983. See Wang Mingdao, *Last Confession*, 212.

26. See Wang Mingdao, *Last Confession*, 138. This article is not available in the People's Daily Archive.

27. Wang Mingdao, *Last Confession*, 239–40. See Chen Yun 陳雲, "Speak the Truth, Don't Talk about Saving Face 只講真理，不要講面子."

28. See Wang Mingdao, *Last Confession*, 98, 99n57.

29. Ying, *Last Confession*, 329.

30. Ying, *Last Confession*, 330. However, something not considered by Wang Mingdao or Ying Fuk Tsang is whether Wang qualified for rehabilitation. If Xu Bin is correct, the corrective action applied only to cadres and intellectuals within establishments. See Xu Bin, "Memory and Reconciliation in Post-Mao China," 53–54.

31. He was so esteemed by overseas Chinese Christians after his release that Calvin Chao (Zhao Junying) 趙君影 (1906–96) wanted to name the seminary he founded after Wang in the early 1980s. Wang refused, and the seminary became known as the Chinese for Christ Theological Seminary 中華歸主神學院, currently located in Alhambra, California. In 1988, Calvin Chao tried to confer on Wang an honorary doctor of divinity degree from the seminary, but again, Wang refused. See Lin and Chang, *An Injured Brave*, 123–24.

32. See Wang Mingdao, *Last Confession*, 78; Lin and Chang, *An Injured Brave*, 93.

33. For example, several leaders in the Beijing Christian Student Association were very vocal in protesting Wang's arrest in 1955 and were subsequently arrested as part of the "clique." See Wing, "The China Inland Mission," 43. The most comprehensive study on this topic is by Leung, *By Faith They Did It*.

34. Although Wang's memory was still sharp in 1983, as can be seen from the massive list of quotations he wrote from memory in his preface, his argument even in the most complete document in the request moves from topic to topic without always being clear to the reader why a transition has taken place. However, although he became repetitive beginning in 1989, his memory for older details remained sharp until 1991 when his memory began to fail. See S. Wang, *The Long Road to Freedom*, 231.

35. Wang Mingdao, *Last Confession*, 195.

36. Wang seems to have made four different drafts of his preface included in the *Last Confession*. The first is found on pp. 179–95, the second on pp. 197–204, the third on pp. 205–10, and the fourth on pp. 255–57.

37. Spence, *The Search for Modern China*, 49.

38. Spence, *The Search for Modern China*, 71–72.

39. Wang Mingdao, *Last Confession*, 195. The English translation is found in Chan, *Faith of Our Fathers*, 255.

40. *The Analects* 15.3.

41. Wang Mingdao, *Last Confession*, 204. This exact phrase that Wang quotes in English has proven difficult to locate. The closest I have been able to find comes from *The Sunday School Helper*, 56. "Be the matter what it may, Always speak the truth: Whether work, or whether play, Always speak the truth. He is but a coward slave, Who, a present pain to waive, Stoops to falsehood; then be brave: Always speak the truth."

42. Wang Mingdao, *Last Confession*, 82.

43. See Murthy, "Deng's 'Civilized' China," 3. Wang does not mention the "Three Loves," which was also part of the policy, which were the love of the motherland, socialism, and the CCP.

44. Wang Mingdao, *Last Confession*, 52, 107. The quote is from *The Book of Rites, The Great Learning*, 2.

45. Wang Mingdao, *Last Confession*, 166. The quote is from *The Book of Rites, The Great Learning*, 11.

46. Wang Mingdao, *Last Confession*, 165. The quote is from *Mencius*, Li Lou I, 1.

47. Wang Mingdao, *Last Confession*, 157.

48. Wang uses the terms "atheism 無神論" and "materialism 唯物主義" interchangeably in his "Rehabilitation Request Manuscript."

49. In a flurry of quotations to prove this point, Wang refers to *Analects* 7.23, *Analects* 9.5, *Analects* 3.13, *Analects* 6.28, *Mencius*, Gaozi II, 35, *Mencius*, Li Lou II, 53, and *Xunzi* 27.66 (Knoblock translation, 224, 27.68).

50. Wang Mingdao, *Last Confession*, 81–82. Mao's quote in Chinese reads, 徹底的唯物主義者是無所畏懼的. See Mao Zedong, *Long Live Mao Zedong Thought*, "Four Sentences for Li Ne."

51. Wang Mingdao, *Last Confession*, 82–83. The breakdown of Chinese moral codes as famine eroded the moral fabric of Chinese society, which led to perversion and destruction during the Great Leap Forward, is tragically described in Dikötter, *Mao's Great Famine*, 258.

52. Wang Mingdao, *Last Confession*, 266.

53. Wang Mingdao, *Last Confession*, 270. Wang does not make mention, or perhaps was not aware, that some of those attacking Confucius at the beginning of the May Fourth Movement were Christians. See Bays, *A New History of Christianity in China*, 107.

54. Wang Mingdao, *Last Confession*, 149–50. The complex motivations for the Criticize Confucius Movement are beyond the scope of this work but are discussed in Williams, "The Succession to Mao," 14:343–47.

55. Mao Zedong, *Long Live Mao Zedong Thought*, 195. Translated into English in Lieberthal, *Governing China*, 71.

56. Wang Mingdao, *Last Confession*, 105, 264. For the story of Xiang Yu and Liu Bang's rebellion against the Qin Empire and the eventual death of Xiang Yu and Liu Bang's establishment of the Han dynasty, see Sima Qian, *The Grand Scribe's Records*, 1:189, 1:207.

57. Wang Mingdao, *Last Confession*, 105.

58. Wang Mingdao, *Last Confession*, 136. Wang also states that the Gang of Four were not responsible for the persecution of the church in China during the 1950s but came to prominence during the Cultural Revolution and lays the blame for the persecution of the church at the feet of the TSPM leaders, chief of whom is Y. T. Wu. A much more sympathetic treatment of Y. T. Wu during this time is provided by Philip Wickeri who indicates that Wu was attempting to remove the foreign influence in the Chinese church while at the same time providing a way for the church to exist in Communist China. See Wickeri, *Reconstructing Christianity in China*, 98. Also, a more nuanced perspective on Wu is provided in Ying, *Christianity's Failure in China*, 67–68.

59. Wang Mingdao, *Last Confession*, 118.

60. Wang Mingdao, *Last Confession*, 54n9. Wang also referred to this memorial book in 1945 in Wang Mingdao, "Their God Is Still Our God," 158. See *North China Christian Union Group Memorial Book*, 9. Z. T. Kuang has an article at the beginning of the memorial book (n.p.) on "Church Unity."

61. *The Analects* 12.22.

62. Wang Mingdao, *Last Confession*, 136.

63. In 1978 at the third plenum of the CCP, Peng Dehuai was rehabilitated. In 1980, Liu Shaoqi was rehabilitated at the fifth plenum of the CCP where it was agreed that the charges against him were false. See Williams, "The Succession to Mao," 386.

64. Wang Mingdao, *Last Confession*, 53. The exact statement in Chinese is 我是基督的門徒，我也是孔子的弟子. In the Chinese Bible, "mentu 門徒" is the term for a disciple of Christ. In *The Analects*, "dizi 弟子" is the term for a disciple of Confucius.

65. The most thorough analysis of this is found in Liang, "Independent Religious Beliefs' Effect on Society," 169–200.

66. Wang Mingdao, *Last Confession*, 120. The quote of Confucius is from *Analects* 5.10. Wang also mentions this advice from Confucius when interviewed about Watchman Nee in 1982. See Ying, "Wang Mingdao Discusses Chinese Church Leaders and Affairs," 80.

67. Wang Mingdao, *Last Confession*, 217.

68. See Williams, "The Succession to Mao," 14:391. The sixth plenum concluded that although Mao had made terrible mistakes during the Cultural Revolution, his contributions as a whole to the People's Republic of China greatly outweighed his mistakes, yet the recognition that Mao was not completely correct in his actions would certainly be viewed by Wang as progress in the right direction.

69. Ying, *Last Confession*, 39; Lin and Chang, *An Injured Brave*, 100; Shi, *Sixty-Three Years*, 123; S. Wang, *The Long Road to Freedom*, 223–24.

70. Liu Jingwen encouraged Wang to be concise if he was going to write the request, but she said he kept deliberating over the wording and including ancient quotes. Due to his deteriorating health along with resistance from his most important relationship, Wang could not finish it. See Ma Feibi, "Wang Mingdao through the Eyes of Mrs. Wang," 8.

71. Ying, *Last Confession*, 39–40 and 46n97.

72. There seems to have been some relational conflict between Liu Jingwen and Wang Tianduo's wife, Yin Wiezhi 殷蔚芷, likely exacerbated while they lived together on Pingjiang Road. See Shi, *Sixty-Three Years*, 125–26. The mother-in-law–daughter-in-law relationship and broader family harmony was also likely improved with the new living arrangements on Wukang Road.

73. Lin and Chang, *An Injured Brave*, 133. This biography of Wang Mingdao presents valuable firsthand information of Wang and Liu Jingwen from 1983 to 1991 from Chang's perspective during the time he lived with them on Wukang Road. Wang's eye surgery was unsuccessful in correcting his glaucoma.

74. Lin and Chang, *An Injured Brave*, 158.

75. S. Wang, *The Long Road to Freedom*, 226.

76. For example, see the talks titled, "A Strong Wall, an Iron Pillar—Wang Mingdao's Testimony"; "Wang Mingdao's Critique of Watchman Nee to Warn Preachers and Christians"; "Wang Mingdao's Sermon 02—Guard against Two Kinds of Leaven; To Serve the Lord One Must Be Holy"; "Wang Mingdao Sermon 02—Come Out from Babylon."

77. S. Wang, *The Long Road to Freedom*, 222–23; *Mencius*, Teng Wen Gong II, 7.

78. S. Wang, *The Long Road to Freedom*, 223. See Matthew 6:14–15.

79. The following references are from the sermons of Wang Mingdao during his days at Wukang Road in Shanghai that were recorded and later transcribed into Microsoft Word documents. They are unpublished and were generously shared with me by Ying Fuk Tsang. Several are untitled, but most, not all, include the date Wang preached the sermon. Wang Mingdao, Untitled Sermon, February 9, 1986.

80. See Wang Mingdao, *Last Confession*, 149.

81. Wang Mingdao, Untitled Sermon, January 28, 1988. Jesus's declaration to love your enemies is found in Matthew 5:43–44. Confucius's statement to "return kindness with kindness and injury with injury" is found in the *Book of Rites*, Biao Ji, 11.

82. *The Analects* 13.6.

83. Wang Mingdao, Untitled Sermon, February 14, 1988. Paul's advice to Timothy that Wang referred to is found in 1 Timothy 4:11–16.

84. See Jeremiah 17:9.

85. Wang Mingdao, "Autobiography 自述," n.d. Bai Juyi's poem that Wang refers to has been translated into English in Gwyther, "Bai Juyi and the New Yuefu Movement," 146.

86. Wei Zheng's biographies are found in *The Old Book of Tang* 舊唐書, book 71, biography 21 of Wei Zheng, as well as in *The New Book of Tang* 新唐書, biography 22 of Wei Zheng. Wang had been impressed with Wei Zheng as early as 1935 and referred to a quote from Wei Zheng's biography in *The Old Book of Tang* in Wang's book, *Look at These Men (Part One)* 看這些人(上), 3.

87. Wang Mingdao, Untitled Sermon on Officials, n.d.

88. See China Knowledge, "Zhenguan Zhengyao 貞觀政要."

89. Wang Mingdao, Untitled Sermon on Officials, n.d. However, the story of Tang Taizong's trip to Nanshan does not appear in the *Essentials*. The story is referred to in the *Fine Stories from the Sui and Tang Dynasties* 隋唐嘉話, 1:11–22. This volume may have been included in the four volumes Wang purchased at the Dongan Market in the 1940s.

90. Wang Mingdao, Untitled Sermon on Officials, n.d. See also Lu Dingyi 陸定一, *Biography of Wei Zheng* 魏徵傳.

91. See Zhong Xuanzao 鍾宣造, "Lu Dingyi's Counter-revolutionary Face Is Revealed from the *Biography of Wei Zheng* 從《魏徵傳》的出籠看陸定一的反革命嘴臉."

92. Wang Mingdao, Untitled Sermon, February 2, 1986.

93. Wang Mingdao, Sermon on "2 Kings 5—Call Naaman 'The Man,'" May 31, 1987. The story of Naaman, a commander in the Syrian army, and the prophet Elisha, who gave him advice on how to heal his skin disease, is found in 2 Kings 5.

94. See Wang's other references to Wei Zheng in Wang Mingdao, *Last Confession*, 51–52, 108, 188.

95. Wechsler, *Mirror to the Son of Heaven*, 119.

96. Wang Mingdao, Untitled Sermon on Officials, n.d.

97. Wang Mingdao, *Last Confession*, 103.

98. Some of the visits to the Wangs on Wukang Road are recorded in Zhao Zhonghui, "Wang Mingdao Recalls Entering Prison for the First Time," 5–7 (1984 interview); Aikman, *Jesus in Beijing*, 47 (1985 interview); Kao, "The Cultural Revolution and the Post-missionary Transformation of Protestantism in China," 192–93 (1988 meeting); Zhao Zhonghui, "An Interview with Mr. Wang Mingdao," 51–56; and Tow, *Wang Ming Tao and Charismatism*, 83–95 (1988 interview).

99. Graham, *Just as I Am*, 604. The Grahams' trip to China was from April 12 to 28, 1988.

100. Graham, *Just as I Am*, 599.

101. Wang Mingdao, "We Are for the Faith!" 151–69. Wang described Ting as an "unbeliever" after reading Ting's statements in K. H. Ting, "Summary of Standing Committee Member K. H. Ting's Speech," 7. Ting would respond to Wang's article with K. H. Ting, "An Earnest Admonishment to Wang Mingdao," 16–20. Philip Wickeri provides Ting's perspective on his conflict with Wang Mingdao in Wickeri, *Reconstructing Christianity in China*, 119–22.

102. Lin and Chang, *An Injured Brave*, 109–10. Wang Mingdao was familiar with and respected Ruth Bell Graham's father, Dr. Nelson Bell, although they never met. Wang had been invited by Dr. Bell to preach in 1937 in Huaiyin 淮陰, Jiangsu Province, when the Bell family was stationed there as Presbyterian missionaries. Wang could not accept the invitation due to a previous commitment and mailed a letter of decline, which Ruth Bell Graham received.

103. Bürklin, *Jesus Never Left China*, 50.

104. Graham, *Just as I Am*, 601.

105. As indicated in an interview of Wang Mingdao and Liu Jingwen on Billy and Ruth Graham's visit in Tow, *Wang Ming Tao and Charismatism*, 88–92.

106. Teng had great respect for Wang Mingdao and believed that Wang had a huge impact on the Chinese church. See Lin and Chang, *An Injured Brave*, 118.

107. As recounted from Chang's perspective in East Gates International, "Rev. Billy Graham's First Visit to China." It is quite possible that Chang was overwhelmed by the fact that the most famous Protestant clergyman in the world, a living legend within the global Christian community, was standing outside his door and he let the Grahams in. The conversation eventually moved to the sitting room as seen in the picture on the website above where the group exchanged scripture verses.

108. Graham, *Just as I Am*, 613–14. There was also an unnamed Englishman present. See S. Wang, *The Long Road to Freedom*, 228. The accounts include contradictory details. Stephen Wang indicates that Wang Mingdao was receiving physiotherapy from his doctor when the Grahams arrived. Since Billy Graham's account was an eye-witness account, his description of events is more reliable, meaning that Wang Mingdao was asleep when the Grahams arrived. Also, in the East Gates International account as recounted by Chang Kuan-Ing, it was Liu Jingwen who was receiving physiotherapy.

109. For example, "Billy Graham in China." Tu Yichao 涂怡超 stated that Graham's aim was "to promote more open and cordial relationships between the Three-Self Church and house churches." See Tu, "Panda Huggers and Dragon Slayers," 5.

110. Tow, *Wang Ming Tao and Charismatism*, 91.

111. Tow, *Wang Ming Tao and Charismatism*, 86.

112. Tow, *Wang Ming Tao and Charismatism*, 92. Liu Jingwen, who said that there was no English translation of this essay for Graham to read, was understandably not aware that in 1963, Francis Jones had translated "We Are for the Faith!" into English in Jones, *Documents of the Three-Self Movement*, 99–114.

113. My summary of the events is based on Spence, *The Search for Modern China*, 739–43.

114. Spence, *The Search for Modern China*, 744.

115. S. Wang, *The Long Road to Freedom*, 228. However, it should be noted that a previous article was written in 1987 in which Wang Mingdao was again invited to join the TSPM by a professor at Nanjing (Jinling) Union Theological Seminary. See Jiang, "An Appeal to Mr. Wang Mingdao," 49–51.

116. Wang Mingdao, "We Are for the Faith!" 169–71. Wang Mingdao grouped Wang Weifan in with the "unbelievers" after reading his article, Wang Weifan, "Although We Are Many, We Are Still One Body," 5–9.

117. See Wang Weifan, "Is It for Faith?" 15–16.

118. See Yao, "Wang Weifan's Evangelical Theology," 3.

119. Wang Weifan, "Wu Yaozong and Wang Mingdao," 37–40.

120. Wang Weifan, "Wu Yaozong and Wang Mingdao," 37.

121. Wang Weifan, "Wu Yaozong and Wang Mingdao," 39.

122. Wang Weifan, "Wu Yaozong and Wang Mingdao," 40.

123. From an interview of Wang Mingdao in 1989 by Yan Liming, "After Reading Wang Weifan's 'Wu Yaozong and Wang Mingdao,'" 120–28. Also, S. Wang, *The Long Road to Freedom*, 229.

124. This unnamed missionary was most likely Doug Sutphen, better known as Brother David or "China's Smuggler" of the missionary organization Open Doors. Sutphen had a special interest in China and would publish a biography of Wang Mingdao in 1989 after visiting him several times in the 1980s. See Brother David and Gilbert, *Walking the Hard Road*, 15.

125. Stephen Wang's biography is available in Zhao Qingzhi 趙清治, "The Life Testimony of a Preacher."

126. The interesting story of these interviews and subsequent writing of *Another Forty Years* is told in S. Wang, "How *Another Forty Years* Was Written."

127. See S. Wang, *The Long Road to Freedom*, 236–39; Lin and Chang, *An Injured Brave*, 136–41. James Hudson Taylor III 戴绍曾, grandson of the famous missionary and frequent guest at the Wang's home in Shanghai, called that morning to inquire about Wang. See Lin and Chang, *An Injured Brave*, 112, 138.

128. Shi, *Sixty-Three Years*, 151–52.

129. See Various Authors, "Mr. Wang Mingdao's 90th Year Special Issue," 32–39.

130. Ying, *Last Confession*, vii. Ying's words are 中國教會最後一位時代巨人離開歷史舞台了!

131. Chao, "A Brief Outline of Mr. Wang Mingdao's Contribution to Chinese Churches," 2–3.

132. Samuel Lamb 林献羔, "The Wang Mingdao I Know," 9–10.

133. See S. Wang, *The Long Road to Freedom*, 54–55. In 1958, Yuan was arrested as a counterrevolutionary and held in the same prison as Wang Mingdao.

See *Biographical Dictionary of Chinese Christianity*, "Allen Yuan." Also, Aikman, *Jesus in Beijing*, 59. Allen Yuan's name in *Another Forty Years* uses the characters 楊襄城 Yang Xiangcheng to protect him at the time since he was still alive when the book was published.

134. Yuan Xiangchen 袁相忱, "Remembering God's Servant Mr. Wang Mingdao," 9–10.

135. Ming Yan 銘言, "Remembering Uncle Wang," 13.

NOTES TO CHAPTER SEVEN

1. See Yao, *The Fundamentalist Movement among Protestant Missionaries in China*, 282, 287.

2. *The Analects* 15.9.

3. *Mencius*, Gaozi I, 10.1.

4. Wang Mingdao, "A Fortified City, an Iron Pillar, a Bronze Wall," 48. Also included in Wang Mingdao, *Fifty Years*, 112–13.

5. Wang Mingdao, "We Are for the Faith!" translated in Jones, *Documents of the Three-Self Movement*, 100–101.

6. As noted by Alexander Chow, email to author, August 31, 2021.

7. Lee, "Cross-Textual Hermeneutics and Identity in Multi-scriptural Asia," 182.

8. *Wang Mingdao's Diary*, 46–47, September 20, 1924.

9. See Wang Mingdao, "Are People Able to Establish God's Kingdom?" 36–46; Wang Mingdao, "How Many Gospels Are There?" 137–38. Also Sun, "Jesus in the Writings of Wang Mingdao," 1146–47.

10. Ng Lee-Ming, *Christianity and Social Change in China*, 163–64.

11. Li, "Wang Mingdao's Contribution to Popular Theology," 21.

12. Liang, "A Reinterpretation of Wang Mingdao's Thoughts on Society," 199.

13. Liang, "A Reinterpretation of Wang Mingdao's Thoughts on Society," 169–200.

14. Liang, "A Reinterpretation of Wang Mingdao's Thoughts on Society," 169.

15. See, for example, Wang's statement in *Wang Mingdao's Last Confession* that Chiang Kai-shek converted to Christianity not out of genuine religious faith but rather to curry favor with the United States. Wang Mingdao, *Last Confession*, 143.

16. Liang, "A Reinterpretation of Wang Mingdao's Thoughts on Society," 199.

17. Liang, "A Reinterpretation of Wang Mingdao's Thoughts on Society," 199.

18. Lam, *Wang Ming-Tao and the Chinese Church*, 233.

19. Lam, *Wang Ming-Tao and the Chinese Church*, 232.

20. Lam, *Wang Ming-Tao and the Chinese Church*, 233.

21. Lam, *Wang Ming-Tao and the Chinese Church*, 235.

22. Lam, *Wang Ming-Tao and the Chinese Church*, 235.

23. Shan, *Major Aspects of Chinese Religion and Philosophy*, v, x.
24. See Ying, "Inner Saint and Outer King."
25. Wang Mingdao, *Last Confession*, 52.
26. Wang Mingdao, *Fifty Years*, 98, 157.
27. Wang Mingdao, *Last Confession*, 149.
28. Wang Mingdao, Untitled Sermon, January 28, 1988.
29. Wang Mingdao, "Taking a Concubine and Divorce," 110. See *Analects* 3.12.
30. Wang Mingdao, "To Glory in Your Shame," 107.
31. Wang Mingdao, "What Does the 'Resurrection of Jesus' Actually Mean?" 51.
32. Wang Mingdao, "Taking a Concubine and Divorce," 110. See *Mencius*, Li Lou I, 26.
33. Wang Mingdao, *Last Confession*, 166.
34. Wang Mingdao, "The Fairest Lesson," 184.
35. Wang Mingdao, *Fifty Years*, 98.
36. Wang Mingdao, "God's Son Jesus (Part 3)," 58.
37. Wang Mingdao, *Fifty Years*, 98.
38. As noted in Ying, "Watchman Nee in the Eyes of Wang Mingdao," 157–58.
39. Li Kaihuan, "Wang Mingdao's Theology," 110.
40. Wang Mingdao, *Last Confession*, 266.
41. Wang Mingdao, *Last Confession*, 136.
42. This way of describing Wesley's theological method was originally theorized by Albert C. Outler. See Outler, "The Wesleyan Quadrilateral in Wesley," 7–18. Also Maddox, *Responsible Grace*, 36–47.
43. See Wang Mingdao, "The Question of Validity of the Last Half of Mark 16," 54–55. Wang refers to annotated notes in *The Scofield Reference Bible*, *The American Revised Version*, and *The Holy Bible: A New Translation* by James Moffatt in this article.
44. *Wang Mingdao's Diary*, 196, April 14, 1934.
45. Mainly articles by George H. Knight and James R. Miller but Wang translated many other authors as well.
46. Wang Mingdao, "The Spiritual Gifts Movement in the Light of Scripture," 229.
47. However, he was not an absolute literalist and entered several theological debates on the proper translation of various theological terms in *The Spiritual Food Quarterly*. On the thorny issue in Chinese theology on how to translate "God," Wang preferred to use "Shen 神," as opposed to "Shang Di 上帝."
48. See Ying, "Watchman Nee in the Eyes of Wang Mingdao," 136.
49. See Wang Mingdao, *Look at These Men (Part One)*, 3. "Jing 經" can be translated as "scripture" or "classic."
50. Wang Gungwu, *China Reconnects*, 61.

51. See also Wang Gungwu's discussion of the importance of the *Four Treasuries* 經史子集 (jing 經 classics or scripture, shi 史histories, zi 子sages, and ji 集 collections) in modern Chinese thought. Wang Gungwu, *China Reconnects*, 52.

52. *Book of Documents*, Instructions of Yi, 1.

53. *Classic of Poetry*, Da Ming, 7.

54. *Classic of Poetry*, Zheng Min, 1.

55. *The Analects* 7.23.

56. *The Analects* 9.5. Wang is mixing his quotes of *Analects* 7.23 and 9.5 together. *Analects* 9.5 reads, "While Heaven does not let the cause of truth perish, what can the people of Kuang do to me?"

57. *The Analects* 3.13.

58. *The Analects* 6.28.

59. *Mencius*, Gaozi II, 35.

60. *Mencius*, Li Lou II, 53.

61. *Xunzi* 27.66 (Knoblock translation III, 224, 27.68). Another way to translate "lord" here is "ruler."

62. Wang Mingdao, *Last Confession*, 81.

63. Mao Zedong 毛澤東, *Long Live Mao Zedong Thought*, "Four Sentences for Li Ne."

64. *The Analects* 16.8.

65. Genesis 39:8–9. Wang Mingdao, *Last Confession*, 81–82.

66. On how many Chinese Christians believe that "Shang Di" and "Shen" are both appropriate terms for God in Chinese, see Eber, "The Interminable Term Question," 154; Peng, *The Translation of the Bible into Chinese*, 119–20.

67. *Wang Mingdao's Diary*, 18, October 10, 1922. See also *Wang Mingdao's Diary*, 28, August 11, 1923.

68. See Louth, *The Origins of the Christian Mystical Tradition*, 73. The Greek word *ousia*, translated into English as "essence" can also be translated as "being" or "substance" and is translated into Chinese as "ti 體."

69. See Wang Mingdao, "Who Is Jesus?" 8–47. The article "Who Is Jesus?" was originally published in *The Spiritual Food Quarterly* in 1927 and revised with the final version in 1947, but Wang published his final edition in 1953.

70. *Wang Mingdao's Diary*, 17, August 6, 1922. See also *Wang Mingdao's Diary*, 28, August 10, 1923.

71. *Wang Mingdao's Diary*, 376, April 25, 1952; *Wang Mingdao's Diary*, 407, July 22, 1952.

72. *Wang Mingdao's Diary*, 413, August 14, 1952; *Wang Mingdao's Diary*, 414, September 1, 1952.

73. The Nicene-Constantinopolitan Creed does not use the phrase "three persons of one essence" translated into Chinese as 三位一體, but the concept is found in the creed. See Percival, "The First Council of Constantinople," 14:163. The phrase

"three persons of one essence" is found in the theological writings of the Cappadocian theologians who were instrumental in constructing the Nicene-Constantinopolitan Creed. See Anatolios, "Discourse on the Trinity," 2:447. The Greek word *hypostases*, translated into English as "person," is translated into Chinese as "wei 位."

74. Wang Mingdao, "The Idols of Christians," 89.

75. Wang Mingdao, "Did Christ Really Rise from the Dead?" 43.

76. *Wang Mingdao's Diary*, 57, June 2, 1925; *Wang Mingdao's Diary*, 79, June 4, 1925.

77. Wang Mingdao, "God's Son Jesus (Part 3)," 58.

78. See Wang Mingdao, "We Are for the Faith!" 153, translated in Jones, *Documents of the Three-Self Movement*, 107.

79. In my recent online presentation on Wang's theology at Princeton Theological Seminary's World Christianity Conference (March 4, 2021), the most frequently asked question was on Wang's theology regarding the Trinity.

80. Louth, *The Origins of the Christian Mystical Tradition*, 36–39. Plotinus described three related *hypostases*: the One, Intelligence (nous), and Soul in his philosophy that later Trinitarian theologians would use to describe three persons (Greek *hypostases*) of one essence (Greek *ousia*) that would inform the theological background on the Godhead, which would be enshrined as orthodox teaching at the Council of Constantinople in 381.

81. See McGuckin, *St. Gregory of Nazianzus*, 135–36. Also Edwards, "The First Council of Nicea," 1:563.

82. Ni, "Sinicizing Jesus," 167.

83. Ni, "Sinicizing Jesus," 171.

84. See Iap, "Bernt Bernsten," 98–99.

85. See *Wang Mingdao's Diary*, 2, January 20, 1921; *Wang Mingdao's Diary*, 4, March 10, 1921; and *Wang Mingdao's Diary*, 8, August 25, 1921. Wang broke with Bernsten over justification by faith on January 27, 1923, and records more tense meetings with Bernsten in *Wang Mingdao's Diary*, 25, February 17 and 18, 1923. There were likely more meetings between the two men, but the published diary is incomplete.

86. *Wang Mingdao's Diary*, 22, January 27, 1923.

87. Iap, "Bernt Bernsten," 100.

88. Gene Ng, "The Shaping Influence of the Chinese YMCA on the Young Wang Mingdao," 190n177. From Wang Mingdao's unpublished diary on December 30, 1921.

89. Iap, "Bernt Bernsten," 101. Paul Wei's currently unpublished documents, kindly shared with me by Iap Sian-Chin, reveal Wei's rejection of the doctrine of the Trinity and Bernt Bernsten's influence. Paul Wei 魏保羅, *True Testimonies of the Holy Spirit* 聖靈真見證冊, 2–3. The True Jesus Church has never accepted the doctrine of the Trinity: "The doctrine of the Trinity, which presents the Godhead

as three persons in one God, neither conforms to the teachings of the Bible, nor the language that it uses." Sun Tao Hsieh, *The Doctrine of the Holy Spirit*, 20.

90. This disagreement over the doctrine of the Trinity is a part of Western Fundamentalist Christianity as well. The doctrine was included as a fundamental Christian teaching in the 1878 Niagara Creed, one of the earliest formulations of Fundamentalist teachings in North America. See Sandeen, *The Roots of Fundamentalism*, 273. However, the extremely influential Fundamentalist Christians John Nelson Darby and Cyrus I. Scofield rejected the doctrine of the Trinity since it could not be inferred from a plain reading of Scripture. See Hempton, *Evangelical Disenchantment*, 52. One of the Bible's Wang Mingdao used for research was *The Scofield Reference Bible*. See Scofield's unsubstantiated comment on the Trinitarian formulation on John 5:7: "it is generally agreed that v.7 has no real authority, and has been inserted." This "general agreement" seems to refer to Scofield's like-minded non-Trinitarian theologians. Scofield, *The Scofield Reference Bible*, 1325.

91. Carnesecca, "Revolution and Religious Reform," 71–72.

92. Tseng, "Revival Preaching," 180.

93. See Anatolios, "Discourse on the Trinity," 2:438.

94. Wang Mingdao, "A Sharp Warning to the Modern Church," 137. Wang writes about Jesus that he is "the head of all things God created 祂是「在神創造萬物之上為元首 的」."

95. Wang Mingdao, "What Is Truth?" 92.

96. See Ni, "Sinicizing Jesus," 177.

97. It is unlikely that Wang would have accepted theological education from Modernist theologians at Yenching University had he been accepted in 1919. The North China Theological Seminary 華北神學院 in Tengxian (modern Tengzhou 滕州), Shandong Province may have been acceptable to Wang due to the school's emphasis on Christian education with the Bible, interpreted from a Fundamentalist theological perspective, having a central place in the curriculum. However, it was only established in 1919, and by the time Wang would have been ready to study there, his rebaptism had secured his decision to move in a direction independent from missionary Christianity. For information on the North China Theological Seminary, see Yao, *The Fundamentalist Movement among Protestant Missionaries in China*, 139–51.

98. As opposed to the brief and tense discussion Wang had with Dora Yu and Jia Yuming in 1925. However, it is quite possible that even if he carefully studied the history of the creation of the Nicene-Constantinopolitan Creed, as well as a thorough exegesis course on John's Gospel, Wang still may have preferred the biblicist position of not accepting words not found in the Bible in theological statements. But since his education was cut short, we will never know.

99. See *Wang Mingdao's Diary*, 426, November 25, 1952. See also Song, "Jia Yuming."

100. See Jones, *Documents of the Three-Self Movement*, 200.

101. In addition to Wang's references to Nee previously referenced in this study, see Lian, *Redeemed by Fire*, 177, and Leung, *Watchman Nee*. Wang's final comments on Watchman Nee, although veiled but clearly referring to Nee, are from a sermon during Wang's Shanghai period in the 1980s. See Wang Mingdao, "Wang Mingdao's Critique of Watchman Nee to Warn Preachers and Christians," at 49:00.

102. Wang Mingdao, "Some Strange Things," 243–45.

103. Wang Mingdao, "Is This a Good Phenomenon or Not?" 82–83.

104. See Shi, *Sixty-Three Years*, 6, and Wang Mingdao, *The Last Fifty Years*, 167–68.

105. Wang Mingdao, "We Are for the Faith!" 174, translated in Jones, *Documents of the Three-Self Movement*, 113–14.

106. Lam, *Wang Ming-Tao and the Chinese Church*, 239.

107. Bays, *A New History of Christianity in China*, 176.

108. See Strauss, "Paternalist Terror," 87–89.

109. See *Biographical Dictionary of Chinese Christianity*, "Wang Mingdao."

110. Wang Mingdao, *Last Confession*, 85.

111. Wang Mingdao, *Last Confession*, 102.

112. As the Five Old Men of Shanghai had done. See S. Wang, *The Long Road to Freedom*, 48.

113. See Bays, *A New History of Christianity in China*, 161–62

114. Wickeri, *Reconstructing Christianity in China*, 121–22.

115. As stated in Jiang, "An Appeal to Mr. Wang Mingdao," 50, and Wang Weifan, "Wu Yaozong and Wang Mingdao," 39.

116. Harvey, *Acquainted with Grief*, 79.

117. Harvey, *Acquainted with Grief*, 79.

118. Wang Mingdao, "We Are for the Faith!" 150–52, translated in Jones, *Documents of the Three-Self Movement*, 104–5.

119. Cui Xianxiang 崔憲祥, "A False Faith Cannot Fool People 信仰的偽裝騙不了人," 14–15, translated in Jones, *Documents of the Three-Self Movement*, 115–16.

120. Wang was also charged with briefly harboring in the Christian Tabernacle former KMT member Liang Lizhi 梁立志 who was later executed as a counterrevolutionary. However, since Wang registered Liang's name in a police registration and the TSPM sought Wang's support even after knowing this, it makes the charge dubious. See S. Wang, *The Long Road to Freedom*, 95–96, 157.

121. Kao, "The House Church Identity," 212–14.

122. China Aid. Sun Yi, "Why We Won't Join the Three-Self Patriotic Association."

123. China Partnership. Wang Yi, "95 Theses." See in particular thesis 95. More recently published in Wang Yi, "Ninety-Five Theses," 123–24.

124. These issues were also central to the April 22, 2015, conference in Vancouver, Canada. See China Aid, "Enduring Faith."

125. The fact that Chinese Christians such as Wang Mingdao and Paul Wei,

who were independent from missionary control and financial dependency, were still connected through close-knit personal networks with Western missionaries is also attested to in Inouye, *China and the True Jesus*, 84.

126. For example, see T. C. Chao's speech, "T. C. Chao on America," in Jones, *Documents of the Three-Self Movement*, 150–51.

127. See Jones, *The Church in Communist China*, 110–11; Bush, *Religion in Communist China*, 217–18; and Lyall, *God Reigns in China*, 134–35.

128. In John 1:1 and 14. For the complex history of the Word (Greek *Logos*) being translated into the Way (Chinese *Dao*) of God in Chinese, see Romano, "Translating and Transplanting the Word of God in China," 184–88.

BIBLIOGRAPHY

For entries published in Chinese, the author (in the first entry), title, publisher, and if applicable, editor will be included in English and Chinese characters. For unnamed author entries, the references are arranged alphabetically by title disregarding the definite (i.e., the) or indefinite (i.e., a/an) article. Chinese classical texts were accessed at the Chinese Text Project online at www.ctext.org.

Adeney, David H. *China: The Church's Long March.* Ventura, CA: OMF Books, 1985.

Adventism in China. "Pilquist E." https://www.adventisminchina.org/individuals/1-expatriates/pilquiste.

Aikman, David. *Jesus in Beijing.* Washington, DC: Regnery, 2003.

Amnesty International Report 1978. London: Amnesty International Publications, 1978. https://www.amnesty.org/download/Documents/POL100011978ENGLISH.PDF.

Anatolios, Khaled. "Discourse on the Trinity." In *The Cambridge History of Christianity: Constantine to c. 600*, edited by Augustine Casiday and Frederick W. Norris, 2:431–59. Cambridge: Cambridge University Press, 2007.

Annual of the Southern Baptist Convention 1930. New Orleans, May 14–18, 1930. http://media2.sbhla.org.s3.amazonaws.com/annuals/SBC_Annual_1930.pdf.

Bashford, James W. *China and Methodism*. Cincinnati: Jennings and Graham, 1906. https://archive.org/details/chinamethodism01bash/page/n4/mode/2up.

Barrington, R. T. "Panel Cites Threat Posed by Marxism." *Oklahoma City Star*, September 14, 1956.

Bays, Daniel H. *A New History of Christianity in China.* Malden, MA: Wiley-Blackwell, 2012.

Becker, Jasper. "The Mystery of Lao She." *South China Morning Post*, September 27, 2001. https://www.scmp.com/article/358800/mystery-lao-she.

Beckwith, Christopher. *Empires of the Silk Road: A History of Central Eurasia from the Bronze Age to the Present*. Princeton: Princeton University Press, 2009.

Beebe, Robert C. "Our Medical Students." *China Medical Missionary Journal* 3, no. 1 (March 1889): 1–4. http://findit.library.yale.edu/bookreader/BookReaderDemo/index.html?oid=11176074#page/2/mode/1up.

Bickers, Robert. Introduction to *The Boxers, China, and the World*, edited by Robert Bickers and R. G. Tiedemann, i–xxi. Lanham, MD: Rowman & Littlefield, 2007.

Bickers, Robert A. "New Light on Lao She, London, and the London Missionary Society, 1921–1929." *Modern Chinese Literature* 8, no. 1/2 (Spring/Fall 1994): 21–39.

"Billy Graham in China: Building Bridges." *Christianity Today*, June 17, 1988. https://www.christianitytoday.com/ct/1988/june-17/billy-graham-in-china-building-bridges.html.

Biographical Dictionary of Chinese Christianity. "Allen Yuan." http://bdcconline.net/en/stories/yuan-allen.

Biographical Dictionary of Chinese Christianity. "Cheng Jingyi." http://bdcconline.net/en/stories/cheng-jingyi.

Biographical Dictionary of Chinese Christianity. "Elisabeth Alden 'Betty' Stam." http://bdcconline.net/en/stories/stam-bette.

Biographical Dictionary of Chinese Christianity. "Francis Price Jones." http://bdcconline.net/en/stories/jones-francis-price.

Biographical Dictionary of Chinese Christianity. (Jia Yuming) "賈玉銘." http://bdcconline.net/zh-hant/stories/jia-yuming.

Biographical Dictionary of Chinese Christianity. "Leslie Theodore Lyall." http://bdcconline.net/en/stories/lyall-leslie-theodore.

Biographical Dictionary of Chinese Christianity. "Wang Mingdao." http://bdcconline.net/en/stories/wang-mingdao.

Biographical Dictionary of Chinese Christianity. (Zhang Yijing) "張亦鏡." http://bdcconline.net/zh-hant/stories/zhang-yijing.

Biographical Dictionary of Chinese Christianity. "Zhao Zichen." http://bdcconline.net/en/stories/zhao-zichen-1.

Bond, Jennifer. "The One for the Many: Zeng Baosun, Louise Barnes and the Yifang School for Girls at Changsha, 1893–1927." *Studies in Church History* 55 (2019): 441–62. http://dro.dur.ac.uk/27013/1/27013.pdf.

Boorman, Howard L. "Cheng Ching-yi." In *Biographical Dictionary of Republican China*. Vol. 1. New York: Columbia University Press, 1967.

Brook, Timothy. "Christianity under the Japanese Occupation." In *Christianity in China: From the Eighteenth Century to the Present*, edited by Daniel H. Bays, 317–37. Stanford: Stanford University Press, 1996.

———. *Collaboration: Japanese Agents and Local Elites in Wartime China*. Cambridge, MA: Harvard University Press, 2005.

Brother David and Lela Gilbert. *Walking the Hard Road—Wang Mingdao*. New York: HarperCollins, 1989.

Bürklin, Werner. *Jesus Never Left China: The Rest of the Story*. Enumclaw, WA: Pleasant Word, 2006.

Bush, Richard C. *Religion in Communist China*. Nashville: Abingdon, 1970.

Cao Jian. "Adoption of Christian Anthropology by Chinese Intellectuals." In *The Oxford Handbook of the Bible in China*, 317–32. New York: Oxford University Press, 2021.

Carnesecca, Cole. "Revolution and Religious Reform: The Indigenous Church Movement in Republican China." *Ching Feng* 12 (2013): 57–74.

Carter, Jimmy. "The United States and China: A President's Perspective." Lecture, Stanford University, Stanford, May 6, 2002. https://www.cartercenter.org/resources/pdfs/news/editorials-speeches/carter-speech-050602-inaugural-oksenberg-lecture-u.s.-and-china.pdf.

Chan Kei Thong. *Faith of Our Fathers.* Shanghai: China Publishing Group, 2006.

Chang, Vincent K. L. *Forgotten Diplomacy: The Modern Remaking of Dutch-Chinese Relations, 1927–1950*. Leiden: Brill, 2019.

Chao, Jonathan 趙天恩. "A Brief Description of Mr. Wang Mingdao's Contribution to the Chinese Church 略述王明道先生對中國教會的貢獻." *China and the Church* 中國與教會 86 (November 1991): 2–4.

———. "The Chinese Indigenous Church Movement, 1919–1927: A Protestant Response to the Anti-Christian Movements in Modern China." PhD diss., University of Pennsylvania, 1986.

———. *A History of Christianity in Socialist China: 1949–1997* 當代中國基督教發展史. Taipei: CMI Publishing Company 中國福音會出版部, 1997.

Chao, T. C. "The Articulate Word—The Problem of Communication (1947)." In *The Collected English Writings of Tsu Chen Chao*, edited by Xiaochao Wang, 485–86. Beijing: Zongjiao Wenhua, 2009.

———. "A Chinese Delegate Looks at Tambaram (1939)." In *The Collected English Writings of Tsu Chen Chao*, edited by Xiaochao Wang, 463–64. Beijing: Zongjiao Wenhua, 2009.

———. "The Indigenous Church (1924)." In *The Collected English Writings of Tsu Chen Chao*, edited by Xiaochao Wang, 177–86. Beijing: Zongjiao Wenhua, 2009.

——— 趙紫宸. *Life of Jesus* 耶穌傳. Shanghai: YMCA Publishing 青年協會, 1935.

Chen Yun 陳雲. "Speak the Truth, Don't Talk about Saving Face 只講真理，不要講面子." *People's Daily*, December 31, 1981.

Cheng Ching-yi 誠靜怡. "Pentecost Era Church 五旬節時代的教會." *China for Christ* 中華歸 116 (May 1931): 2–7.

Cheng, Marcus 陳崇桂. "A New Commandment (The Eleventh Commandment) 新誡命 (第十一條誡命)." *Tianfeng* 485 (October 1955): 15–16.

Chiang Kai Shek 蔣介石. "The Principles of Jesus concerning National Salvation 耶穌為救國的標準." *Evangelism* 佈道雜誌 6 (January–February 1933): 5–8.

China Aid. "Enduring Faith: Wang Mingdao and the Emergence of the House Church Movement in China." https://www.fcnabc.org/files/poster/20150626WangMindao-spk.pdf.

China Aid. Sun Yi. "Why We Won't Join the Three-Self Patriotic Association." Translated by Rachel Ritchie, China Aid. https://chinaaid.org/why-we-wont-join-three-self-patriotic/.

China Knowledge. "Wen Tianxiang 文天祥." http://www.chinaknowledge.de/History/Song/personswentianxiang.html.

China Knowledge. "Zhenguan Zhengyao 貞觀要." http://www.chinaknowledge.de/Literature/Historiography/zhenguanzhengyao.html.

China Partnership. Wang Yi. "95 Theses: The Reaffirmation of Our Stance on the House Church." Unnamed Translator. https://www.chinapartnership.org/blog/2015/08/95-theses-the-reaffirmation-of-our-stance-on-the-house-church.

China's Young Men. National Committee of the YMCA of China: Shanghai, 1906–16. Gale Primary Sources, Nineteenth Century Collections Online: Asia and the West.

Chinese Ancient Poetry. Chen Ziang 陳子昂. "On a Gate Tower at Yuzhou 登幽州臺歌." https://fanti.dugushici.com/ancient_proses/4035.

Chinese Ancient Poetry. Du Mu 杜牧. "EFang Palace 阿房宮賦." https://fanti.dugushici.com/ancient_proses/47516.

Chinese Ancient Poetry. Zhang Jie 章碣. "Book Burning Pit 焚書坑." http://fanti.dugushici.com/ancient_proses/35894.

The Chinese Classics, vol. 5. Translated by James Legge. London: Trubner, 1872. https://babel.hathitrust.org/cgi/pt?id=uc1.b000970398&view=1up&seq=9.

The Chinese University of Hong Kong. "Chung Chi Campus Newsletter." May 16, 2019. https://www.cuhk.edu.hk/ccc/publications/newsletter/pdf/newsletter20190516.pdf.

Ching, Julia. *Confucianism and Christianity: A Comparative Study.* Tokyo: Kodasha International, 1977.

Chirot, Daniel. Modern Tyrants: *The Power and Prevalence of Evil in Our Age.* Princeton: Princeton University Press, 1996.

Chu, Samuel C. "Early 20th Century Chinese Christian Writers and the Church Indigenization Movement." *Bulletin of the Institute of Modern History: Academia Sinica* 12 (1983): 195–217.

Cohen, Paul A. "Christian Missions and Their Impact to 1900." In *The Cambridge History of China*, edited by John K. Fairbank, 10:543–90. Cambridge: Cambridge University Press, 1978.

———. *History in Three Keys: The Boxers as Event, Experience, and Myth.* New York: Columbia University Press, 1997.

———. "Humanizing the Boxers." In *The Boxers, China, and the World*, edited by Robert Bickers and R. G. Tiedemann, 179–98. Lanham, MD: Rowman & Littlefield, 2007.

"Confucius Kills Shao Zhengmao 孔子殺少正卯." *People's Daily*, August 7, 1973.

Cook, Richard R. "Fundamentalism and Modern Culture in Republican China: The Popular Language of Wang Mingdao, 1900–1991." PhD diss., University of Iowa, 2003.

———. "Wang Mingdao and the Evolution of Contextualized Chinese Churches." In *Contextualization of Christianity in China: An Evaluation in Modern Perspective*, edited by Peter Chen-Main Wang, 209–23. Sankt Augustin, Germany: Institut Monumenta Serica, 2007.

Covell, Ralph R. *Confucius, the Buddha, and Christ*. Maryknoll, NY: Orbis, 1986.

Criticism Group of the Military and Political University 軍政大學大批判組. "The Gun Must Always Be in the Hands of the Party and the People—Criticizing Lin Biao's Crimes against the Party's Absolute Leadership over the Army 槍杆子要永遠掌握在黨和人民手裡—批判林彪反對黨對軍隊絕對領導的罪行." *People's Daily,* November 13, 1974.

"Criticize Confucius's Reactionary Thought and Take the Road of Uniting the Workers and Peasants 批判孔子反動思想走與工農相結合的道路." *People's Daily*, September 28, 1973.

Cui Xianxiang 崔憲祥. "A False Faith Cannot Fool People 信仰的偽裝騙不了人." *Tianfeng* 477–78 (August 1955): 14–15.

"Day Schools in Chihli." *Educational Review* 3, no. 11 (November 1910): 14.

Dikötter, Frank. *Mao's Great Famine*. New York: Walker, 2010.

Dong, Madeleine Yue. *Republican Beijing: The City and Its Histories*. Berkeley: University of California Press, 2003.

Dunch, Ryan. "Science, Religion, and the Classics in Christian Higher Education to 1920." In *China's Christian Colleges: Cross-Cultural Connections, 1900–1950*, edited by Daniel H. Bays and Ellen Widmer, 57–82. Stanford: Stanford University Press, 2009.

East Gates International. "Rev. Billy Graham's First Visit to China." https://eastgates.org/rev-billy-grahams-first-visit-to-china/.

Eastman, Lloyd E. "Nationalist China during the Nanjing Decade." In *The Cambridge History of China*, edited by John K. Fairbank, 13:116–67. Cambridge: Cambridge University Press, 1986.

———. "Nationalist China during the Sino-Japanese War 1937–1945." In *The Cambridge History of China*, edited by John K. Fairbank, 13:547–608. Cambridge: Cambridge University Press, 1986.

Eber, Irene. "The Interminable Term Question." In *Bible in Modern China: The Literary and Intellectual Impact*, edited by Irene Eber, Sze-Kar Wan, and Knut Walf, 135–61. Sankt Augustin, Germany: Institut Monumenta Serica, 1999.

Edwards, Mark. "The First Council of Nicea." In *The Cambridge History of Christianity: Origins to Constantine*, edited by Margaret M. Mitchell and Frances M. Young, 1:552–67. Cambridge: Cambridge University Press, 2006.

Elison, H. B. "Japan Wars on Mr. Wu." *Saturday Evening Post*, May 13, 1939.

Encyclopedia Knowledge. "Caolanzi Prison Former Site 草嵐子監獄舊址." https://www.easyatm.com.tw/wiki/%E8%8D%89%E5%B5%90%E5%AD%90%E7%9B%A3%E7%8D%84.

Ewing, Charles, and Bessie Ewing. *Death Throes of a Dynasty*, edited by E. G. Ruoff. Kent, OH: Kent State University Press, 1990.

Feng Chunxiang 馮春祥. "Criticizing Confucius's Fallacy of Studying and Being an Official 批判孔子的讀書做官的謬論." *People's Daily*, December 10, 1973.

Feng Youlan 馮友蘭. *A History of Chinese Philosophy* 中國哲學史. Shanghai: Commercial Press 商務印書館, 1934.

———. *On Confucius* 論孔丘. Beijing: People's Publishers 人民出版社, 1973.

Furth, Charlotte. "Intellectual Change: From the Reform Movement to the May Fourth Movement, 1895–1920." In *The Cambridge History of China*, edited by John K. Fairbank, 12:322–405. Cambridge: Cambridge University Press, 1983.

Glüer, Winfried. "The Legacy of T. C. Chao." *International Bulletin of Missionary Review* 6, no. 4 (October 1982): 165–69.

———. "T. C. Chao Revisited: Questions about His Later Years." *Ching Feng* 11, no. 2 (2012): 171–96.

Goldin, Paul R. "Xunzi." In *The Stanford Encyclopedia of Philosophy*, edited by Edward N. Zalta. Stanford: Stanford University, 2018. https://plato.stanford.edu/entries/xunzi/.

Goldman, Merle. "The Party and the Intellectuals." In *The Cambridge History of China*, edited by John K. Fairbank, 14:218–58. Cambridge: Cambridge University Press, 1987.

Goldman, Merle, and John K. Fairbank. "The Post-Mao Reform Era." In *China: A New History*, 406–56. Cambridge, MA: Harvard University Press, 2006.

Goldman, Merle, and Leo Ou-fan Lee, eds. *An Intellectual History of Modern China*. Cambridge: Cambridge University Press, 2002.

Goossaert, Vincent, and David Palmer. *The Religious Question in Modern China*. Chicago: University of Chicago Press, 2007.

Graham, Angus C. *Poems of the West Lake: Translations from the Chinese*. London: Wellsweep, 1990.

Graham, Billy. *Just as I Am: The Autobiography of Billy Graham*. New York: HarperCollins, 1997.

Gu Shouhai 穀守海. "Lin Biao Cursed Qin Shihuang as an Attack on the Dictatorship of the Proletariat 林彪咒罵秦始皇就是攻擊無產階級專政." *People's Daily*, February 27, 1974.

Guo Jingwei 郭經緯. "Protestant Christian Elementary Education in China—A Discussion on the Establishment of Universal Elementary and Middle School Education 基督教新教在華基礎教育—興辦普及,特殊中小學教育商榷." In *Setting the Roots Right—Christian Education in China and Taiwan* 將根紮好—基督宗教在華教育的檢討, edited by Wang Chen-Main 王成勉, 617–40. Taipei: Liming Publishers 黎明文化, 2007.

Gwyther, Jordan A. "Bai Juyi and the New Yuefu Movement." MA thesis, University of Oregon, 2013. https://core.ac.uk/download/pdf/36687766.pdf.

Harvey, Thomas Alan. *Acquainted with Grief: Wang Mingdao's Stand for the Persecuted Church in China*. Grand Rapids: Brazos, 2002.

———. "Challenging Heaven's Mandate: An Analysis of the Conflict between Wang Mingdao and the Chinese Nation-State." PhD diss., Duke University, 1998.

———. "Sermon, Story, and Song in the Inculturation of Christianity in China." In *Sinicizing Christianity*, edited by Peggy Brock, 138–66. Leiden: Brill, 2017.

Hawkes, David. *Chu Tzu: The Songs of the South.* Oxford: Clarendon, 1959.

Hempton, David. *Evangelical Disenchantment.* New Haven: Yale University Press, 2008.

The History of Western Medicine in China. Indiana University Library. "Hopkins Memorial Hospital." http://www.ulib.iupui.edu/wmicproject/node/511.

"Hopkins, N. S. North China." Missionary Files: Methodist Episcopal Church Missionary Correspondence, 1846–1912 (China), 1887–1904. General Commission on Archives & History, United Methodist Church. Gale Primary Sources, Nineteenth Century Collections Online: Asia and the West.

"Hopkins, Nehemiah S., M.D., Passes." Missionary Bio, Madison, NJ, 1954, Drew University Methodist Episcopal Church Archives. Gale Primary Sources, Nineteenth Century Collections Online: Asia and the West.

Hopkins, N. S., and G. D. Lowry. "Hospital Reports: Peking Medical Work." *China Missionary Medical Journal* 20, no. 3 (May 1906): 148–49. http://findit.library.yale.edu/bookreader/BookReaderDemo/index.html?oid=11354884#page/51/mode/1up.

Hu Suh. "Intellectual China in 1919." *Chinese Social and Political Science Review* 4, no. 4 (December 1919): 345–55.

Iap Sian-Chin. "Bernt Bernsten: A Prominent Oneness Pentecostal Pioneer to North China." In *Global Renewal Christianity: Asia and Oceania*, edited by Vinson Synan and Amos Yong, 91–106. Lake Mary, FL: Charisma House, 2016.

Inouye, Melissa Wei-Tsing. *China and the True Jesus: Charisma and Organization in a Chinese Christian Church.* Oxford: Oxford University Press, 2018.

"In Remembrance: J. Walter Lowrie." *Chinese Recorder* 61, no. 3 (March 1930): 181–82.

Internet Encyclopedia of Philosophy. "Feng Youlan." https://iep.utm.edu/feng/.

Ireland, Daryl R. *John Song: Modern Chinese Christianity and the Making of a New Man.* Waco: Baylor University Press, 2020.

James, Alfred Francis. *Reports on Deputation of Australian Churchmen to Mainland China*. New York: Far Eastern Office, 1957. https://archive.org/details/reportsondeputat00jame/mode/2up.

Jia Heng 嘉衡 and Chun Shu 春樹. "The Reactionary Essence of Lin Biao and His Group Advocating for 'Determining Power' 林彪一夥鼓"決定動力"的反動實質." *People's Daily*, August 10, 1975.

Jiang Hua. "On the Work of the Supreme People's Court, June 7, 1983." In *The People's Republic of China, 1979–1984, a Document Survey*, edited by Harold C. Hinton, 1:295–300. Wilmington, DE: SR Scholarly Resources, 1986.

Jiang Peifen, "An Appeal to Mr. Wang Mingdao." *Chinese Theological Review* 3 (1987): 57–59.

Jones, Francis P. *The Church in Communist China: A Protestant Appraisal*. New York: Friendship Press, 1962.

———. *Documents of the Three Self-Movement: Source Materials for the Study of the Protestant Church*. New York: National Council of the Churches of Christ in the USA, 1963.

Kao Chen-yang. "The Cultural Revolution and the Post-missionary Transformation of Protestantism in China." PhD diss., University of Lancaster, 2009.

———. "The House Church Identity and Preservation of Pentecostal-Style Protestantism in China." In *Christianity in Contemporary China: Socio-cultural Perspectives*, edited by Francis Lim, 207–19. Oxford: Routledge, 2012.

———. "Reassembling Christianity: Fuzhou Protestantism under China's Cultural Revolution from the Perspective of Life-History Research." *Sino-Christian Studies*, no. 31 (2021): 7–44.

Ketler, Isaac C. *The Tragedy of Paotingfu: An Authentic Story of the Lives, Services and Sacrifices of the Presbyterian, Congregational and China Inland Missionaries Who Suffered Martyrdom at Paotingfu, China, June 30th and July 1, 1900*. New York: Fleming H. Revell, 1902.

Knechtges, David R., and Taiping Chang. *Ancient and Early Medieval Chinese Literature: A Reference Guide, Part One*. Leiden: Brill, 2010.

Knight, George H. *In the Cloudy and Dark Day: God's Message of Peace to the Weary, the Sorrow-Laden, the Troubled, and the Tired*. London: Hodder and Stoughton, 1910. https://babel.hathitrust.org/cgi/pt?id=yale.39002088449765&view=1up&seq=9.

———. *In the Secret of His Presence: Helps for the Inner Life When Alone with God*. London: Hodder and Stoughton, 1906. https://babel.hathitrust.org/cgi/pt?id=yale.39002088449658&view=1up&seq=5&q1=in.

Krabbendam, Hans. "Three-Way Chess: Arie Kok and the Failure to Expand American Fundamentalism in Europe." *Church History and Religious Culture* 94 (2014): 227–58.

Kwok Wai Luen. "The Christ-Human and Jia Yuming's Doctrine of Sanctification: A Case Study in the Confucianisation of Chinese Fundamentalist Christianity." *Studies in World Christianity* 20 (August 2014): 145–65.

———. "Sola Scriptura's and the Chinese Union Version Bible's Impact upon Conservative Christian Leaders: The Case of Watchman Nee and Wang Mingdao." *Journal of the Royal Asiatic Society* 30, no. 1 (2020): 93–103.

———. "Theology of Religions and Intertextuality: A Case Study of Christian-Confucian and Islamic Confucian Dialogue in the Early 20th-Century China." In *Christian Literature in Chinese Contexts*, edited by John T. P. Lai, 62–74. Basel: MDPI, 2019.

Lacy, Walter N. *A Hundred Years of Chinese Methodism*. New York: Abingdon-Cokesbury, 1948.

Lam Wing-hung. *Chinese Theology in Construction*. Pasadena: William Carrey Library Publishing, 1983.

———. "The Emergence of a Protestant Christian Apologetics in the Chinese Church during the Anti-Christian Movement in the 1920s." PhD diss., Princeton Theological Seminary, 1978.

———. *A Half Century of Chinese Theology 1900–1949* 中華神學五十年. Hong Kong: China Graduate School of Theology 中國神學研究院, 1998.

——— 林榮洪. *Wang Ming-Tao and the Chinese Church* 王明道與中國教會. Hong Kong: China Graduate School of Theology 中國神學研究院, 1982.

Lamb, Samuel 林献羔. "The Wang Mingdao I Know 我所認識的王明道先生." *China and the Church* 中國與教會 86 (November 1991): 9–10.

Lee, Archie C. C. "Cross-Textual Hermeneutics and Identity in Multi-scriptural Asia." In *Christian Theology in Asia*, edited by Sebastian C. H. Kim, 179–204. Cambridge: Cambridge University Press, 2008.

Lee, Moses Kung Yu. "Aspects of the Emergence of the Chinese Church from the Missionary Movement, 1900–1949." ThD diss., University of South Africa, 2000, chap. 5.

Lee, Samuel Mau Cheng. "A Comparative Study of Leadership Selection Processes among Four Chinese Leaders." DMiss diss., Fuller Theological Seminary, 1985, chap. 7.

Leung Ka-lun 梁家麟. *By Faith They Did It: Beijing Christian Student Association and Chinese Christian Evangelistic Band* 他們是為了信仰－北京基督徒學生會與中華基督徒佈道會. Hong Kong: Alliance Bible Seminary Press 建道神學院, 2001.

———. *Wandering between Christianity and Confucianism* 徘徊於耶儒之間. Taipei: Cosmic Light Publishing House 宇宙光出版社, 1997.

———. *Watchman Nee: His Glory and Dishonor* 倪柝聲的榮辱升黜. Hong Kong: Alliance Bible Seminary 建道神學院, 2003.

Li Boxiong 李柏雄. "Wang Mingdao's Contribution to Popular Theology" 王明道對大眾神學的貢獻. *China and the Church* 中國與教會 9–10 (May–June 1980): 19–22.

Li Kaihuan 李開煥, ed. "Wang Mingdao's Theology 王明道的神學." *Jiang He* 江河 28 (August 1948): 110.

Li Siqun 黎斯群. "Wu Han—The Zealot of the Jiang [Chiang Kai-shek] Dynasty, Deputy of American Imperialism 吳晗-蔣家王朝的策士, 美帝的幫辦." *People's Daily*, April 27, 1966.

Li Tang and Martha Smalley. "A Chinese Christian Leader Revisited: The John Sung Papers at Yale Divinity Library." *Journal of Religious and Theological Information* 15, no. 3–4 (2016): 90–106.

Li Zipeng 黎子鵬. "Late Qing Chinese Christian Literature: The Narrative Features of the Peep of Day, 1864 晚清基督教文學：《正道啟蒙》(1864) 的中國小說敘事特徵." *Dao Feng Chinese Theological Journal* 道風 35 (July 2011): 279–97. https://repository.lib.cuhk.edu.hk/en/item/cuhk-531011.

Lian Xi. *Redeemed by Fire, The Rise of Popular Christianity in Modern China*. New Haven: Yale University Press, 2010.

Liang Shouhua 梁壽華. "Independent Religious Beliefs' Effect on Society: A Reinterpretation of Wang Mingdao's Thoughts on Society 超然信仰的社會實效性—王明道社會觀的再詮釋." *Dao Feng Chinese Theological Journal* 道風漢語神學學刊, no. 9 (1998): 169–200. https://repository.lib.cuhk.edu.hk/en/item/cuhk-530524.

Lieberthal, Kenneth. *Governing China: From Revolution through Reform.* New York: Norton, 2004.

Lim, C. E., I. C. Yuan, H. P. Chu, P. Z. King, and C. U. Lee. *National Medical Association of China Medical Guide, 1928*. Beijing: Chinese Medical Association, 1928. https://indianamemory.contentdm.oclc.org/digital/collection/WMIC/id/410/rec/1.

Lim Ka-Tong. *The Life and Ministry of John Sung*. Singapore: Genesis Books, 2012.

Lin Chiu-Hsiang 林秋香 and Chang Kuan-Ing 章冠英. *An Injured Brave* 受傷的勇士－王明道的一世紀. Taipei: CCLM Publishing Group 華宣出版社, 2006.

Ling, Samuel D. "The Other May Fourth Movement: The Chinese 'Christian Renaissance,' 1919–1937." PhD diss., Temple University, 1981.

Lo Ping-cheng. "Confucian Ethic of Death with Dignity and Its Contemporary Relevance." *Annual of the Society of Christian Ethics* 19 (1999): 313–15.

Louth, Andrew. *The Origins of the Christian Mystical Tradition: From Plato to Denys*. Oxford: Oxford University Press, 2007.

"Lowry, George D. North China." Missionary Files: Methodist Episcopal Church Missionary Correspondence, 1846–1912 (China), 1894–1901. General Commission on Archives & History, United Methodist Church. Gale Primary Sources, Nineteenth Century Collections Online: Asia and the West.

Lu Dingyi 陸定一. *Biography of Wei Zheng* 魏徵傳. Beijing: Chinese Book Company 中華書局, 1962.

Lu Wantian 鹿完天. "Record of the 1900 Beijing Incident 庚子北京事變紀略." In *The Boxers* 義和拳. Shanghai: Shenzhou Guoguang Publishing 神州國光社, 1951. https://ctext.org/library.pl?if=en&res=87389.

Lui, Hing Hung Otto. "Development of Chinese Church Leaders—A Study of Relational Leadership in Contemporary Chinese Churches." PhD diss., Fuller Theological Seminary, 2011, chap. 5.

———. *Development of Chinese Church Leaders*. Carlisle, UK: Langham Monographs, 2013.

Lutz, Jessie G. "Middle Schools—The Roots of Christian Education in China and Taiwan." In *Setting the Roots Right—Christian Education in China and Taiwan*, edited by Wang Chen-Main, 1–18. Taipei: Liming Publishers, 2007.

Lyall, Leslie T. *Come Wind Come Weather: The Present Experience of the Church in China.* Chicago: Moody Press, 1960.

———. *God Reigns in China*. London: Hodder and Stoughton, 1985.

———. *Three of China's Mighty Men.* London: Overseas Missionary Fellowship Books, 1973.

———. *Three of China's Mighty Men* 中國教會三巨人. Translated by Zhang Linmanmei 張林滿鎂. New Taipei City: CCLM Publishing Group 華宣出版社, 2012. (Chinese translation of the 1973 English version)
———. *Watchman Nee, David Yang, Wang Ming-tao: Steadfast in Faith*. Translated by Jürg Klemenz and Irma von Puskas. Giessen, Germany: Brunnen, 1974. (German translation of *Three of China's Mighty Men*.) https://info2.sermon-online.com/german/LeslieTheodoreLyall/Zeugen_Des_Gegenwaertigen_Gottes_Band_202_Watchmann_Nee_David_Yang_Und_Wang_Ming_Tao_1974.pdf.
Ma Feibi 馬非比. "Wang Mingdao through the Eyes of Mrs. Wang 王師母眼中的王明道." *China and the Church* 中國與教會86 (November 1991): 8.
Maddox, Randy L. "The Recovery of Theology as a Practical Discipline." *Theological Studies* 51 (1990): 650–72.
———. *Responsible Grace: John Wesley's Practical Theology*. Nashville: Kingswood Books, 1994.
Madsen, Richard. *China and the American Dream*. Berkeley: University of California Press, 1995.
Main, Duncan. "Hospital Reports." *China Medical Missionary Journal* 2, no.4 (December 1888): 183–88. Section on "Students." http://findit.library.yale.edu/bookreader/BookReaderDemo/index.html?oid=11153634#page/38/mode/1up.
Mann, Susan. "Scene-Setting: Writing Biography in Chinese History." *American Historical Review* 114, no. 3 (June 2009): 631–39.
Mao Zedong 毛澤東. "Four Sentences for Li Ne 送給李訥的四句話." In *Long Live Mao Zedong Thought* 毛澤東思想萬歲! Beijing: n.p., 1968. https://www.marxists.org/chinese/maozedong/1968/5-064.htm.
Marchal, Kai. "Lü Zuqian's Political Philosophy." In *Dao Companion to Neo-Confucian Philosophy*, edited by John Makeham, 197–222. Heidelberg: Springer Netherlands, 2010.
Matsutani, Yosuke. "Wang Mingdao, Counter-revolutionary Chinese Evangelist, Has Yet to Restore His Honor." [In Japanese.] *China 21* 48 (2018): 119–46.
———. "Yanaihara Tadao and China: His Article, 'The Ideal of the Nation' and His Visit to Wang Mingdao." [In Japanese.] *Sociological Studies* 25 (2012): 97–123. http://www.ritsumei.ac.jp/acd/re/ssrc/result/memoirs/kiyou25/25-05.pdf.
McGuckin, John A. *St. Gregory of Nazianzus: An Intellectual Biography*. Crestwood, NY: St. Vladimir's Seminary Press, 2001.
"Medical Education in China." *China Medical Missionary Journal* 1, no. 3 (September 1887): 127–29. http://findit.library.yale.edu/bookreader/BookReaderDemo/index.html?oid=11107971#page/39/mode/1up.
"Member of the Standing Committee of the Fifth National People's Congress, Chairman of the Committee for the Chinese Christian TSPM, a Memorial Service for Mr. Y. T. Wu Was Held in Shanghai 五屆人大常委、中國基督教三自愛國運動委員會主席吳耀宗先生追悼會在上海舉行." *People's Daily*, September 27, 1979.

"Members of the Educational Association of China, 1910." *Educational Review* 3, no. 4 (April 1910): n.p.

Miller, James R. *In Green Pastures.* London: Thomas Nelson, 1904. https://web.archive.org/web/20060207200904/http://in-green-pastures.jr-miller.com/.

———. *A Life of Character.* New York: Thomas Y. Crowell, 1894. https://www.gracegems.org/Miller/a_life_of_character.htm.

Ming Yan 銘言. "Remembering Uncle Wang—Recalling the Death of Wang Mingdao 懷念王伯伯一 並憶述王明道逝世過程." *China and the Church* 中國與教會86 (November 1991): 13.

"Missionary News: Pao-ting-fu Memorial Services." *Chinese Recorder* 32, no. 5 (May 1901): 264–66.

Moser, Michael J., and Yeone Wei-Chih. *Foreigners within the Gates: The Legations at Peking*. Chicago: Serindia Press, 2006.

Mühlhahn, Klaus. "Remembering a Bitter Past: The Trauma of China's Labor Camps, 1949–1978." *History and Memory* 16, no. 2 (Fall/Winter 2004): 108–39.

Mullowney, J. J. "Report of the Peking Hospital, October, 1910." *China Missionary Medical Journal* 25, no. 3 (May 1911): 206–9. http://findit.library.yale.edu/bookreader/BookReaderDemo/index.html?oid=11194955#page/71/mode/1up.

Murthy, Sheela. "Deng's 'Civilized' China of 'Five Disciplines, Four Graces, and Three Loves.'" *China Report* 19, no. 6 (November 1983): 3–11.

Naquin, Susan. "Funerals in North China: Uniformity and Variation." In *Death Ritual in Late Imperial and Modern China*, edited by James L. Watson and Evelyn S. Rawski, 37–70. Berkeley: University of California Press, 1988.

Nature Index. "Ten Institutions That Dominated Science in 2015." https://www.natureindex.com/news-blog/ten-institutions-that-dominated-science-in-twenty fifteen.

Neal, James B. "Medical Teaching in China." *China Medical Missionary Journal* 11, no. 2 (June 1897): 89–91. http://findit.library.yale.edu/bookreader/BookReaderDemo/index.html?oid=11240513#page/3/mode/1up.

Nedostup, Rebecca. *Superstitious Regimes: Religion and the Politics of Chinese Modernity*. Cambridge, MA: Harvard University Press, 2009.

Ng, Gene 吳劍麗. "The Shaping Influence of the Chinese YMCA on the Young Wang Mingdao 中國基督教青年會對少年王明道的信仰形塑." In *I Believed; Therefore, I Spoke: Essays in Honor of Leung Ka-lun at the Occasion of His 60th Birthday* 我信，所以說話：梁家麟院長六秩壽辰紀念祝賀文集, edited by Zhang Yunkai 張雲開 and Chen Zhiheng 陳智衡, 159–94. Hong Kong: Alliance Bible Seminary 建道神學院, 2018.

———. "The Situation of the Christian Tabernacle and Wang Mingdao's Preaching during the Chinese Civil War (1945–1949) 內戰時期基督徒會堂的處境及王明道的傳道事業 (1945–1949)." In *Instant in Season, Out of Season: The Chinese Church during the Civil War Period* 務要傳道——內戰時期的中國教會,

edited by Huang Wenjiang 黄文江, Zhang Yunkai 張雲開, and Chen Zhiheng 陳智衡, 233–54. Hong Kong: Alliance Bible Seminary 建道神學院, 2019.

Ng Lee-Ming, "Christianity and Social Change: The Case in China, 1920–1950." PhD diss., Princeton Theological Seminary, 1971, chap. 2.

——— 吳利明. Christianity and Social Change in China 基督教與中國社會變遷. Hong Kong: Chinese Christian Literature Council 基督教文藝出版社, 1981.

———. "Wang Ming-Tao: An Evaluation of His Thought and Action." *Ching Feng* 16, no. 2 (1973): 51–80.

Ni Huiliang, "Sinicizing Jesus in the First Half of the Twentieth Century: How Chinese Christians Understood Jesus." PhD diss., Claremont Graduate University, 2008, chap. 4.

Norden, Bryan Van. "Mencius." In *The Stanford Encyclopedia of Philosophy*, edited by Edward N. Zalta (Fall 2019). https://plato.stanford.edu/entries/mencius/.

North China Christian Union Group Memorial Book 華北中華基督教團成立周年紀念冊. Beijing: North China Union Group 華北教團, 1943.

The North China Famine of 1920–1921 with Special Reference to the West Chihli Area. Beijing: Peking United International Relief Committee, 1922.

Onsager, Lawrence W. "On Fire for China, the Story of Erik Pilquist, Pioneer Adventist Missionary to China." Unpublished manuscript. No date. http://www.sdahistorians.org/uploads/1/2/3/6/12365223/onsager_paper.pdf.

"On the Field." *Chinese Recorder* 57, no. 5 (May 1926): 373–79.

Outler, Albert C. "The Wesleyan Quadrilateral in Wesley." *Wesleyan Theological Journal* 20, no. 1 (1985): 7–18. https://wtsociety.com/files/wts_journal/1985-wtj-20-1.pdf.

Payk, Christopher. "Revisiting the Life and Theology of the Confucian-Christian Wang Mingdao." PhD diss., National Chengchi University, 2021. https://ah.nccu.edu.tw/retrieve/223758/650501.pdf.

"Peking Gives Wu Pei-Fu, China's Honest War Lord, a Fine Princely Funeral." *Life*, March 4, 1940, 30–32.

Peking Lassies: A Sketch of Life and Work in an LMS Girls' Boarding School. Beijing: London Missionary Society, 1910.

Peking University and Tsinghua University's Criticism Group 北京大學; 清華大學大批判組. "On the Violence of Qin Shihuang 略論秦始皇的暴力." *People's Daily*, January 21, 1974.

Peng, Ann Cui'An. *The Translation of the Bible into Chinese*. Eugene: Pickwick Publications, 2021.

"Peng Dehuai and His Backstage Crimes Cannot Escape 彭德懷及其後台罪責難逃." *People's Daily*, August 16, 1967.

Percival, Henry R. "The First Council of Constantinople." In *The Seven Ecumenical Councils: Nicene and Post-Nicene Fathers*, edited by Philip Schaff and Henry Wace, 1:161–90. Peabody MA: Hendrickson Publishers, 1994.

"Personal Notes." *China Missionary Medical Journal* 14, no. 4 (October 1900): 308–12. https://findit.library.yale.edu/bookreader/BookReaderDemo/index.html?oid=11243818#page/86/mode/1up.

Political Imprisonment in the People's Republic of China. London: Amnesty International Publications, 1978. https://www.amnesty.org/download/Documents/204000/asa170151978en.pdf.

Porter, Henry D. "The Boxers and the Hospitals." *China Missionary Medical Journal* 14, no. 4 (October 1900): 292–96. http://findit.library.yale.edu/bookreader/BookReaderDemo/index.html?oid=11243818#page/72/mode/1up.

Rainey, Lee. "Confucianism and Tradition." In *Historicizing "Tradition" in the Study of Religion*, edited by Steven Engler and Gregory P. Grieve, 227–44. Berlin: De Gruyter, 2005.

Rawski, Evelyn S. "Elementary Education in the Mission Enterprise." In *Christianity in China: Early Protestant Missionary Writings*, edited by Suzanne W. Barnett and John K. Fairbank, 135–52. Cambridge, MA: Harvard University Press, 1985.

"Rehabilitation of Rightists Announced in China." *Amnesty International Newsletter*, July 1978. https://www.amnesty.org/fr/wp-content/uploads/2021/06/nws210071978en.pdf.

"Religion: A Church That Would Not Die." *Time*, September 10, 1979. https://content.time.com/time/subscriber/article/0,33009,920617,00.html.

Ren Zhongxiang 任鐘祥. *A Brief History of the Shanghai Christian Local Church* 上海基督徒聚會處簡史. Shanghai: Shanghai City Christian TSPM Committee 上海市基督教教務委員會, 1996.

Renshaw, Michelle. "Accommodating the Chinese: The American Hospital in China, 1880–1920." PhD diss., University of Adelaide, 2003.

"Rev. James W. Lowrie." *New York Times*, January 29, 1930. https://www.findagrave.com/memorial/151373378/james-walter-lowrie#view-photo=127381955.

Reynolds, Arthur. *Pathway to Glory: The Voice of China's Christians*. London: Overseas Missionary Fellowship, 1968.

———. *Strength for the Storm.* Singapore: OMF Books, 1988.

Romano, Monica. "Translating and Transplanting the Word of God in China." In *Sinicizing Christianity*, edited by Peggy Brock, 167–94. Leiden: Brill, 2017.

Rourke, Mary. "Jonathan Chao, 65; Missionary Who Tracked the Development of Christianity in China." *Los Angeles Times*, January 20, 2004. https://www.latimes.com/archives/la-xpm-2004-jan-20-me-chao20-story.html.

Sandeen, Ernest R. *The Roots of Fundamentalism.* Chicago: University of Chicago Press, 1970.

Schwartz, Benjamin J. "Themes in Intellectual History: May Fourth and After." In *The Cambridge History of China*, 12:406–50. Cambridge: Cambridge University Press, 1983.

Scofield, C. I. *The Scofield Reference Bible*. New York: Oxford University Press, 1917. https://babel.hathitrust.org/cgi/pt?id=uc1.l0071259550&view=1up&seq=5.

Shan Chun. *Major Aspects of Chinese Religion and Philosophy: Dao of Inner Saint and Outer King*. Berlin: Springer, 2012.

Shavit, David. *The United States in Asia: A Historical Dictionary.* New York: Greenwood, 1990.

Shaw, Yu Ming. *An American Missionary in China: John Leighton Stuart and Chinese-American Relations*. Cambridge, MA: Harvard University Press, 1992.

Sheridan, James E. *Chinese Warlord: The Career of Feng Yu-hsiang.* Stanford: Stanford University Press, 1966.

———. "The Warlord Era: Politics and Militarism under the Peking Government: 1916–1928." In *The Cambridge History of China*, 12:284–321. Cambridge: Cambridge University Press, 1983.

Shi Meiling 施美玲. *Sixty-Three Years—Walking the Narrow Road with Mr. Wang Mingdao* 六十三年—與王明道先生窄路通行. Hong Kong: Spiritual Rock Publishers 靈石出版社, 2006.

Sima Qian. *The Grand Scribe's Records*. 2 vols. Translated by Tsai-Fa Cheng et al. Edited by William H. Nienhauser Jr. Bloomington: Indiana University Press, 1994.

———. *Records of the Grand Historian: Han Dynasty I.* Translated by Burton Watson. New York: Columbia University Press, 1993.

"The Situation in the North." *China Missionary Medical Journal* 14, no. 4 (October 1900): 275–78. http://findit.library.yale.edu/bookreader/BookReaderDemo/index.html?oid=11243818#page/54/mode/1up.

So Yuen Tai 蘇遠泰. "An Analysis of Wang Mingdao's Perspective on the Bible and Hermeneutics 析王明道的聖經觀與釋經學. *Jian Dao Journal* 建道學刊, no. 12 (July 1999): 297–323.

Song Baiyu Andrew. "Christ against Culture? A Re-evaluation of Wang Mingdao's Popular Theology." *Journal of Global Christianity* 3, no. 1 (February 2017): 48–64. https://trainingleadersinternational.org/jgc/75/christ-against-culture-a-re-evaluation-of-wang-mingdaos-popular-theology.

———. "Jia Yuming—A Chinese Keswick Theologian: A Theological Analysis of Christ-Human Theology in Jia's Total Salvation." *Journal of Global Christianity* 4, no. 1 (February 2018). https://trainingleadersinternational.org/jgc/102/jia-yuming-1880-1964-a-chinese-keswick-theologian-a-theological-analysis-of-christ-human-theology-in-jias-total-salvation.

Song Shangjie. *The Diary of John Sung: Extracts from His Journals and Notes.* Translated by Thng Pheng Soon. Singapore: Genesis, 2012.

Song Tian-Zhen 宋天真. *The Diary of His [John Sung's] Spiritual Life* 靈歷集光. Hong Kong: Eng Yu Evangelistic Mission 恩雨宣道, 1995. http://cclw.net/soul/linglijiguang/index.htm.

Spence, Jonathan. *The Search for Modern China.* New York: Norton, 1990.

Starr, Chloë. *Chinese Theology*. New Haven: Yale University Press, 2016.

Sterba, James P. "Carter, Ending China Trip, Stresses Taiwan Issue." *New York Times*,

September 4, 1981. https://www.nytimes.com/1981/09/04/world/carter-ending-china-trip-stresses-taiwan-issue.html.

Strauss, Julia C. "Paternalist Terror: The Campaign to Suppress Counterrevolutionaries and Regime Consolidation in the People's Republic of China, 1950–1953." *Comparative Studies in Society and History* 44, no. 1 (January 2002): 80–105.

Stuart, Leighton. "Yenching University." *Educational Review* 25, no. 1 (April 1918): 90.

Sun, Poking J. "Jesus in the Writings of Wang Mingdao." In *The Chinese Face of Jesus Christ*, edited by Roman Malek, 3a:1137–48. Sankt Augustin, Germany: Institut Monumenta Serica and China-Zentrum, 2005.

Sun Tao Hsieh. *The Doctrine of the Holy Spirit*. Anaheim: True Jesus Church, 2008.

Sun Yusheng 孫玉升. "Wu Han, What Qualifications Do You Have to Represent the People 吳晗，你有什麼資格代表人民？" *People's Daily*, May 6, 1966.

The Sunday School Helper. February 25, 1883. https://babel.hathitrust.org/cgi/pt?id=hvd.ah6ax1&view=1up&seq=454&q1=Always%20speak.

Szuma Chien (Sima Qian). *Selections from Records of the Historian*. Translated by Yang Hsien-yi and Gladys Yang. Beijing: Foreign Language Press, 1979.

Tang Xiaowen 唐曉文. "What Does Confucius's Killing of Shao Zhengmao Tell Us 孔子殺少正卯說明了什麼?" *People's Daily*, January 4, 1974.

Taylor, Jay. *The Generalissimo: Chiang Kai-Shek and the Struggle for Modern China*. Cambridge, MA: Harvard University Press, 2011.

Thompson, Larry C. *William Scott Ament and the Boxer Rebellion*. Jefferson, NC: McFarland, 2009.

Thorkelson, Willmar. "More Saloons than Churches Reported." *Minneapolis Star*, October 8, 1955.

Thrapp, Dan L. "Faction Blamed in China Arrest." *Los Angeles Times*, October 8, 1955.

———. "Southland Parish." *Los Angeles Times*, December 10, 1955.

Tiedemann, Rolf G. "The Advance of Pentecostalism in China, 1907–1937." In *Ecumenism and Independency in World Christianity*, edited by Alexander Chow and Emma Wild-Wood, 195–220. Leiden: Brill, 2020.

———. *Handbook of Christianity in China, Volume Two: 1800–Present*. Leiden: Brill, 2010.

———. *Reference Guide to Christian Missionary Societies in China: From the Sixteenth to the Twentieth Century*. New York: Routledge, 2009.

Ting, K. H. 丁光訓. "An Earnest Admonishment to Wang Mingdao 正告王明道." *Tianfeng* 447–48 (August 1955): 16–20.

———. "Summary of Standing Committee Member K. H. Ting's Speech 丁光訓常委發言摘要." *Tianfeng* 457 (March 1955): 7.

Tsai Yen-zen. "Scriptures and Their Popularization: The Case of the *Lun-yu* and *Hsiao-ching* in the Han Dynasty." *Journal of Humanities East/West* 18 (December 1998): 137–65. http://nccur.lib.nccu.edu.tw/bitstream/140.119/6604/1/relig15.pdf.

Tseng, Gloria S. "Bathsheba as an Object Lesson: Gender, Modernity and Biblical

Examples in Wang Mingdao's Sermons and Writings." *Studies in World Christianity* 21, no. 1 (2015): 52–65.

———. "Revival Preaching and the Indigenization of Christianity in Republican China." *International Bulletin of Missionary Research* 38, no. 4 (October 2014): 177–82.

Tu Yichao. "Panda Huggers and Dragon Slayers: Billy Graham, American Evangelicals, and Sino-American Relations." Billy Graham Center Annual Lecture, September 25, 2013. https://www.wheaton.edu/media/billy-graham-center-archives/2013-Annual-Lecture-Transcript.pdf.

Vala, Carsten T. "Failing to Contain Religion: The Emergence of a Protestant Movement in Contemporary China." PhD diss., University of California, Berkeley, 2008, chap. 3.

Various Authors. "Mr. Wang Mingdao's 90th Year Special Edition 王明道先生九秩高壽特輯." *Chinese Churches Today* 今日華人教會 (November 1990): 32–39.

Wang Gungwu. *China Reconnects: Joining a Deep-Rooted Past to a New World Order.* Singapore: World Scientific Publishing, 2019.

Wang Kung Lee. "China's Mineral Industries in 1967: Victims of the Cultural Revolution." *Asian Survey* 9, no. 6 (June 1969): 425–37.

Wang Mingdao 王明道. "Are People Able to Establish God's Kingdom 人能建設天國麼?" *The Spiritual Food Quarterly* 靈食季刊 17 (Spring 1931): 36–46.

———. "Be Faithful to God and Not Concerned about People's Feelings 向神盡忠莫顧人情." *The Spiritual Food Quarterly* 112 (Winter 1954): 231–38.

———. "Can We Trust That the Miracles in the Bible Are True 聖經中的奇事是可信 的麼?" *The Spiritual Food Quarterly* 11 (Fall 1929): 141–44.

———. "Christ's Second Coming 基督再來." *The Spiritual Food Quarterly* 5 (Spring 1928): 13–20.

———. "A Conscientious Girl 一個盡職的小女子." *The Spiritual Food Quarterly* 87 (Fall 1948): 17–80.

———. "The Cross of Christ 基督的十字架." *The Spiritual Food Quarterly* 1 (Spring 1927): 19–26.

———. "Did Christ Really Rise from the Dead 基督果真復活了嗎?" *The Spiritual Food Quarterly* 33 (Spring 1935): 32–45.

———. "Does Dr. Sherwood Eddy Preach the Gospel 艾迪博士是傳福音的麼?" *The Spiritual Food Quarterly* 32 (Winter 1934): 245–47.

———. "The East Will Sing 東方將明歌.". *The Spiritual Food Quarterly* 2 (Summer 1927): 75–76.

———. "Editor's News 編者的消息." *The Spiritual Food Quarterly* 1 (Spring 1927): 69–70.

———. "Editor's News 編者的消息." *The Spiritual Food Quarterly* 6 (Summer 1928): 116.

———. "Editor's News 編者的消息." *The Spiritual Food Quarterly* 11 (Fall 1929): 186.

———. "Editor's News 編者的消息." *The Spiritual Food Quarterly* 75 (Fall 1945): 115–20.
———. "Editor's News 編者的消息." *The Spiritual Food Quarterly* 85 (Spring 1948): 75.
———. "The Evils of the Modern YMCA 現代基督教青年會的罪惡." *The Spiritual Food Quarterly* 34 (Summer 1935): 94–106.
———. "The Fairest Lesson 最公平的教訓." *The Spiritual Food Quarterly* 80 (Winter 1946): 183–89.
———. "God's Son Jesus (Part 3) 神的兒子耶穌(續)." *The Spiritual Food Quarterly* 97 (Spring 1951): 53–58.
———. "The Gospel in Genesis 5 創世紀第五章的福音." *The Spiritual Food Quarterly* 24 (Winter 1932): 185–97.
———. "How Many Gospels Are There 一共有幾個福音呢?" *The Spiritual Food Quarterly* 23 (Fall 1932): 131–38.
———. "The Human Heart 人心." *The Spiritual Food Quarterly* 90 (Summer 1949): 104–5.
———. "The Idols of Christians 基督徒的偶像." *The Spiritual Food Quarterly* 6 (Summer 1928): 80–90.
———. "In Memory of Mother 追念母親." *The Spiritual Food Quarterly* 84 (Winter 1947): 258–78.
———. "Is This a Good Phenomenon or Not 這是不是好現象呢?" *The Spiritual Food Quarterly* 50 (Summer 1939): 82–87.
———. "Jesus's Virgin Birth 基督的童女誕生." *The Spiritual Food Quarterly* 9 (Spring 1929): 12–16.
———. *Look at These Men (Part One) 看這些人(上)* (1935). Reprint. New Taipei City: CCLM Publishing Group 華宣出版社, 2013.
———. "Look at These Ninevites 看這些尼尼微人." *The Spiritual Food Quarterly* 85 (Spring 1948): 13–16.
———. "Martin Luther's Prayer 路德馬丁的一篇禱文." *The Spiritual Food Quarterly* 1 (Spring 1927): 17.
———. "Maxims for Believer's Conduct in Society 信徒處世格言." *The Spiritual Food Quarterly* 59 (Fall 1941): 170–71.
———. "The Meaning of [the Word] Church 教會的意義." *The Spiritual Food Quarterly* 58 (Summer 1941): 87–102.
———. "More Important than Work 比工作更重要的事." *The Spiritual Food Quarterly* 85 (Spring 1948): 24–39.
———. "Mr. Song Shangjie [John Sung] Has Died 宋尚節先生去世了." *The Spiritual Food Quarterly* 71 (Fall 1944): 149–57.
———. "My Confession 我的檢討." *Tianfeng* 515 (October 1956): 7–9.
———. "My Opinion of Spiritual [Ministry] Work 靈工芻言." *The Spiritual Food Quarterly* 56 (Winter 1940): 224–26.
———. "New Year's Letter from Wang Mingdao 王明道新年來信." *Evangelical Communications* 音文宣社通訊 31 (1981): 1–2.

———. "Publication Announcement 出版露佈." *The Spiritual Food Quarterly* 1 (Spring 1927): 9.

———. "The Question of Validity of the Last Half of Mark 16 馬可福音地十六章後 半質疑." *The Spiritual Food Quarterly* 101 (Spring 1952): 54–55.

———. "The Resurrected Christ 復活的基督." *The Spiritual Food Quarterly* 1 (Spring 1927): 27–39.

———. "Saints Who Fall Ill Should Remember This 患病的聖徒當留意的一件事." *The Spiritual Food Quarterly* 76 (Winter 1945): 166–71.

———. "Scared to Death 還是嚇死的多." *The Spiritual Food Quarterly* 53 (Spring 1940): 51–57.

———. *Selections from Wang Mingdao's Diary* 王明道日記選輯. Hong Kong: Spiritual Rock Publishers 靈石出版社, 1997.

——— (Wang Ming-tao). *Shaped by the Hand of the Master*. Translated by Thomas Order. Thoune, Switzerland: Christian Library CLC, 1998. (French translation of *A Stone Made Smooth*)

———. "A Sharp Warning to the Modern Church 現代教會的棒喝." *The Spiritual Food Quarterly* 3 (Fall 1927): 133–51.

———. "A Small Elm Tree on the City Wall 城墻上的一株小榆樹." *The Spiritual Food Quarterly* 48 (Winter 1938): 232–36.

———. *The Spiritual Food Quarterly* 靈食季刊 (1927–55). Reprint. New Taipei City: CCLM Publishing Group 華宣出版社, 2012–14.

———. "The Spiritual Gifts Movement in the Light of Scripture 聖經光亮中的靈恩運 動." *The Spiritual Food Quarterly* 28 (Winter 1933): 213–32

———. *The Spiritual Gifts Movement in the Light of Scripture* 聖經光亮中的靈恩運動. Beijing: Spiritual Food Quarterly Press, 1934.

——— (Wong Ming-Dao). *The Spiritual Gifts Movement*. Translated by Arthur Reynolds. Southampton: Mayflower Christian Books, 1990. (Translation of *The Spiritual Gifts Movement in the Light of Scripture*)

——— (Wong Ming-Dao). *A Stone Made Smooth*. Translated by Arthur T. F. Reynolds. Southampton: Mayflower Christian Books, 1981. (Translation of *The Last Fifty Years*)

——— (Wang Ming-tao). *A Stone Made Smooth*. Unnamed Translator. Bielefeld: Christian Literature Distribution: 1991. https://clv.de/W.-Ming-tao-Ein-Stein-wird-geschliffen/255323. (German translation of *A Stone Made Smooth*)

———. "The Story of Zhang En and Wang Yi 王恩與張義的故事." *The Spiritual Food Quarterly* 12 (Winter 1929): 235–40.

———. "A Strong Wall, an Iron Pillar—Wang Mingdao's Testimony 堅城鐵柱-王明 道見證." Sermon. No date. https://www.youtube.com/watch?v=NbYbk3vrmr4&list=PLeyV8uWMaMm0TfMS- koWZ3JEaveoadkqC&index=3.

———. "Taking a Concubine and Divorce 納妾與離婚." *The Spiritual Food Quarterly* 62 (Summer 1942): 103–13.

———. "Their God Is Still Our God 他們的神仍是我們的神." *The Spiritual Food Quarterly* 76 (Winter 1945): 144–63.

———. "Their Sorrows Shall Be Multiplied That Hasten after Another God 以別神代 替耶和華的他們的愁苦必加增." *The Spiritual Food Quarterly* 51 (Fall 1939): 134–40.

———. "This Is the Lord Jesus's Disciple 這才是主耶穌的門徒." *The Spiritual Food Quarterly* 65 (Spring 1943): 29.

———. "To Glory in Your Shame 以自己的羞辱為榮耀." *The Spiritual Food Quarterly* 86 (Summer 1948): 104–12.

———. "To Neglect a Warning Is to Court Disaster 輕忽了警告遭遇了禍患." *The Spiritual Food Quarterly* 95 (Fall 1950): 158–64.

———. "The Uncompromising Christ 不妥協的基督." *The Spiritual Food Quarterly* 66 (Summer 1943): 68–72.

———. "A Very Important Role 一件極重要的本分." *The Spiritual Food Quarterly* 53 (Spring 1940): 19–23.

———. "Wang Mingdao Sermon 02—Come Out from Babylon 王明道講道 02 - 從巴 比倫出來." Sermon. No date. https://www.youtube.com/watch?v=lWenH5ndAAE.

———. "Wang Mingdao's Critique of Watchman Nee to Warn Preachers and Christians 王明道講道指責倪柝聲給傳道人與基督徒的警戒." Sermon. No date. https://www.youtube.com/watch?v=HiXhBUy4ZZ0&list=PLeyV8uWMaMm0TfMS- koWZ3JEaveoadkqC&index=4.

———. *Wang Mingdao's Last Confession* 王明道的最後自白. Edited by Fuk Tsang Ying 邢福增. Hong Kong: Logos Publishers 基道出版社, 2013.

———. "Wang Mingdao's Sermon 02—Guard against Two Kinds of Leaven; To Serve the Lord One Must Be Holy 王明道讲道 02 - 防備兩種酵;侍奉主要聖潔." Sermon. No date. https://www.youtube.com/watch?v=Dz_wQ7_by1g&list=PLeyV8uWMaMm0TfMS- koWZ3JEaveoadkqC&index=5.

——— (Wang Ming Tao). *Wang Ming Tao and Charismatism.* Translated by Timothy Tow. Singapore: Christian Life Publishers, 1989. https://www.febc.edu.sg/v15/assets/pdfs/febc_press/Wang%20Ming%20Tao%20&%20Charismatism.pdf.

———. "Watch Out for Thieves 謹防竊賊." *The Spiritual Food Quarterly* 11 (Fall 1929): 172–78.

———. "We Are for the Faith 我們是為了信仰!" *The Spiritual Food Quarterly* 114 (Summer 1955): 134–74.

———. "What Does the 'Resurrection of Jesus' Actually Mean 耶穌復活究竟是甚麼意思呢?" *The Spiritual Food Quarterly* 85 (Summer 1948): 42–71.

———. "What Is Truth 真理是甚麼呢?" *The Spiritual Food Quarterly* 102 (Summer 1952): 88–93.

———. "Who Is Jesus 耶穌是誰?" In *Our Lord* 我們的主, 8–47. (1953) Reprint. New Taipei City: CCLM Publishing Group 華宣出版社, 2012.

Wang, Stephen 王長新. *Another Forty Years* 又四十年. Scarborough, ON: Gospel Publishing House 福音出版社, 1997.

———. "How *Another Forty Years* Was Written 又四十年是怎樣寫成的." *Christian Life Quarterly Digest* 生命季刊 18 (June 2001). https://www.cclifefl.org/View/Article/559.

———. *The Long Road to Freedom: The Story of Wang Mingdao*. Translated by Ma Min. Tonbridge, UK: Sovereign World, 2002. (Translation of *Another Forty Years*)

Wang, Thomas 王永信. "'Faithful unto Death': Wang Mingdao and the Rise of China's House Churches 2015 Conference Main Session (1) The Chinese Church's Man of Character by Rev. Thomas Wang「至死忠心」王明道與中國家庭教會的興起2015研討會主題信息（一）華人教會的大丈夫_王永信牧師." July 7, 2015. Sermon, 28:40. https://www.youtube.com/watch?v=qVJw5hkil4I&list=PL4ySDlhAUh_gbxfNPTm91dR41dk_2ex0F&index=1&t=427s.

Wang Weifan 汪維藩. "Although We Are Many, We Are Still One Body 我們雖多, 乃是一個身體." *Tianfeng* 465 (May 1955): 5–9.

———. "Is It for Faith 是為了信仰麼?" *Tianfeng* 473–74 (July 1955): 15–16.

———. "Wu Yaozong and Wang Mingdao." *Chinese Theological Review* 5 (1989): 44–48.

Wang Xiaojing. "The Church Unity Movement in Early Twentieth-Century China: Cheng Yingyi and the Church of Christ in China." PhD diss., University of Edinburgh, 2012.

Wang Yi. "Ninety-Five Theses: The Reaffirmation of Our Stance on the House Church." In *Faithful Disobedience: Writings on Church and State from a Chinese House Church Movement*, edited by Hannah Nation and J. D. Tseng, 104–24. Downers Grove, IL: InterVarsity Press, 2022.

Watchman Nee. "Not Wider than a Locality." Living Stream Ministry. https://www.ministrybooks.org/SearchMinBooksDsp.cfm?id=2F2307FA82. [Subscription required for access]

———. "The Orthodoxy of the Church." Living Stream Ministry. https://www.ministrybooks.org/books/reader.php?id=M_kmjLntGl9E. [Subscription required for access]

——— 倪柝聲. *The Spiritual Man* 屬靈人. Shanghai: Shanghai Gospel Bookroom 上海福音書房, 1928.

Wechsler, Howard J. *Mirror to the Son of Heaven: Wei Cheng at the Court of T'ang T'ai-tsung*. New Haven: Yale University Press, 1974.

Wehrle, Edmund S. *Britain, China, and the Antimissionary Riots 1891–1900*. Minneapolis: University of Minnesota Press, 1966.

Wei Jin 衛今. "Looking at the Book Burning of Qin Shihuang from the Yinqueshan Bamboo Slips 從銀雀山竹簡看秦始皇焚書." *People's Daily*, July 9, 1974.

Wen Tianxiang 文天祥. "The Song of the Spirit of Righteousness 正氣歌." Translated by Feng Xinming 馮欣明. http://tsoidug.org/Literary/Spirit_Righteousness_Comp.pdf.

Wesley, John. *John Wesley*. Edited by Albert C. Outler. New York: Oxford University Press, 1964.

West, Philip. *Yenching University and Sino-Western Relations, 1916–1952*. Cambridge, MA: Harvard University Press, 1976.

Whyte, Martin K. "Death in the People's Republic of China." In *Death Ritual in Late Imperial and Modern China*, edited by James L. Watson and Evelyn S. Rawski, 289–316. Berkeley: University of California Press, 1988.

Wickeri, Philip L. *Reconstructing Christianity in China: K. H. Ting and the Chinese Church*. New York: Orbis, 2007.

Wikipedia. "Arthur T. F. Reynolds." https://en.wikipedia.org/wiki/Arthur_T._F._Reynolds.

Wilcox, Holly C. "Psychiatric Morbidity, Violent Crime, and Suicide among Children and Adolescents Exposed to Parental Death." *Journal of the American Academy of Child & Adolescent Psychiatry* 49, no. 5 (May 2010): 514–23.

Williams, Leroy B. "The Succession to Mao and the End of Maoism." In *The Cambridge History of China*, edited by John K. Fairbank, 14:303–401. Cambridge: Cambridge University Press, 1987.

Wing Yui So. "The China Inland Mission and the Chinese Christian Student Movement in 1937–1956." Unpublished manuscript, 2017. https://sosir.org/sites/sosir.org/files/attachments/The%20China%20Inland%20Mission%20and%20The%20Chinese%20Christian%20Student%20Movement%20in%201937-1956.pdf.

Witness Lee. *Watchman Nee: A Seer of the Divine Revelation in the Present Age*. Anaheim: Living Stream Ministry, 1991.

Wong, Hin. "The Formal Opening of Yenching University." *Educational Review* 21, no. 4 (October 1929): 348–52.

World Missionary Conference 1910, Report of Commission II: The Church in the Mission Field. Edinburgh: Oliphant, Anderson, and Ferrier, 1910. https://archive.org/details/reportofcommiss00unknuoft/page/n5/mode/2up?view=theater.

Wright, Tim. *Coal Mining in China's Economy and Society 1895–1937*. Cambridge: Cambridge University Press, 1984.

Wu Chang Shing 吳昶興. "Searching Modern Christian Identities during an Anti-Christian Movement: A Case Study of Timothy Tingfang Le 非基督教育運下現代基督徒身分的索：以劉廷芳為例." *Sino-Christian Studies* 漢語基督教學術論評 17 (2014): 36–37.

Wu, Dongsheng John. *Understanding Watchman Nee: Spirituality, Knowledge, and Formation*. Eugene: Wipf & Stock, 2012.

Wu Jingzi. *The Scholars*. Translated by Yang Hsien-yi and Gladys Yang. New York: Columbia University Press, 1992.

Wu, Y. T. 吳耀宗. *Darkness and Light* 黑暗與光明. Shanghai: YMCA Publishing 青年協會, 1949.

———. "Where Is God 上帝在那裡?" *Tianfeng* 22 (November 1945): 7–10.

Xie Jiapeng and Su Yuxiao. "Chinese Translations of John Bunyan's *The Pilgrim's Progress*." *Bunyan Studies* 22 (2018): 114–41.

Xu Bin. "Memory and Reconciliation in Post-Mao China: 1976–1982." In *Routledge Handbook of Memory and Reconciliation in East Asia*, edited by Kim Mikyoung, 47–60. London: Routledge, 2016.

Xunzi. *Xunzi: A Translation and Study of the Complete Works*. Vol. 3. Translated by John Knoblock. Stanford: Stanford University Press, 1994.

Yamane, David. "Narrative and Religious Experience." *Sociology of Religion* 61, no. 2 (Summer 2000): 171–89.

Yan Liming 嚴立明. "After Reading Wang Weifan's Article on Y. T. Wu and Wang Mingdao 讀汪維藩吳耀宗與王明道後." *Hu Han Journal* 呼喊季刊, no. 58 (February 1990): 120–28.

Yao Xiyi. *The Fundamentalist Movement among Protestant Missionaries in China, 1920–1937*. Lanham, MD: University Press of America, 2003.

———. "Wang Weifan's Evangelical Theology." In *Yearbook of Chinese Theology 2016*, edited by Paulos Z. Huang, 3–16. Leiden: Brill, 2016.

Ying Fuk Tsang 邢福增. *Anti-imperialism, Patriotism, and the Spiritual Man—A Study on Watchman Nee and Local Church* 反帝, 愛國, 屬靈人—倪柝聲與基督徒聚會處研究. Hong Kong: CSCCRC 基督教中國宗教文化研究社, 2005.

———. *Christianity's Failure in China? Essays on the History of Chinese Communist Movement and Christianity* 基督教在中國的失敗? 中國共產運動與基督教史論. Hong Kong: Logos and Pneuma Press 道風書社, 2008.

———. "A Counterrevolutionaries' Final Words—Wang Mingdao's Plea to Redress a Mishandled Case Posthumous Manuscript Analysis 反革命分子的最後聲音一王明道平反文稿論析." In *Pondering before the Cross: Textual Analysis and Scriptural Interpretation* 十字架前的思索：文本解讀與經典詮釋, edited by Wang Chen-Main 王成勉, 319–54. Taipei: Dawn Culture Publishers 黎明文化事業出版, 2010.

———. "Counter-revolution in the Revolutionary Era: A Preliminary Study on the Case of 'Wang Mingdao's Counter-revolutionary Clique' 革命時代的反革命： 基督教「王明道反革命集團」案始末考." *Journal of the Institute of Modern History, Academia Sinica* 中央研究院近代史研究所集刊 67 (March 2010): 97–147.

———. "Inner Saint and Outer King: Rethinking the Mission of Chinese Christians from a Historical Perspective 內聖與外王——從歷史角度再思華人基督徒的信仰使." Presentation at the Forum on Christian Faith of Chinese Intellectuals, Los Alamos, August 4–6, 2016. https://forumcfci.org/forum2016/sites/default/files/Proceeding/Ch3_art4.pdf.

———. "Wang Mingdao and the North China Christian Union Group—Enemy Occupied Area Church Leader's Resistance and Cooperation Case Studies 王明道與華北中華基督教團一淪陷區教會人士抵抗與合作的個案研究." *Jian Dao Journal* 建道學刊, no. 17 (January 2002): 1–56. Revised and expanded in *Conflict and Assimilation: Modern Chinese Christian History Research* 衝突與融合——近代中基督教史研究論集. Taipei: Universal Light Publishers 宇宙光出版社, 2006.

———. "Wang Mingdao Discusses Chinese Church Leaders and Affairs—An Annotated Analysis of a Conversation in the 1980s 王明道談中國教會的人與事－1980 年代的一次談話考釋." *Journal of the History of Christianity in Modern China* 近代中國基督教史研究集刊 8 (December 2009): 80–91.

———. "Watchman Nee in the Eyes of Wang Mingdao 巨人愛恨—王明道所認識的倪柝聲." *Ching Feng* 景風 15, no. 1/2 (2016): 131–58.

Young, Ernest P. "Politics in the Aftermath of Revolution: The Era of Yuan Shih-kai, 1912–1916." In *The Cambridge History of China*, edited by John K. Fairbank, 12:208–55. Cambridge: Cambridge University Press, 1983.

Yu, Anthony C., trans. *The Journey to the West*. Vol. 3. Chicago: University of Chicago Press, 1980.

———. *The Monkey and the Monk: An Abridgement of* The Journey to the West. Chicago: University of Chicago Press, 2006.

Yuan Xiangchen (Allen) 袁相忱. "Remembering God's Servant, Mr. Wang Mingdao 憶神僕王明道先生." *China and the Church* 中國與教會86 (November 1991): 11–12.

Zhang Jing 張靜. "The Spread and Development of Early Christianity in Baoding during the Late Qing Dynasty 清末民初基督新教在保定的傳播與發展." Taipei: Independent Author, 2015. https://www.jintian.net/today/?action-viewnews-itemid-69890.

Zhang Yifei 張益飛. "The Great Traitor Liu Shaoqi Will Be Expelled from the Party Forever 把大叛徒劉少奇永遠開除出黨大快人心！" *People's Daily*, November 3, 1968.

Zhang Zhiyi 張執一. "Speech of the Deputy Minister of the United Front Work Department of the CCP Central Committee Zhang Zhiyi at the National Christian Conference 中共中央統戰部張執一副部長在基督教全國會議上的講話." *Tianfeng* 2 (1981): 19.

Zhao Qingzhi 趙清治. "The Life Testimony of a Preacher: Remembering Elder Wang Changxin 傳道人的生命見證：緬懷王長新長老." *Christian Life Quarterly Special Article* 生命季刊微信專稿 (February 2017). https://www.cclifefl.org/View/Article/5342.

Zhao Zhonghui 趙中輝. "A Visit with Mr. Wang Mingdao 王明道先生訪問記." *Faith and Life* 信仰與生活156 (October–November 1988): 53.

———. "Wang Mingdao Recalls Entering Prison for the First Time 王明道憶述第一次進監情形." *China and the Church* 中國與教會 86 (November 1991): 5–7.

Zhong Xuanzao 鍾宣造. "Lu Dingyi's Counter-revolutionary Face Is Revealed from the *Biography of Wei Zheng* 從《魏徵傳》的出籠看陸定一的反革命嘴臉." *People's Daily*, November 9, 1967.

Zia, H. L. (Xie Honglai) 謝洪賚, ed. *Friendly Talks with Students* 修學一助. Shanghai: National Committee of the YMCA of China 中華基督教青年會組合, 1914.

———. *The Protestant Missions in China: Selected Works of Xie Honglai* (H. L. Zia) 中國耶穌教會小史：謝洪賚文選. Edited by Zhao Xiaoyang 趙曉陽.

New Taipei City: CCLM Publishing Group 華宣出版社, 2020.
———. *World Leaders* 後進楷模. Shanghai: National Committee of the YMCA of China 中華基督教青年會組合, 1912.

INDEX

Page numbers in italics refer to figures and tables.

CHRISTOPHER PAYK

is a chaplain at Morrison Academy Taipei in New Taipei City, Taiwan.
He is the author of *Grace First: Christian Mission and Prevenient Grace in John Wesley*.